The Temple Woman Within Series

Seeking The Lost Temple of Julie

by
Julie Biro

The Temple Woman Within Series
Book 1

Seeking The Lost Temple of Julie
The Temple Woman Within Series
Book 1

Copyright © Julie Biro 2022

The right of Julie Biro to be identified as the author of this work (Seeking The Lost Temple of Julie) has been asserted by her under the Copyright Amendment (Moral Rights) act 2000.

First published as *Basket of Hurts* 2018
Revised edition - 2022

This work is copyright.
Apart from any use as permitted under the Copyright Act 1968, no part may be reproduced, copied, scanned, stored in a retrieval system, recorded or transmitted in any form or by any means, without the prior written permission of the author.

Cover design by Birology Books.
birologybooks.com.au

The Temple Woman Within Series

Note

'Seeking The Lost Temple of Julie' is a work of creative non-fiction. Names, places, characters, and incidents are either a product of my memory or are used creatively to relate actual events. The events in this story are true. The effects on me, the principal character are real. The views expressed in this memoir are solely mine.

This book contains references to suicide, sexual abuse, addiction and mental illness. I have written in a way that this aspect of the subject matter in my story is dealt with as an exploration of the themes associated with these issues and their impact on me. As such at times I have put words in the characters' mouths that reflect the issues of these themes rather than what we actually said to each other, to best tell the story. These themes may be troubling to some readers.

In order to safeguard the privacy of individuals who are still alive at the time of publishing this book and for me to be still able to tell my story, I have used different names and identifying characteristics and where possible occupations where it was appropriate to do so. All settings in my story with the exception of my trip overseas named only because they are integral to my story, are deliberately general so as not to associate characters in my book with any specific location to further safeguard their privacy.

Introduction

We are all born into a family narrative we inherit that is passed down through the generations. This narrative shapes who we are and what we become and we hand it down to the next generation.

Family narratives can and often support the growth of a budding child into adulthood on a chosen path that reflects their natural talents and dispositions as a human being; creating healthy and productive people able to embrace the challenges and setbacks of life and still continue to thrive. And then there is the rest of us ... We carry a basket of hurts in our hearts full of unresolved family trauma inherited from our parents. These baskets are passed down through the generations to us creating an environment in which the trauma is perpetuated.

This family narrative supports the growth of a broken child who is mired by the weight of the basket they carry in their hearts, making them ill equipped to negotiate the challenges and setbacks life brings them.

We are all born with a story in us waiting to be told, its seeds in stories lived before this one, our own personal myth we craft over the course of a lifetime. Sometimes we need to step out of our family narrative and onto our own pathway to discover it, as I have done.

Julie Biro

ACT 1
childhood memories

setting: under the budding child's willow tree of dreams
    scene 1: the flower girl
    scene 2: playing ouija
    scene 3: seeds of ancient memories

setting : in the broken child's cave of sorrows
    scene 4: when is dad coming home?
    scene 5 : mr and mrs jones
    scene 6. susan and ray
    scene 7: the family argument
    scene 8: the loony bin
    scene 9: we were a footy family

setting: under the budding child's willow tree of dreams
    scene 10: the last day of primary school

setting: in the broken child's cave of sorrows
    scene 11: the last day of primary school

ACT 2
awkward adolescence

setting: under the budding child's willow tree of dreams
    scene 1: first kiss
    scene 2: first date
    scene 3: my cheesecloth dress

setting: in the broken child's cave of sorrows
    scene 4: drinking
    scene 5: looking for love

setting : under the budding child's willow tree of dreams
    scene 6: teaching

setting: in the broken child's cave of sorrows
    scene 7: love found

ACT 3
finding the temple woman within

setting: in the broken child's cave of sorrows
   scene 1: getting married

setting: leaving the budding child's willow tree of dreams
   scene 2: wedding day

setting: the budding child enters the broken child's cave of sorrows
   scene 3: married life
   scene 4: louise
   scene 5: my sister's wedding

setting: in julie's tent of travels
   scene 6: overseas
   scene 7: pompeii
   scene 8: nana
   scene 9: paris
   scene 10: the tour
   scene 11: amsterdam
   scene 12: india
   scene 13: the tarot cards
   scene 14: a doorkeeper and an astrologer
   scene 15: marriage breakup
   scene 16: the school in the bush

setting: in the broken child's cave of sorrows
   scene 17: a hole in my pyjamas
   scene 18: the family picnic
   scene 19: a new squabble
   scene 20: something really bad happened to me

setting: julie's camp by the river
   scene 21: befriending the broken child

setting: the path by the river
   scene 22: the women's circle
   scene 23: our picnic
   scene 24: consulting my life map

scene 25: my dream tour
scene 26: moving on
scene 27: back in the cave of sorrows
scene 28: the christmas tree
scene 29: meeting the temple woman within

time: years later....
scene 30: the final betrayal

The Temple Woman Within Series

Cast of Characters

Main Characters

Narrator: Julie in the voices of ...
The Budding child
The Broken child
The Temple Woman

Julie's sister

Julie's mother's side of the family
Her siblings Joyce, Eileen, Bob and Grace
Joyce's family- husband Alan, sons Jack, Colin and Terry
Eileen's family- husband Harry; children Phil, Cathy, Jane and Ian
Bob's family- wife Gwen and three children
Julie's Nana Lil
Julie's Grandad Jack
Julie's great grandmother
Julie's biological grandmother May

Julie's father's side of the family
His sister Bev
Julie's grandfather Pa
His wife Auntie Win
Julie's grandmother

Julie's husband and family
Julie's husband Neil
Julie's in-laws Margaret and Richard
Julie's brother-in law Barry and wife Carol

Minor Characters

Julie's wished for parents
Susan and Ray

Julie's wished for family
Mr and Mrs Jones
Leanne her best friend and her sister

Julie's Grade 6 teacher

Julie's godmother Auntie Helen

Julie's girlfriends
Tammy
Vicki
Louise
Carolyn
Kim

Julie's boyfriends
Mark
Gary
Paul
Tad
Chris
Glen

Julie's Temple Woman Awakeners
Rose the Tarot Card Reader
Lois the Doorkeeper to a Soul's Awakening
Colleen the Clairvoyant
Marie the Astrologer
Adele the Natural Therapist
Anna, Claudia, Joan and Alice the Women's Circle

Julie's Happy Ending
Laci

The Seeking Begins

$\mathcal{A}s$ a little girl Julie lived her life split in two. Inside her lived a budding child and a broken child. She knew them very well. These two children carried a basket each. The budding child's was a flower girl's basket filled with the seeds of her life's promise. Despite her best attempts to plant them in her garden, they struggled to take root and grow. The broken child's was a picnic basket weighed heavy with the rotting seeds of hurts, despite her best attempts to shed them from her basket.

Though I knew them both very well, Julie's budding child and the broken child didn't know me at all. The budding child caught her first glimpse of I, the Temple Woman, standing in a garden within the ruins of a temple in Pompeii. A long, narrow road pitted with dark shadows and paved by the stories of others who came before Julie, brought her to Pompeii one sunny day.

Until that day, Julie had been walking around in a family story that made no sense to her, believing it to be her own. As a child she had no understanding of this inheritance. In her teens she still believed it to be her story and by then she'd lost all hope of writing herself out of it. On that day walking amongst the ruins in Pompeii, she had a glimpse of a new life story. A twist in time let in a chink of light that shone on the ruins of a temple bringing it to life in its full glory. Though she didn't know it, the budding child living inside Julie had just opened the doorway to her temple a crack where I, The Temple Woman dwelt, allowing the light to shine onto her basket she'd been carrying in her heart for the last twenty-seven years. The seed of Julie's essence stirred in that chink of light, a part of her she hadn't known she was seeking. It lay nestled in amongst other seeds of ancient memories warming in the budding child's basket along with the tendrils of memories Julie's travels were stirring within her, beckoning her to find me, the Temple Woman within.

I took the unripened seed of Julie's essence out of the budding child's basket and placed it back in mine. My basket was made of mother of pearl inlaid with clear quartz crystals that also formed the handle of the basket. From the deep pockets of my long white shift I took out two small clear quartz crystals. Lifting them to my tiara made of eagle feathers with a large crystal point that

The Temple Woman Within Series

sat between my eyes, I tapped them against it and looked up to the stars. I placed one crystal in the budding child's basket adding a feather from my tiara, then reached into my own basket, took out a pack of tarot cards and placed them in her basket with the crystal and the feather.

With the seed of Julie's essence tucked away safely in my basket it was time to return the budding child to her realm under the willow tree, where she'd been walking around lost in amongst its branches until that day in Pompeii. The seeds of her own life story were contained in the day dreams she enjoyed under the willow tree in the front garden of her childhood home, their memories still held with fondness in her heart. She needed to reacquaint herself with them to enable her to orient herself toward the path of I, The Temple Woman where her life story lay.

The broken child who also lived inside Julie needed to return to her realm, the cave; a dark place in Julie's heart, the bad memories buried in her mind she needed to find and face, a consequence of living within her family's story. Julie's temple door closed. It wouldn't open again until the budding child had befriended the broken child. That was the only way Julie would be able to reclaim the lost part of herself she was seeking, the Temple Woman within.

As I'd done for the budding child, I placed the other crystal and a feather from my tiara into the broken child's basket adding for her from my basket a triangle made out of clear quartz crystal on each side. Written in golden light were three words. At the top, 'Beauty'. In one corner at the base, 'Respect', the other corner, 'Care'. Though it lay on top of her basket, little light penetrated the darkness of her cave; the realm of all her unhealed trauma and pain. This meant she would not be able to see the triangle until she had shed some of the rotting seeds of hurt that her basket contained.

setting
the budding child looks into the broken child's cave

The story inherited from her mother's family overshadowed Julie, demanding attention every day of her life, thwarting the budding child's attempts to plant her seeds in her garden then watch them flourish and grow. That one story, sad and full of loss, spawned many more whose origins began in generations past and were handed down. It was a story that echoed round the walls of the broken child's cave. Julie's budding child clothed in a long turquoise silk dress, her basket filled with the seeds of her life's promise clutched tight in her hand, stood at the entrance to the cave.

Peering into the dim light of the cave, I knew I couldn't enter. I had to protect my seeds.

Awareness is their nourishment, tears their water, emotion their juice. Consciousness is their flesh, awakening their sunlight, Julie's bodily temple the vessel they flourish in. The seeds wait for the perfect combination of Julie, time and place for them to bear fruit. It is a mother's task to tend them with loving care and provide a garden for them to grown in.

I saw a child kneeling in front of a wicker picnic basket, dressed in blue flannelette pyjamas with little white daisies all over them and a hole in the crotch. She took out a football, a pair of underpants stained with blood, her handkerchief with pretty pink and blue flowers on it also stained with blood. A white envelope fluttered about the basket in amongst some empty beer bottles. The child grabbed it, plonking the football over it so it wouldn't blow away. Then she set about straightening the plates and cutlery behind buckled straps coming away from the seams.

As my eyes adjusted to the dim light, I saw Nana walking the thin edge between the light and darkness inside the cave. She was picking up citrines and chipping away old shells, bones and feathers that were encrusted in the walls and rocks that stuck out of the floor of the cave. There were baskets filled with dirty laundry, their handles worn, alongside other battered ones, some filled with beer bottles. One large cane basket bleached and dried with age but as sturdy as the day it was bought, stood out amongst them; Nana's basket. Nana knocked it over as she tried to lift her leg up to step over it. A bunch of yellowed papers fell out. She picked up a handful of them, flipping through the telegrams and letters until she stopped at one with a governmental letter head. As she stared at it, I heard a familiar squabble I knew well that Nana had heard over and over between my mother and her brother and sisters when they were growing up but could never settle.

"You're not my sister," my mother said.

"Yes I am," said her sister Eileen.

"Joyce is my sister", my mother shot back.

"She's mine too", said Eileen. "She was my sister before you came along. If it wasn't for you, me and Bob wouldn't be living with Nana. It's all your fault. I wish you were never born then Mum would still be here. I want my mother". Eileen burst into tears. Bob started crying too. "Bob and I are poor. You and Joyce have everything. It isn't fair. Everything was perfect before you came along. You took my sister away from me. Why couldn't Nana look after you so me and Bob and Joyce all got to stay together and live with Auntie", Eileen sobbed.

My mother, their baby sister, the centre of their squabble, burst into tears too. This squabble didn't belong in Nana's basket but she adopted it along with two of her sister's children, my mother and her sister Joyce.

An elderly woman dressed in a navy cotton frock and black lace-up shoes, her hair in a bun, sat on a large flat rock, a small sturdy hamper in her lap. Nana came over, sat beside her and asked, "What could we do Mum? We tried so hard to make the children feel they weren't missing out. Eileen and Bob felt they had and their sisters hadn't, despite our best efforts to share the love between them the same".

"All we could do was show them love, care, and kindness Lil", her mother replied.

Nana and her mother watched my mother and her siblings standing there looking lost and apart even though they were together. Nana went up to them, pulled a white hankie out of her pocket and dried their tears. Both the women gave each child a hug and a smile, then sent them off to play amongst the crystals and feathers. They wrapped their arms round each other's waists and watched the children clamber over some rocks, their squabble forgotten for now.

Nana bent over the fire poking at the ashes with a stick, while her mother filled the kettle from the stream. Once the kettle was on, I heard Nana call the child in the pyjamas over to the fire. The child took out some plates and cutlery from her picnic basket laying them beside

Nana's pot of tea and enamel mugs. Nana held her in her arms stroking her hair as they sat on the rock together.

Men's voices ... Grandad. My father's. Uncle Alan. There were others too, Grandad's mates from the war. The men stood in a small circle with him beers in their hands, listening to another one of Grandad's war stories.

The child in the pyjamas called out, "Where's my sister?" the question shrilling throughout the cave making Nana and her mother look up. She was making a fairy ring, her teddy bear propped up beside her against a rock, oblivious, hidden in the shadows though close enough to be in Nana and her mother's sight. Her thick wavy brown hair fell across her round, pale face as she fossicked in her lolly bag. She pulled out a jelly baby and a strawberry kiss which she popped into her mouth.

Auntie Eileen from the other side of my mother's split-in-two family joined Nana who she called Auntie Lil and her grandmother who raised her, by the fire. She accepted a cup of tea from them with a smile. My cousins Kathy and Jane who had the same thick wavy hair and blue eyes as their mother, put the skipping rope they'd been playing with back in Auntie Eileen's basket. They took a little cake out of the metal tin offered by our great-grandmother and a plate from the child in the pyjamas to put it on, looking pleased, as such a treat was not often shared by both sides of the family.

Kathy and Jane looked around for their two aunties, Joyce and my mother I guess to see if they were going to join them. I saw them. They were in another part of the cave unaware of the afternoon tea, doing the washing and mending. Empty pill bottles rolled about them gathering speed in the breeze, until they were lifted and deposited in amongst the empty beer bottles lying near the men's feet.

A slippery pyramid of beer bottles lay stacked up against the wall of the cave between the circle of men where the war stories were being told and the kitchen table where my father's family were having their get together. There was my father tall and tanned, dressed in a brown suit with matching hat and shiny brown lace up shoes he wore to work as a detective at an inner city police station, alternating between the two locations. He took the empties to add to the pyramid, bringing more beer to the circle and to his family at the table, their drunken voices bouncing off the walls of the cave.

Listening to the squabbling of my mother's family and hearing the drunken voices of my father's, I pulled my basket of seeds to my heart wondering how I was going to keep them safe, knowing I had to find a way. I walked back to the willow tree that stood beside the cave, parted the branches and stepped inside with my basket.

ACT 1

childhood memories

... scene 1 ...

the flower girl

setting
under the budding child's willow tree of dreams

In the weeping green softness that draped to the ground in a curtain of invisibility, the sun peeked through its veil of quiet and into the earth, warming my grey blanket I laid on the ground. Looking around I eyed my childhood treasures with delight, eager to hold them once again and revisit the pleasurable memories that were joined to them that filled my heart with joy. Under my willow tree in the front garden where I escaped to from the house as a child I was free to daydream about all the possibilities for my future life and who I might become within them.

My favourite ballet books and pale pink ballet shoes lay together under my colored pencils, a book of hairstyles I'd sketched and cut out of the Women's Weekly magazine beside them. My ballet case was filled with Barbie doll clothes, my jewellery box with the ballerina who danced inside it, in a tangle of necklaces and rings. A Vegemite glass full of paper letters, numbers and a pen for playing 'Ouija', sat on an unwanted school desk my mother had organised for me to use to play my favourite game 'School' at home. On top of the pile on the desk, stood a globe of the world that needed pumping up, broken pieces of chalk that had fallen out of the box onto it making it dusty. My blackboard was clean though, standing on its wooden easel with its duster. A hairbrush with a white handle and a small round mirror encased in a pink swirled patterned handle lay under the easel.

The long strands of green leaves shivered as they danced along the ground. Caught in the sunlight rays of copper flecked with the colors of the rainbow filtered through the spaces in the branches making me stop to follow their flickering. Out of their hue a smiling face appeared ringed in that copper light.

My beloved Susan stood there dressed in her going away outfit she wore the day she married; a smart two-piece suit with matching coat, hat and bag in warm brown tones. I put my basket down on the desk and smiled back at Susan like she did when the photographer had asked her to on Susan's wedding day. For me that was an extra special day.

Across the hall in the other half of Nana and Grandad's house rented from them where she lived with her parents, Susan stood at the lounge room window in a full length white satin dress, a long train stretched across the small room like a pool of shiny water. Her hair was curled up around her short veil attached to a ring the same as mine.

The willow tree leaves swished across my head. I took off my flower girl's gloves and picked up the silk turquoise ring out of my jewellery box that had crowned me flower girl for the day. I swung it over and over my fingers spinning it like my insides were spinning with nerves on Susan's wedding day.

I'd held Susan's hand as we stood in front of the pot plant on its tall wrought iron stand, a wedding present from our family. The photographer asked us to look at each other and smile. That was easy. I loved Susan.

I loved Auntie Helen too. She'd come over to Nana's house to do my hair. She opened up her beauty case on the polished dining room table setting up her combs, bobby pins, brushes and hairspray in a neat row. With a smile she asked me to sit, which I did by lowering myself with great care because I didn't want to crease or catch my long silk turquoise colored dress on Nana's chair. Mum who'd helped dress me watched and told me to stay still until Auntie Helen finished.

She brushed my long brown hair with light strokes and threaded it through the donut shaped ring pulling it up to the top of my head. Weaving my hair through the ring, she pinned and sprayed in a smooth rhythm that didn't jerk my head about like when Mum did my hair. Satisfied the bun sat in place Auntie Helen picked up the matching silk turquoise ring and placed it over my top knot, crowning me flower girl for the day. She held up a mirror, leaned in close to me and showed me how my hair looked. It looked like a grown-ups. Nana came in looking pleased with how I looked asking me to follow her to her bedroom so I could have a look at myself in her full length mirror. I looked as beautiful as Auntie Helen did in her pale blue bridesmaid's dress in Mum's wedding album.

Auntie Helen looked like my Barbie doll she'd bought for me. My Barbie stood with perfect posture on a stand by my bed dressed in different outfits Auntie Helen had bought for her. Each night I brushed Barbie's blonde hair back and placed a blue band over it after I'd dressed her for bed wearing a powder blue full length negligee with matching sheer brunch coat and slippers with high heels and pompoms on them. Barbie looked as beautiful as Auntie Helen did.

Just before we left for the church, Mum handed me a pair of short turquoise gloves to put on as I hopped into a long white car with white ribbons tied to it and sat in the back beside Susan's bridesmaid. As we drove off I waved out the window at the neighbours standing on the footpath there to have a look, just like the Queen did on the way to a ball.

I loved playing 'Queen'. I'd reach up on the top shelf of Mum's wardrobe and pull down Nana's old hat and a pair of her gloves, go through Mum's shoes, clothes and jewellery box choosing what took my fancy. I needed something to tie around my waist for a train for this game. An old sheet from the hall cupboard did the job.

My little sister was walking her pram filled with dolls around the garden. "Stop your play and carry my train", I ordered. She left her dolls and picked up the train. Following behind me as I walked down the driveway with my head held high, she kept bumping into me when I stopped for a moment here and there to speak to my subjects and hurry my ladies-in-waiting along.

"My dolls are crying", she said eager to end the game, dropping my train and rushing to them, picking one up out of the pram. She rocked the baby in her arms to comfort her then changed her, wrapping her up tight in a soft baby blanket Mum had once wrapped her in. She kissed the baby and placed her with tenderness back in the pram.

When I entered the church, I strode straight down the aisle holding my small woven basket of creamy fragrant gardenias without waiting for Susan. Mum whisked me back to the entrance, the guest's smiling at me. I waved to my sister who was sitting on Nana's knee. I hadn't planned to upstage the bride. When Susan stood arm in arm with her Dad Paddy at the start of the aisle, this time I led the procession as rehearsed, back straight, head in the air, step by slow measured step to the altar where Ray and his best man were waiting in black suits.

> After the service, Julie and her mother posed for a photo outside the church. She wore black gloves, a fascinator, and a weariness round her mouth that showed in a thin smile that didn't reach her dull blue eyes, nor match the bright sheen of her smart green dress which Julie, though only a young child was old enough to notice.

I picked up my worn down pencils their lead broken, that lay on top of my sketch book of hairstyles brushing the willow branches away that scraped my desk. Dropping the pencils back into the torn box I flipped the lid over them and put them on my desk. I slid to one side of my desk opening my sketch book. A blue hair roller split apart fell out of it. Rollers. Ouch! My head prickled at the thought of them. All those mornings of concert nights when Mum put my hair in rollers before school and a scarf over them to make sure they didn't fall out. She'd arrive at school at lunchtime unannounced with her head full of rollers covered in a scarf too. I'd see her striding across the netball court in the direction of the shelter sheds so I'd duck behind them and head for the steps to the bottom oval but she'd get there first and cut me off. I was caught. I wanted to run away to play with the boys but I couldn't. I had to suffer for my art, the dance, just like Dame Margot Fonteyn. Mum whipped off my scarf and pulled, yanked, twisted and pinned the rollers back in place, then fastened the scarf tight around my head again. They cut into my scalp by the end of the day and the scarf rubbed making my head hot and itchy. I couldn't wait to get to the concert hall to pull them out.

On concert nights Mum was in charge of hair. She commanded backstage with a mouthful of bobby pins, a thick comb and can of hairspray. "Stand still!", she ordered. She combed, teased, pinned and sprayed the girls' hair until they looked as beautiful as the mothers who came to my house to have their hair done after school.

After escorting a mother from down the road to the salon; a kitchen chair set up in the lounge room, I wrapped the plastic sheet over her dress and clipped it around her neck. Mum chatted to her while I watched, ready to pass the papers and rollers lying in the plastic tray when she put out her hand. She even let me rinse the perm while the mother stood with her head tipped forward over the bathroom basin. It left a stain even after a good scrubbing. Mum and I worked our way around the mother removing the soggy papers and rollers after the final rinse. The smell burnt my nostrils and made my eyes water but it didn't matter because I loved being Mum's apprentice. I passed her the comb and brush, then the hairspray from a tray behind the chair. Sometimes she let me do the final spray after the mother agreed her hair was done to her liking. Once she'd inspected it at Mum's dressing table mirror, the mother smiling as she turned her head from side to side pleased with her new hairdo, Mum and I smiled too.

Picking up my sketch book of hairstyles off the dusty desk under my willow tree I flipped through the hairdos I'd cut out of the Women's Weekly, my source of inspiration. I came to the ones I'd drawn myself and smiled. There was that style with the blonde hair, scribbled curls done with yellow pencil faster and faster round the woman's face until they ended on the top of her head. Using a brown pencil I'd drawn a fancy clip to hold the do together. The other style was on a brunette. I'd given her long hair flowing down the page with a little curl on the end. I'd sip on orange cordial taking another biscuit from my plate as I admired the fabulous hairdos I'd created.

Lost in the creation of my hairstyles, I'd jumped when Mum parted the leaves of my willow tree leaned in and told me to come inside: the only way I would leave my tree before dark. When she saw what I was doing with the hairdos, she snatched the book out of my hands. "There's no money in hairdressing. It's long hours for little pay and you have to stand all day. You need a secure job. Come inside". Annoyed she'd interrupted me, I gathered up my things in a stink and followed Mum to the front door.

Sitting on my grey blanket I went through the rest of the hairdos in my sketch book the pictures brittle with age and faded now, the hairstyles dated. I pulled my long turquoise dress up my legs a little way to make myself more comfortable. A book with a photo of a ballerina on the front caught my eye. It was my prized book about Dame Margot Fonteyn. I closed my book of hairdos and opened the other book looking for my favourite page. I turned the pages one by one that I'd studied with the different movements and costumes my favourite ballerina would wear for the ballets she performed in. I found the page I was looking for, Dame Margot en pointe with full poise and grace in a short white tutu, her hair pulled back tight just like my flower girl's bun. I'd tried my friend Debbie's points on once and ended up wobbling all over the place. Dancing was hard to do. I wanted to be the best ballerina in the world just like Dame Margot.

Putting my book down, curling and swaying in my flower girl's dress, my arms reaching up towards the top of my tree, neck outstretched as graceful as a swan's I rose on my tippy toes, making an arch over my head and fluttered my feathers like the swans I'd fed bread to with Susan at the Botanical Gardens in the city. They were elegant and graceful like Dame Margot Fonteyn with their long white necks and the way they glided across the water.

My love of ballet began only because the doctor told Mum I was too skinny and needed to build my legs up. I was glad he had. I loved ballet. Susan knew I did too. She took me to the ballet for a special performance as a surprise, my very first.

Susan and I sat in our seats for the afternoon matinee at the grand old theatre in the city. The red velvet curtains swept back and the conductor deep in the orchestra pit waved his baton and flipped the pages of his music as the ballerinas in long tutus and feathered caps glided across the stage en pointe.

A woman in a short tutu appeared in the spotlight. I grabbed Susan's hand and stared in wonder as Dame Margot Fonteyn began to dance, even more beautiful than in the pictures of my ballet book, Nureyev even more handsome and strong as he partnered my idol.

My presence, the Temple Woman, began to form within the budding child expressed in the graceful movements of the ballerina dancing under the branches of the willow tree and in the shaft of sunlight that lit her way down the aisle on the day Susan and Ray were married.

The budding child was oblivious to me because Susan was her light for whom she shone brightest and best then. She was the effervescence that spilled over into her life like bubbles in a lemonade that quenches a big thirst on a hot summer's day. Fizzy bubbles that popped with chatter and laughter, giggles and playful fun every happy childhood needs.

Being her mother's apprentice as she watched the school mother's primp and preen in front of the mirror after their hair was done and being Susan's flower girl fostered the desire to pluck these seeds of femininity from her basket and plant them in her garden to grow her inner beauty. The opportunity was snatched away as the budding child's mother snatched away her book of hairdos and demanded she leave the intimacy of her weeping green world where she began to express my essence; the Temple Woman she would one day become.

... scene 2 ...

playing ouija

Kneeling up to put my treasured ballet book back on my dusty old desk I knocked over the Vegemite glass full of paper letters and numbers from my 'Ouija' game. I lay them down on top of my desk in a semi-circle, with the words 'Yes' and 'No' above them and put the glass over them. As I did, the air swirled through my willow tree, the branches dipping and swaying like swishing tulle petticoats under a fancy dress. I jumped up stomping my feet. I was a gypsy girl strutting and twirling, the ends of my embroidered skirt flashing a hint of white petticoats in a whirl of bangles and jangles with the rest of my dance troupe. Falling down laughing, righting the paper numbers and letters from my 'Ouija' game with one hand, I scrambled to sit up again.

Oh how I loved playing games. I had Scrabble and Monopoly, my sister had Mouse Trap and Ker Plunk. All my friends were given Twister for their birthdays. We played it at their parties. It was fun. I wanted Twister too.

Debbie had a new game her Mum and Dad gave her for her birthday. I didn't know what I was in for when she invited me to go and play it with her that day after school.

The back fence of Debbie's house ran along the driveway where the teachers parked their cars. The yard was filled with an orchard of lemon, apple and orange trees. Debbie's mother let me pick some fruit sometimes which she put into a brown paper bag. She flipped it over and made two handles in the corners to help me to carry it home.

You couldn't go in her front door as the hallway overflowed with boxes of material. The lounge room was the sewing room with a table piled high with colorful sequins, tulle, satins and ribbons. Dad called her 'Dancing Debbie'. Her mother was always making costumes for her and other members of our dance troupe, including me. She competed in the big ballet competitions as well as the ones we entered in with our dance troupe. She was short like me so even en pointe she would never make a ballerina but she was graceful like one. Debbie's mother made some room at the end of the table to set the game up and we sat down. It had all the letters of the alphabet on it and numbers from one to ten in a semi-circle across it. At the top were the words 'Yes' and 'No'.

As Debbie set it up, I asked her about it.
"What's this game called?"
"Ouija ".
"What a strange name. How do you play it?"
"You ask questions and you get answers. It really works".
"But how?"
"We think of a question, then we put our hands on the disc and wait for it to go to the letters to spell the answer".

A spelling game. Goodie! I loved spelling.

Debbie placed the black plastic horseshoe shaped disc on the board, put her hand on it and said to me, "Put your hand on mine. So what are we going to ask? I know. Will we win our ballet competition?"

I thought that was a good one because Debbie and I were in the same dances. We'd been rehearsing them for weeks. Debbie asked the question. I waited. I didn't take my eyes off the board. Nothing happened. This was dumb. As I started to pull my hand away, the disc started moving.

"You did that!", I accused.

"No I didn't!"

This game was making me nervous

"Let's do it again". Before I could say no, Debbie placed her hand over mine. She asked again, "Will we win our ballet competition?" This time the disc started to move a bit jerkily to the letters 'y' then 'e', then 's'. I wasn't pushing it and Debbie said she wasn't. "See it works". Debbie looked pleased with herself.

"That's spooky". My tummy felt all funny. I pulled my hand away.

"Do you want another turn?" Debbie had our hands on the disc before I could answer and asked, "Does Craig like Julie?" I didn't want to know. "Y-e-s". This time the disc slid to the letters. "Yuk". I pulled a face.

Lucky for me Debbie's Mum came in and interrupted us as I didn't want to know any more about Craig. She said to Debbie, "Pack that game away. I have to finish sewing your costume and I need all the table".

Not long after that game with Debbie, I'd made good use of a wet Saturday afternoon that'd left me wondering what to do. I pulled the grey blanket off the top of the kitchen table and crawled out from under my cubby with my coloring book and pencils, tired of drawing. I decided to play that Ouija game even if it was a bit scary. I went to the junk drawer and found some scrap paper, scissors and a blue pen. Sitting up at the kitchen table, I cut the paper into small squares and wrote the letters of the alphabet on them, then the 'yes' and 'no' and the numbers from one to ten arranging them in a semi-circle on the table. I needed something to put my hands on to move to the letters. A Vegemite glass slid well on the kitchen table because the surface was very shiny and slippery. Opening the cupboard the glasses were kept in I found one up the back corner and put it on the table.

Now I needed my sister. She turned her shoulder when I tried to pull her up by the arm away from the TV.

"Come on you'll like it". I turned off the TV.

"Don't ... Mum!"

"You can have some lollies after".

That got her moving. She followed me to the kitchen as I explained how the game worked. Sitting at the table, she put her hand on the glass over mine as I asked,

"What's the name of my sister's teacher?"

The glass felt stuck, then it started kangaroo hopping, then gliding like Dame Margot Fonteyn to all the letters that made Miss Brown. My sister's eyes grew big and she said, "Do it again".

We did over and over while Mum ironed. She liked it when we played well together, so she was happy too. It was our new game. We played it after school, on weekends and when Mum and Dad had friends over. When Dad wasn't working Friday night was the night friends were invited over for drinks.

After tea, Mum busied herself in the kitchen, sliding a combination of cheese cubes and pickled onions onto tooth picks. She stood them up in the middle of a circle of asparagus spears wrapped in white bread and prunes wrapped in bacon all pierced with toothpicks too. Vol-au-vents filled with canned salmon and tinned corn soup mixture were baking in the oven, along with some party pies. She got out a small cane basket, lined it with a couple of white serviettes and tipped a large bag of potato chips into it for the children. Glasses were lined up on the bench, the fridge filled with pineapple and raspberry lemonade for us, beer for the men and ginger beer for the ladies to go with their Cinzano.

"Julie, look after your guests", Mum said as she closed the kitchen door. I went straight to the junk drawer to get the Ouija letters and torch then some matches and candles from the cupboard, placing the candles around the room in some Vegemite jars and lighting them. My sister spread the letters on the table. She knew what to do now. I turned to my guests, "Come on everyone. Sit down. We're going to play a game". As they sat down at the table I popped the basket of chips in the middle. It was a squash, some of the littler ones had to kneel up on their chairs to see what was going on. I turned off the kitchen lights. The shadows the candlelight made danced up the walls. Big pairs of eyes were looking at me. Turning on the torch I stuck it under my chin making spooky noises and my scariest face. A couple of the kids squealed. One asked, "Let me have a turn". I gave the torch to the girl next to me and said, "Let's see who can pull the scariest face". I wanted them to have fun. Everyone had a turn. There were lots of giggles and more squeals. "Now we're going to play the game. Put your hands on the glass". They did as I asked and all leaned forward so they could reach it. I stood the torch on the table. It lit up the ceiling. I looked at their faces flickering in the candlelight. It was so spooky. One of the candles hissed and spat. We all jumped. This was fun.

"I'm going to ask a question and the glass is going to move to the letters and spell the answer. They nodded at me. "How many boys are there in the room?" The glass started to jerk and lurch all over the table. My guests started to accuse each other.

"You did that".

"No, you did".

"Stop it. You're wrecking the game".

Their squabbling was annoying me. "Quieten down you lot". They did as I asked. We tried again. The glass warmed up, wandering all over the table. The squeals got louder as the glass went faster. I heard footsteps. I blinked when the kitchen light switched on.

"What's going on here Julie? Pack that game away now".

"Yes Mum". The night's excitement was over. Asking my guests who wanted a lemonade I set to pouring them drinks, then with my sister's help packed the game away.

It wasn't long before my sister and I found the opportunity to play 'Ouija' again. Mum popped over the road for a chat with a neighbour while Dad was in bed asleep after a night shift. We didn't want our parents to know what we were asking about. We wanted to know if the three children who'd been abducted, were still alive. It'd been all over the papers and on the TV. The two girls were close to the same age as us. I'd be so scared if that happened to me. Mum and Dad told us not to talk to strangers. Our teachers did too. They told us lots of times.

I set up the kitchen table with the letters and we placed our hands on the glass. We both asked, "Are those three children who were abducted, still alive?" The glass started to move under our hands as usual. We let it wander all over the table. All of a sudden a cold wind whooshed into the room. There were no windows open in the kitchen and the doors were closed but the kitchen window started rattling hard. It was a hot day so the outside blinds were down to keep the room cool. The glass flew out from under our hands and smashed into little pieces on the floor. We never played that game again. We never talked about it either.

I, the Temple Woman knew how to wield this power of inner sight and inner knowing as would the budding child one day. I also knew this was not a frivolous game for children to play. The two sisters were at a tender age, too young to understand the power of seances and the forces they could unleash in the wrong hands but old enough to know now that Ouija wasn't another harmless childhood game they could enjoy playing together. The use of the Ouija board was a connection to a realm with a life of its own and to be avoided unless approached with the awareness and knowledge of the clairvoyant who knew how to wield it.

There were gentler ways for Julie's mother to nurture the budding child's seeds of inner sight and inner knowing with loving care so she may plant them in the garden her mother provided for her, than leaving her to play Ouija with her sister while she ironed their clothes.

... scene 3 ...

seeds of ancient memories

I stuffed the pieces of paper and the pen back in the Vegemite glass. Laying them beside me, I lifted the lid of my desk pushing some leaves away from my tree that'd blown in over it, tickling my flower girl's bun. My school books were stacked up in a pile to one side of the desk. The brown paper Mum bound them in just before the start of each school year still felt smooth as I picked up each one. I admired the now crinkled different photos of my favourite birds, animals and flowers I'd cut out of the Women's Weekly pasting them on with great care at the end of the summer holidays.

I wanted to be a teacher when I grew up because I loved playing 'School'. Mum encouraged it as Dad had wanted to be a teacher but he didn't have the education, leaving school early.

When the principal said they were going to throw out some old desks Mum asked if she could have one for me. My own desk. It would be just like school!

She organised for a couple of boys in my class to bring the desk to my house one night after school. Standing at the front gate waiting for it to arrive I wished the boys would hurry up as I wanted to play my favourite game before tea. My footy mates Craig and Andy appeared at the bottom of the street. They dropped the desk at their feet using the opportunity to have a rest and catch their breath.

They kept dropping it as they made their way up the street yelling at each other as it fell on their toes, so funny to watch. I ran inside to get Mum. She wiped her hands on her apron and followed me outside. I stood behind her letting her do the talking.

"Come on boys this way. You're doing a good job". They brought it around to the back of the house and dropped it on the playroom floor, red faced and puffing. I rushed into the lounge room to tell my sister.

"Hey the desk's arrived!" Of course she didn't even look up so I danced in front of the TV. "Come on. You've had your turn watching the telly. Come and play with me". She never wanted to but who else was going to be the student? I'd played with a pretend student until she was big enough to know how to. That wasn't half as much fun. I wasn't going to let her get away with it. I pulled her away from the TV and she followed me to the playroom where I pointed at the desk. "Look. That will be better to sit in than the kitchen chair. Help me put the books in. Which side do you want?" I slid in beside her. "You be the teacher for a change. I want to sit in the desk".

"I don't know what to do".

"Yes you do. You go to school. Go on". She started to tap the board with the ruler and say the tables. "No. I'm supposed to say the tables not you. Just point". I started to say them but she joined in. It was no good. "Go and sit down. I'll do it". I grabbed the ruler pointing at the three times table and she repeated it after me. "Well done. Now we are going to do some spelling". I wrote cat on the blackboard with the white chalk. I pointed to it and she spelt it, c-a-t. "Get out your book and write it down then draw a picture". She lifted the lid of the desk taking out the exercise book and a box of colored pencils.

"Hurry you're too slow. We have lots to get through today". I loved using my big teacher's voice.

"Can I go when I have?" As usual it didn't take long for her to be sick of the game.

"Not until you're dismissed". She hung her head scribbling another picture. "Come and show the class".

As she slid out of the desk Mum came into the room. "Julie pack that game away and help me set the table for tea".

"Class dismissed", I said to my sister's back. I heard the lounge room doors shut and the man on the TV talking through the wall. I couldn't wait to play 'School' tomorrow.

I went through the stack of school books inside my desk looking for my Social Studies books, the dust between them rising up through the rays of sunlight filtering down from the top of my tree. Social Studies was one of my favourite subjects. I found the one I was looking for, my Grade 3 one. It had a photo of a kangaroo on it hopping across the desert like in the movie reels at school.

Every Friday afternoon my teacher Miss Pritchard took our class to the projection room to watch a movie. Sitting on the rotting floorboards in a draught I'd clapped my quiet happy clap to myself when I saw an aboriginal face flicker on the screen.

The children laughed playing out in the hot sun in the dirt and dust. Some of them ran down to the water hole to join their cousins for a swim, making me want to laugh with them and I did, inside. They were having so much fun. They didn't stop laughing even with all those blowflies crawling up their noses and into their eyes, not even trying to shoo them away. Blowflies were the enemy in my house. Mum rushed for the fly swat as soon as one appeared. Or she made me do the swatting. All that flapping about for a fly!

Those children were so lucky. They got to run about in bare feet all the time. I fiddled with the buckles of my sandals. They were digging into my feet and gave me blisters even when I wore socks. Mum said that would help but it didn't, it just made my feet sweat more. Putting a Band-aid over them didn't stop the rubbing either. I hated it when I went outside to play and Mum said "get something on your feet". I'd wait until she couldn't see me and throw my shoes on the ground. I liked to let my feet get used to the hot road. "Ooch, aach", I said as I hopped from one foot to the other. I was dancing like the aborigines. They called it a corroboree. The aboriginal people didn't wear much. It was so hot. Lucky them. Bathers and bare feet, my favourite way to dress.

The mothers and grandmothers smiled a lot but the fathers and grandfathers didn't. That's because hunting was hard work. They had to walk a long way to find food to bring back to camp for the women and children. They threw their boomerangs to knock down kangaroos and emus which they killed with their spears.

The women gathered vegetables and berries in wooden dishes they called a coolamon, carrying them on their heads back to camp. They found white worms called witchetty grubs dropping them into their mouths while they were still wriggling! We all squealed. Miss Pritchard told us to "shoosh".

I really liked the houses they lived in - called mia-mias, made out of the bark of trees. They peeled it off and put sheets of it over branches from the same tree then tied them all together. Everyone helped make them even the children. The mia-mia's had a dirt floor and an opening just like a tent. In the summer I loved sleeping outside in my Cowboys and Indians tent.

Back in the classroom Miss Pritchard said we had a special project to do. She told us to go home and build a picture in a shoebox about the movie and show the class how we made it. I was going to make a mia-mia! At afternoon recess I ran down to the bottom oval to the gum trees looking for bits for it. Some twigs and bark lying around were just right. I put them in my school bag on the way back to class. I couldn't wait to get home and start my picture. Miss Pritchard let me choose some cellophane, so I took red and yellow for the fire. She said we could take our colored pencils home too, which I did.

I jigged up and down behind Mum trying to look over her shoulder as she pulled out towels and lifted blankets in the hall cupboard looking for a shoebox. I emptied the contents of my school bag onto the kitchen table and stood the box on its side staring at the empty space. Cutting the cellophane into smaller squares I scrunched them up and pasted them to the bottom, twisting the tops so the flames leapt from the fire. I liked it. It looked good. I glued, stuck and tied the string to the bark and twigs so my mia-mia could stand up all on its own at the back behind the fire. Next, how to get it into the box. Oh no! I was squashing the fire so I took it out. It was all a mess. I wanted to get it all done so I could leave it next to my bed and look at it before I went to sleep. I cut out some aborigines from the lid of the shoebox. I found my brown pencil and drew their faces putting big smiles on all of them.

Miss Pritchard liked my diorama so much she asked me to leave it on display on the table at the front of the blackboard. I couldn't stop looking at it and forgot to listen to her. I was with the aboriginal children laughing and playing in the hot sun in the places at the top of my jigsaw map of Australia.

Remembering the aboriginal movie I'd watched at school and the diorama Miss Pritchard liked so much made me think about when I used to visit Pa in the country with my family and that picnic on a cold winter's day. I lay down on my grey blanket under my tree wriggling to get comfortable. I closed my eyes and the aroma of warm bread filled my nostrils. The fog hadn't lifted and thick white frost covered the ground when we'd set off that morning. We'd stopped at a large lake on the way. The wind rushed over it making little waves on the water. The small boats tied to the bottom of the lake were empty and no fishermen stood at the water's edge. It was cosy and warm inside the bakery across the road from the jetty. The white loaves of bread were just out of the oven. The lady had wrapped them in white paper stuck with sticky tape. I used one of them for hand and cheek warmers until Mum told me to get that bread off my face and stop being silly.

"I'm cold."

"Well get in the car then". I did as I was told.

The seats, the ground and the trees at the picnic spot were dripping wet, the air fresh and clean, the sun starting to come out from behind the clouds. My sister and I blew fog out of our mouths. I said, "Let's see who can blow the furthest". She started blowing harder.

"Go and get some wood for the fire", Auntie Win called to us. She pulled her knitted beanie over her short permed hair. Her glasses fogged up as she sipped on some hot coffee from the thermos. We wrapped our coats around our jumpers and check slacks, pulled our gloves on tight, then started looking for twigs on the ground near the picnic bench.

Auntie Bev, Dad's sister, took the blackened large tin can out of the boot of the car, used over the fire on picnics many times. Dad made billy tea in it. Auntie Bev carried it down to the stream filling it up with fresh water. She put it down beside the fire pit clapping her hands to try and keep them warm. She took a packet of cigarettes out of her coat pocket offering one to my father lighting it, then hers. They didn't look like brother and sister, Auntie Bev short with a fair complexion and blue eyes like Pa.

Dad scrunched up the newspaper he'd taken out of the boot and laid it on the ashes in the barbecue pit. I liked it when he poked the fire with a stick and the newspaper caught fire from the ashes like the aborigines did in the movie reels at school. They'd rubbed a stick fast in their hands between some gum leaves until they caught fire. Auntie Bev sprinkled a handful of tealeaves into the billy and put the lid on.

Dad and Pa took it in turns to flip the meat over on the barbecue with a metal slide. The fire hissed and spat as the fat from the meat sank through the metal griddle and dripped into the fire. Mum and Auntie Win busied themselves putting the lettuce, cheese and tomato salad they'd made at home on plates. My sister and I were more interested in gobbling up the fresh bread with a burnt sausage and some 'dead horse', Dad's word for tomato sauce.

Auntie Bev picked up the tea towel, lifted the billy lid and said, "Tea's ready".

My sister and I stood back holding hands. This was the scary bit. The others stood back too while Dad lifted the billy off the fire. He removed the lid, spinning the boiling billy in circles by its blackened handle. He stopped and said, "Tea's ready". I let out a deep breath. He never spilled a drop. How did he do that? We all sipped the hot tea out of old tin mugs. It tasted smoky good.

After lunch was the best part of the day, the boomerang throwing competition. Dad went first. He cocked his arm and with a big throw sent the boomerang flying through the air. I chased after it but by the time I'd turned around it'd already landed at my father's feet. How did he do that? "Show me. Show me. When is it going to be my turn?"

"In a minute. Out of the way. You'll know all about it if it hits you on the head".

I did as I was told for a second and then was off chasing it again. At last it was my turn. I cocked my arm just like Dad and threw it up in the air as hard as I could. Plop. It landed just past my feet. I tried again. It dropped on my feet. Ouch. It hurt! Even with desert boots on. That made the others laugh, and me even more determined to do it right. I tried again and again. It was such a heavy piece of wood for a little girl like me to throw but I threw it further and further with each try even though it didn't còme back. I gave it one last go. This time it worked! It flew through the air and landed at my feet just like it did for Dad even if I hadn't thrown it as far as he could. My family clapped and cheered.

Dad gave me a glass of lemonade as a reward for all my hard work. Wait till I tell all my friends back at school!

I opened my eyes and stretched on my grey blanket looking up to the top of my tree. It could be a mia-mia just that mine was made out of willow leaves. That holiday visit was a special one because after the picnic Pa promised he'd take me to see the cave paintings again before we went home, a place just a few white people knew about and had permission to visit.

Dad had left very early in the morning to go rabbit shooting with his mates. Auntie Win was leaving for work as I went into the kitchen to have breakfast. Pa had already eaten and was getting his old faded yellow FJ Holden with the cracked red leather seats, started.

After breakfast, my sister and I climbed in the back, Mum in the front beside Pa. My tights caught in the cracks when I wriggled in my seat to get comfortable. The seats smelt liked the old worn red leather punching bag that hung on a broken beam in the wooden lean-to that passed for a carport. Pa used it after work. I stood and watched as he got his eye in and took aim and the bag banged about with his blows. Dad said he used to be a boxer.

The site with the cave paintings was a short way out of town on a large property. We always stopped at the farmhouse first to say hello and let the owners know we were going to visit the caves. They gave my sister and I biscuits and lemonade, Mum and Pa a cup of tea in their rundown kitchen.

The caves were right down the back of the property through several paddocks with cows and bulls. My sister and I knelt up on the back seat looking for bulls while Pa hopped out, opened the gate and drove into the paddock closing the gate behind us. Mum kept watch too. The bull was walking towards the gate with some of the cows following him. "Hurry up Pa, he's coming!" we yelled through the open windows banging on the back window in case he hadn't heard. He had. He ran to the car slamming the door shut. Lucky Pa was a sprint champion when he was young. When we came to the last gate it was shut too but I jumped out first as usual and opened it looking around at this place I loved. The tall gum trees, the big old boulders all shining in the sun, the smell of fresh manure and the soft loving eyes of the cows watching us as we hurried across the paddock to the caves. I couldn't see any bulls. Pa left the car running and the doors open just in case we had to make a quick dash when we'd finished exploring. I hoped the car wouldn't run out of petrol. Then we'd be stuck. I sprinted to the boulders as fast as I could. Running must have been in my family's blood. I was a sprint champion too like Pa. It was too hard for me to get up on the boulders so I waited for the others to get a hand up. I wished they'd hurry!

Pa gave me a leg up. He gripped each of our hands until we were all standing up on the ledge. I turned around and there were the paintings. Kangaroos, emus, stick people. I drew stick people too when Miss Pritchard asked us to draw a picture with people in it. I wasn't very good at drawing.

It was cool in the cave no matter what time of the year we visited it. I could feel the walls close in on me giving me a chummy hug. I hugged them back with my heart.

Pa told us, "These paintings were done a long time ago. They are made with the colors of dirt and rocks. The aborigines ground them into a paste and painted the people and animals on these walls that were special to them. They tell the story of their people for others to see who visit this site. If you know how to read these paintings, they can tell you where to find food and what sort, where the closest waterhole is and to make sure there's plenty of food and shelter for all their people. The paintings tell about The Dreamtime and show a map to find the way back to the stars".

I never tired of hearing these stories even though I didn't know what it all meant. To me it sounded like a wonderful adventure like the aboriginal children had in the movie reels at school. I never wanted to leave when Pa said it was time to go. The only way I would was with a promise of a next time which Pa always made and kept.

"Bye cows! Bye paintings! Bye mountains!" I waved at them all from my rocky lookout high on the ledge. My voice grew bigger and louder and you could hear it all over the place. So I did it again.

Stepping back into the daylight the sun was so strong it made me blink. I ran to the car looking out for bulls and hopped in watching out the back window until the boulders were a dot in the distance. I sat back in my seat keeping an eye out the window for more bulls until the farmhouse appeared.

I sat up on my grey blanket the aroma of warm bread still in my nostrils. I rubbed my eyes, the images of the paintings on the cave walls still there. As my eyes adjusted to the shafts of sunlight pouring down from the top of my tree, I knelt up and rummaged about inside my desk. Wedged in amongst a ruler and bits of chalk I found pieces of my jigsaw map of Australia, their edges worn. Picking up the board they fitted into and laying the pieces on top, I sat back on my blanket stretching my legs, my turquoise shoes peeking out of the entrance. Laying the board on my lap I chose one of the worn pieces I'd found, looking to see where it fitted. I'd done that jigsaw over and over again on a winter's day sitting on the floor in the lounge room my back to the warmth of the briquette heater. When I'd finished it I'd run my hands over the smooth pieces looking at all the names of the places on the top of the map I knew off by heart. Wyndham, Broome, Derby, The Kimberley. I wondered what it was like up there because my friend Dawn came from that part of Australia. She is aboriginal. Mum and Dad's friend's the Brady's adopted her when she was young because her family couldn't afford to look after her, Dad told me. Mr Brady could because he was a lawyer. They lived on a farm not that far away from our house.

We drove past the old stone church on the corner of their road and went down the steep hill. When I saw their gate I hoped Dawn was waiting outside for me but she wasn't this time. I looked around the yard as we drove in. She was down by the chicken coop. I wound down the window and called out to her. She'd seen me too. We waved to each other.

Sitting in the lounge room we smiled at each other while our parents talked about us, waiting for them to say we could go out to play. I followed Dawn to the chicken coop. We dug our hands into the dirt and hay on an egg hunt as the chickens scattered clucking and flapping about making us giggle. I loved the smell but I didn't like getting the poo on my hands. Dawn didn't care. She was really good at finding the eggs. We brushed the hay and dirt off ourselves before putting the eggs in a bucket which Dawn carried up to the house. Our parents were talking in the lounge room so they didn't hear the back fly-wire door open and the two of us putting the eggs in a green bowl on the kitchen table and sneak outside again.

I liked it when my sister played at a friend's place so it was just Dawn and me when we visited. Dawn was just like the girls in the movie reels at school but even more beautiful than them. She had big brown eyes, short curly hair and smooth chocolate colored skin. When she smiled her teeth looked whiter than mine. Her eyes sparkled sometimes when we played. Most of the time she didn't say much. She was a bit shy.

As the sun dropped down over the yard Dawn and I sat on the fence holding hands watching the kangaroos feeding on the stumpy grass in the paddocks, looking to the mountains beyond. I asked Dawn if she missed her parents. She started to cry. I put my arm around her. I didn't want to go home. I wished she lived with me. The kookaburras said goodbye to the day with their long throaty laughter as the chickens settled into their box in the coop. Our parents came out to the car, mine saying it was time to go. I couldn't wait till the next time I visited Dawn.

My heart warmed with the memories of the times I'd shared with Dawn. I took the board off my lap putting the completed puzzle back up on my desk. I lay down on my blanket, its warmth equal to the warmth in my heart returning to my day dreams about those places at the top of

Australia I wanted to visit one day, far away from where I lived way down at the bottom.

My day dreaming was broken by my globe of the world being swept off my desk by a willow branch. I blew into the air valve as hard as I could and my globe was plump and round again. I grabbed it spinning it hard the countries whizzing by, then put it on my knees, stopped it spinning and found Italy following its boot with my finger until I found Pompeii. I knelt down, put the globe at the entrance to my tree, spun it again stabbing my finger at Greece. My fingers walked over Athens and to the islands, tracing the shapes of them with my fingertip. I pulled some bangles in all colors of the rainbow out of my jewellery box stringing them up each arm, the sunlight coming in through the branches of my tree splashing on the sparkling flecks of color in each bangle. I found my black and gold Buddha necklace with the chunky metal chain and put it round my neck, my bangles and Buddha catching my globe as I wiggled to get more comfortable. Turning my globe I found India. Spinning it within the weeping green softness of my tree I was travelling around the world.

'Around The World' was the name of the game my friend Jenny had made up to play at lunchtime with our other friends on the school's bottom oval. She'd found a big stick that dropped from the gum trees near the wire fence and drew a circle in the gravel. She divided it up into sections that represented different countries. We ran around it until the one with the stick said the name of a country. The first to jump into the section that matched that country won a point. Then it was their turn to take the stick. The one with the most points at the end of the game won a flight to the country of their choice. There were so many countries I wanted to visit making it hard to decide where to fly to first; Greece, Italy, France, India, England, Spain. Portugal, Holland, or Austria from where Nana and Grandad brought me back a walking doll dressed in the national costume. I brushed her blonde hair each night before I went to sleep and lay her next to me in bed.

In Grade 6, we had to do a talk on a country for Social Studies. My teacher made a timetable listing the country and the presenter for that week. We were given two weeks to research our talk then he gave us a mark out of ten based on presentation and information.

Snuggled in bed before lights out, Mum read me 'Heidi', one of my favourite story's. After a talk on Switzerland I wanted to visit the wooden house high up in the Alps in the green fields with white daisies where Heidi lived. Debbie went overseas to New Zealand lucky thing. She showed us her Maori doll and tiki made of green jade when she gave her talk. Wendy's Dad went on a business trip to Fiji. She had a doll to show us like Debbie's but it didn't have marks on its face. It had woolly black hair with a yellow flower in it called a hibiscus. She showed us photos of palm trees and colorful fish. The water was so clear you could see them swimming along on the bottom of the sea. The people had happy smiling faces and they said "bula" when they said hello. She passed a coconut around the class that had fallen from a palm tree. Wendy's Dad told her the tropics had lots of different flowers with special smells like frangipani. What a beautiful name for a flower. Our class knew a bit about the tropics because our teacher sent tapes from our class to our sister class in Hawaii. We told them all about the outback, the kangaroos, koalas and what we did at school. They sent back tapes telling us about volcanoes, whales and dolphins and the huge waves people surfed with dolphins over there. Now I wanted to go to Hawaii and Fiji. If Debbie had been to New Zealand then I wanted to go there too.

My talk was on the Aborigines. A boomerang, coolamon, bullroarer and digging stick were kept on top of the kitchen cupboards at home. Pa had been given them by a tribe in Darwin, up there at the top of my jigsaw map when he was there with his battalion during the war, real ones that'd been used once. Dad said he'd let me take them to school for my talk if I promised to look after them. I wrapped them up in separate plastic bags. They didn't fit in my school bag so Mum drove me to school on the morning of my talk.

When India was the country of the month, I cut the picture of the Taj Mahal from the out of date brochure I'd been given for free by the travel agents Mum took me to after school. I pasted it in my Social Studies book then drew a cow under it because they are sacred to the Indian people my teacher told the class.

When Greece was country of the month I learned it was a warm, sunny place. Those were the places I liked best. There were volcanoes in Greece too. I loved looking at pictures of volcanoes. The lava was red and orange and ran like a river. It bubbled like the toffee Mum made in a pot on the stove. I loved Mum's toffee. She poured it into white patty pans then put it in the fridge to cool. I liked it best when it was soft and really chewy. I pretended I was eating hot lava.

There was a place in Italy called Pompeii where a volcano called Mt Vesuvius erupted one day a long time ago burying the whole city in ash. I'd seen it in the magazine Mum bought from the newsagent every month, full of pictures and information about all sorts of things that had happened in the history of the world. I stared in horror at pictures of animals and people trapped in the lava and when it cooled, stuck in it forever. That was too scary to think about. Still, I was going to visit there one day and see it for myself. The buildings were so old they were falling to bits. Those bits left on the ground our teacher told us, were the ruins of temples. They were so big they reached way up into the blue sky. In one of the magazines there were statutes with arms missing and women in long pleated dresses like I wore but mine were shorter. They had their hair in a bun like my flower girl hairdo.

Within the soft embrace of my tree I dropped deeper into dreaming of faraway places on the other side of the world. Enticed by the gentle swaying of the branches against my legs I put down my globe, flipped off my turquoise shoes and slid my feet into my ballet shoes, flexing my toes. I stood up straight placing my feet together in first position, head up, eyes staring through the spaces between the willow tree branches. It was me pretending to be a pretty, sophisticated French girl taking her poodle for a walk down the Champs Elysée. I'd had my pink ballet flats on as I promenaded around the local hall doing my best ballet walk, feet pointing out in first position, toe, heel, toe heel, one measured step after the other. My back was straight because good posture was very important for a ballerina Miss Robinson told us every week. My chin was up, my eyes looked ahead and I remembered to smile. My pink plastic poodle on a blue lead matched the black ones walking around the hem of the pink and white candy striped dress Mum had bought me. The poodles on my dress, walked past a black ink drawing of the Eiffel Tower and a café on the Champs Elysée. I wanted to win the fancy dress competition at the end of year ballet break up, and with my performance I did. I also wanted to go to Paris and stroll along the Champs Elysée one day. And I wanted a black poodle too.

'Take Me Back to Sorrento'. That tune kept going around in my head as I put my turquoise shoes back on and sat back down on my blanket under my tree humming it trying to remember the words of the song. When I visited Nana, the tune escaped when she lifted the shiny polished lid of the small table with gold flecks sparkling in it. I'd run my hands over the shiny surface while the tune played.

Nana and Grandad's house was filled with strange smells from all over the world. Skins from Morocco, leather work from Egypt, smooth wooden carved busts of slaves from their journey through the Suez Canal. I sat on the couch with Nana as she turned the pages of a thick leather photo album with a plaited spine. She let me lift the thin rice paper protecting the photos giving me time to look at them in detail and ask lots of questions. There were camels and men in dresses with funny hats. Nana said the hat was called a fez. They had one. I lifted it off the window sill and stroked its silken tassel as Nana kept turning the pages of the album. "I'm going to Morocco when I'm grown up". Nana smiled, patted me on the head then we went out to the kitchen to make some scones for afternoon tea.

The seeds of ancient memories quivered in the budding child's flower girl basket with the stories of faraway places her classmates brought to the classroom with their talks on different countries. They quivered seeing the photos and artefacts of her grandparents travels.

There was one seed that warmed a little more than the others as two little girls with different colored skin collected eggs and sat together as the sun dropped down over the yard. It was warmed further by the fire beside the mia-mia in her diorama and kept warm by visits to her father's family in the country.

All these seeds of ancient memories were asking to be planted in her garden. I, the Temple Woman took the seeds and put them in my basket until the perfect combination of Julie and time and place arose for them to bear fruit.

... scene 4 ...

when is dad coming home?

setting
in the broken child's cave of sorrows

Julie's broken child walked over to the kitchen table where her father's family were having their gathering across the stream. She turned up a discarded kitchen chair and sat on it.
As they argued she lifted a bottle out of her picnic basket and stood it on its end, an empty and silent witness to the pastime of drinking. The bitterness was preserved in the brown walls of the glass long after the last beer was downed, and the conversation it encouraged long forgotten. In that empty bottle was the story of the broken child's pain.
The necks of some of the bottles protruded from holes in the thinning weave of her basket and knocked against her ankles. Wisps of smoke rose out of them, stubs of cigarettes smouldering in their bubbled bottoms. The ash settled there, mixed with the warm dregs.
Drops of amber fluid dripped onto the broken child's toes. Curling them up she let them trickle away. Looking down at her feet she found patches of ash stuck to them in a mottled pattern. She picked them off, then flicked them onto the mossy floor of the cave, pushing the basket away. Her father lurched past and threw another empty into her basket. It rattled and rolled about until it settled against the other empties, their labels faded and curled at the corners.
Eddying around and around inside the empty bottle standing on its end at her feet was her lament, "when is Dad coming home?" Her mother had four answers to that question she'd ask every day. Soon. Later. I don't know. Not till tomorrow. There was one answer she didn't offer - Never. The one she dreaded and hoped she wouldn't ever hear.

I stared at the empty beer bottle, the same old pictures of family life tumbling around inside it as I'd lived them over and over, always the same question coming out of it,

"When is Dad coming home?"

"Soon", Mum said.

I was so excited the times when he came home sober in time for tea. He'd sit up in his big gold velvet comfy chair and light up a cigarette. Then he'd pull out the paper from the magazine rack by his chair and turn to the crossword. I loved doing crosswords too. I stood beside him watching him through the smoke swirling around the chair waiting for him to ask me to hop on his knee. But he never did. The need for a cuddle was greater than the invitation for one. So I climbed onto his knee anyway pushing the paper into his chest. He folded the newspaper back to get a better look at the crossword, its breeze fanning the smoke about my face.

"I want to help". I wriggled closer to look at the clues.

His pen dug into 4 down and 3 across. He drew his cigarette to his lips sucked on it then blew the smoke out, it making circles between our faces. Putting the cigarette back in the ash tray he took a sip of froth from the head of his beer. Smoke and beer. I didn't like the smell of either but that was Dad's smell.

"That's enough. Hop off. I want to relax".

I held on tight to the arms of his chair gritting my teeth. He lifted one arm then the other off. I pushed them back on again. Could we turn it into a game? My only hope of staying.

"Did you hear me. Get off!" He pushed me hard with his hands. I fell on to the carpet as he adjusted the newspaper and had another sip of his beer then writing in the answer to the next clue on the crossword. My sister sat in front of the TV, her nose all but pressed against it looking up at the flickering images not aware I'd passed by, let alone in tears.

"When is Dad coming home?"

"Later", Mum said.

Dad had promised he'd be home in time to take us to my ballet concert when I'd asked Mum about it that afternoon. He hardly ever came to them. When he did, he kept going outside for a smoke. He even missed one of my dances the last time he did that. He wanted to go home as soon as it was over. This was my big night tonight. I was doing my first solo. I peeped out to see if Susan and Ray were there yet.

"Come away from there. You have to get ready, practice your steps", Mum hissed.

"I can't see them".

"Come away will you". Mum pulled me away from the curtains.

I kept sneaking a peep while Mum kept busy teasing another girl's hair.

There they were! I waved and called to them until they noticed me. They waved back. I was happy now. Susan and Ray promised to come to my ballet concerts. They always kept their word. I searched the audience from the side of the stage to check if Dad had arrived. I looked out again during the first dance I was in with the rest of the troupe. He wasn't there. Susan and Ray stood up smiling, clapping hard. He was probably on his way. He wasn't there for the next one either. Susan and Ray sat in their chairs smiling, clapping again. Another costume change and I was on. I looked for Dad but he wasn't there. I put on my brightest smile and best singing voice but my insides ached with disappointment as I danced across the stage dressed as Little Boy Blue singing his song. Susan and Ray clapped and waved a big wave as I left the stage.

I pretended I was asleep when Dad tiptoed into my room in the early hours of the morning and put something on the white bedhead behind my pillow. Whatever it was, I didn't want it. I wanted him at my ballet concert. Nothing else would do.

In the morning he'd already gone to work. Sitting beside the photo I kept of Dad, stuck with yellowed tape to the bed head, I found a box of chocolates with a hand written note on a card with pink hearts. It said, "To My Little Ballerina. Love from Dad". I tore the card up throwing it in the bin on the way to school. I kept the chocolates and shared them with my sister.

"When is Dad coming home?"

"I don't know", Mum said.

I'd watched the stove, watched the clock, set the table. The three of us ate our tea, the place set for my Dad, empty. His plate of stew covered with another plate on top of the big pot on the stove. The water boiled dry, his tea burnt dry. I dried the dishes and put them away. That was now tomorrow night's tea, or another tomorrow's for when he came home.

Sirens woke me up in the early hours of the morning with their warnings of danger. I jumped out of bed and stood at the kitchen window watching for more police cars with their flashing lights to go past in the distance on the main road not far from my house. He still wasn't home. Was he okay? Where was he? Was he in danger? What if something had happened to him? Who would look after us? If he came home, what was going to happen? Not another fight. I hated it when Mum and Dad fought. What if he'd been hurt?

Too cold to stand there watching out the window any longer, I climbed back into bed. Lying there these unanswered questions pumped to the beat of my pounding heart until the rattling keys jabbed at the lock, the door a thin barrier keeping him at bay. I pulled my pillow tight over my ears, closed my eyes and curled into a ball under the covers.

I was never ready for the sound and the drink stink of him soaking the house.

The dim glow of the hall light reached the foot of my bed. In this tiny space of open wooden doors round one of the slanging match began. Mum charged out of their bedroom hissing and spitting a barrage of fear and frustration my pillow earmuffs failed to deaden. Dad ducked and swayed about Mum's verbal onslaught with as much comprehension as a punch drunk boxer.

With each round of their fight my gut was pummelled with their shouted punches. The kitchen door slammed. Another blow to my gut. Their bedroom door slammed. An upper cut to my heart. I looked over at my sister in the bed across from me. Her eyes were closed, her breathing even. I wondered how she could sleep through all this noise. The pipes banged in the wall as the toilet flushed. The fridge door banged, then the plates rattled in the cupboard. Mum's sobs reached through their closed bedroom door. The kitchen door banged shut, then the bathroom door. He was getting ready for bed.

I removed the pillow from my ears and lay still holding my breath not daring to breathe in case he noticed. I was awake bursting to go to the toilet. I would rather pee my pants than risk getting up and going even one round with him. He'd take any one on in this state. That foul mouth always had plenty left in it. Their bedroom door opened and slammed shut on tonight's bout.

The cold lino stung my toasty warm tiptoes as I pressed my bedroom door "ssh" closed and crept back to bed. I picked up the family cat, Tabs, from the end of the bed and snuggled her into my stomach. Her purrs soothed my burning gut but not my thumping heart. There was light coming in my bedroom window. Soon it would be time to get up for school. I'd hold off going to the toilet till then. I cried under the blankets waiting for it to go quiet in their bedroom. My bed was the only refuge left for me in this boxing ring I called home.

"When is Dad coming home?"

"Not till tomorrow", Mum said.

"Why not?"

"He has to work", Mum replied.

Work. Humph. I bet he's out drinking again, not on nightshift the same old answer Mum gives me when I'd ask when Dad is coming home. I took myself off to bed.

Day shift, nightshift, afternoon shift but it was the double shift of a siege that brought me to my parent's double bed to sit and examine his gun one morning not long after the siege.

There are some things children need to do when their parents are out. I needed to see what a gun was really like. I knew it was kept between shifts on the top shelf of Dad's side of the wardrobe with his handcuffs and baton.

I lay its heaviness on the bed beside me, its oily greasy smell fresh in my palms that I tried to wipe away on my dress, but it stayed. I toyed with the trigger, daring my finger to pull it back knowing I shouldn't in case it was loaded. Picking up the dry, cracked, brown leather holster stained with perspiration, I played with the wide straps that went over Dad's shoulders. Now I knew what was hidden under his detective suit. I pushed my arms through the straps heaving it on and looked at myself in the mirror of Mum's white dressing table. I slid the gun in and out of the holster using both hands because it was so heavy. Now I knew what a gun was really like. A man pointed a gun like this at Dad during that siege and he grabbed it off him even though there were bullets in it!

"Look up at your father. Look proud. Smile". The flash went off in my face and there we were, the whole family in the newspaper next morning looking at Dad's Certificate of Bravery awarded by the Police Commissioner at a ceremony the day before. All because of a gun. I never wanted to see a gun again. What if that man had shot Dad? It meant the possibility of 'never' when I asked Mum when Dad was coming home. Guns. I hated them.

My ears already hurting, I winced at the sound of another empty bottle being tossed onto the pyramid by my father creating a clanging, banging out of tune song that rattled and shook my nerves. Kicking the legs of the kitchen chair hard over and over I squeezed my hands even harder over my ears pressing my eyes shut, trying to block out the arguing of Dad's family in the cave and the ringing of Mum and Dad's arguments in my ears. Why couldn't our family be like Mr and Mrs Jones's family?

> In asking that question, Julie's broken child didn't realise that what she was asking was why couldn't her family nurture the budding child, the child she didn't know and needed to befriend if the Lost Temple of Julie was to be found.

... scene 5 ...

mr and mrs jones

Mr and Mrs Jones were just like Darren and Samantha in 'Bewitched' my favourite TV program. Mrs Jones wore beautiful clothes and shoes and loved to cook for Mr Jones's business clients just like Samantha. Mr Jones had a position high up in an accountancy firm in the city where he travelled to on the train dressed in a very expensive suit. She attended cookery school where she learned how to prepare gourmet food for the dinner parties she hosted. Her kitchen shelves were lined with cook books she took down looking at them for ages at the kitchen bench when deciding on a dish to cook. Mrs Jones let me help with the cooking because she was teaching Leanne and her little sister how to cook. She showed us the steps in the recipe book and explained the measurements, then how to mix them in a bowl with her Mixmaster turning the different combination of ingredients into delicious cakes, slices, biscuits, casseroles and baked dinners. We were allowed to lick the bowl after we placed what we had made into the oven before we started washing up the bowls, beaters and the utensils we'd used to create the dishes. Mrs Jones let us have sneak peeks to see how our recipe was going, the aroma filling the kitchen making us eager to have what we'd made out of the oven cooked so we could have a taste.

I wished Mum would let me help her in the kitchen.

Unlike Mrs Jones comfortable life as a wife of an accountant where she enjoyed activities at home of a domestic nature, making do and making ends meet tied Julie's mother to the house wearing her manicured hands and nerves down. She'd filed and painted the nails of the wives of dignitaries and diplomats doing their hair for a ball or the races. Now those hands were put to work in the endless, repetitive chores of domesticity and their attendant frustrations.

After school Julie would often find her mother out the back in the vegetable garden she'd prepared in the corner of the backyard tending it out of economic necessity. A policeman's wage didn't stretch too far in the first place, let alone one that also financed a regular and hefty drink bill.

The routine after school was; put my school bag down on the bench, empty it of books, my lunch box and drink bottle, get changed out of my uniform, help myself to a drink and a couple of biscuits out of the tin then stand watching Mum chop some vegetables she'd just picked from the garden.

She'd say, "Go outside and play".

"I want to help".

"Go outside and play. You're in my way".

"I want to help".

"You have years and years ahead of you when you have to cook. Make the most of it while you can when you don't have to. Now out of my kitchen".

"I don't want to".

"Outside *now*!"

"Make me". I'd had enough of all the times she's said no when I asked to help her in the kitchen even after being given an explanation this time.

Mum threw open the junk drawer in the kitchen, pulled out the wooden spoon and waved it at me. I poked out my tongue and ran out the door straight to the vegetable patch, leaping over the lettuces. I turned around to see Mum coming at me with a large saucepan in her hand. She held it up ready to strike, yelling at me as she tried to catch me. We played chasey round the edge of the patch and when Mum got too close I ran faster angering her even more. She aimed for my bottom and took a swing. I leapt across the carrots then back over the pumpkins then around the patch again. A whoosh of air went around my legs as the saucepan brushed past. I kept running through the carport, grabbed my basketball off the front lawn and ran down the road to the school to shoot some hoops. That was way too close this time. I wasn't going home until she'd calmed down.

Cupping my hands over my ears I tried to deaden the sound of Mum and Dad's arguments still fresh in them. They competed with the one going on with Dad's family while he staggered between it and the gathering of men listening to war stories of Grandad's. All their voices banging off the walls of the cave grew louder with each glass of beer they drank. What was wrong with my family?

Mr Jones was home for tea at 6pm every night and all weekend too except when he went away on business overseas.

When I asked Mum why Dad couldn't be home for tea at 6pm like Mr Jones she said he was working long hours to look after us and not to be so ungrateful. I wished my Dad was home for tea at 6pm every night.

Dinnertime was quiet at Mr and Mrs Jones's house.

I wished it was at mine.

Sometimes there were cross words. Mr Jones frowned reminding my best friend Leanne and her sister about their manners when they answered their mother back at the dinner table. My father knocked me off my chair with a backhander when I answered Mum back. I wished Dad would never hit me again. Mr Jones smiled at his children and wife a lot while they were eating dinner. I wished Dad did that.

Mr Jones played games with his children after tea and on weekends.

I liked Chinese Checkers and dominoes best. My sister and I played games a lot at Susan and Ray's. Mum played with us at home sometimes. I wished Dad played games with me. Leanne had the latest toys and games. When I asked Mum would she buy me Twister she said what she usually did; we couldn't afford it.

I wished we could afford it.

Mr Jones helped Leanne with her homework.

I wished Dad helped me with mine.

Leanne won a scholarship to a private school. She travelled there on the train. Her parents set up a study for her with her own desk. When I asked Mum if I could sit for a scholarship too she said we couldn't afford a private school, even with a scholarship. I missed Leanne, my best friend since kindergarten. I wished we could afford for me to go to Leanne's private school.

Mrs Jones was very good at needlework. She taught Leanne and her sister how to sew. Leanne made beautiful tapestries, knitted, and sewed for her dolls and for herself. I watched her cut out patterns turning them into clothes on her mother's sewing machine.

Mrs Jones decided I needed to learn to sew too, giving me some brown paper to practice with first. No matter how hard I tried, the lines ran all over the place. In despair she decided she'd help me make a dress for my Barbie doll. She gave me a scrap of material and showed me how to put a dart in after she cut out the dress to fit my doll. I was delighted to see I'd sewn a straight line. I showed Mrs Jones. She laughed. I was puzzled and hurt. She said it was a perfect dart, except I'd sewn it in upside down. I laughed too. I wished Mum liked sewing so she could teach me how to sew.

Mrs Jones was an expert knitter. Mum knitted jumpers each winter for my sister and I. I liked to knit but being left handed, I kept picking it up the wrong way. Mum had tried to help me until she gave up on me being able to knit right handed. Mrs Jones sat with me watching, ready to correct my mistakes until I'd turned into a right handed knitter like everyone else. I knitted Barbie a trendy suit and for me, a jumper and matching scarf. I was so pleased with myself being able to do something

Leanne could do. I wished Mum had the patience to teach me how to knit.

Mrs Jones and Leanne went shopping for the best quality clothes and shoes, which they chose together. I came home and found clothes on the bed to wear because Mum didn't like to go shopping with me even when I asked her if we could. I wanted the same clothes as Leanne but Mum said we couldn't afford it. I wished we could afford it and that Mum would go shopping for clothes with me.

When Leanne and I rode together on her three-wheeler bike Leanne pedalling, me standing on the back, we were the same. We screamed through the bends down the hills past the new brick houses on the estate where she lived. We were two best friends who loved to giggle and have fun together.

... scene 6 ...

susan and ray

Why can't my parents be like Susan and Ray? It was so much fun at Susan and Ray's. When Mum said I was going to stay at Susan and Ray's for the weekend or even better in the school holidays my heart raced with both relief and excitement. I got to do all the things I wished I could do with Mum and Dad when I visited at their place. One of my favourite things was doing the crossword with Ray. He sat in his chair in the lounge room of their small two bedroom flat and opened the paper. I hopped on his knee waiting for him to find the page with the crossword. He helped me with the clues I couldn't read myself. Sometimes he started writing in the word for me but left gaps so I could fill in the rest as I worked it out. He was so kind. I liked that feeling when someone was kind to me. I could relax and think. He could be strict and used a firm voice sometimes so I knew he meant what he said. I didn't blame him. I did get a bit silly when I visited. I couldn't help it. It was all the happiness escaping out of me I couldn't let out at home. That happiness spilled over when Ray said we were going to the fairground on the esplanade by the sea not far from their flat.

The Ghost Train rattled along on its tracks jolting the car as slimy green ghouls and ghosts popped out at us with spooky cackles. Doors opened and closed, cobwebs tickled our hair. I clutched Susan and Ray by the arm screaming and laughing as we all bumped about in the car. Susan screamed and laughed with me. Ray laughed at us. I looked over at my sister. Her face was white with fright.

The pink fairy floss on a long wooden stick was sticky sugary sweet in my mouth as I bit into it walking along to the Scenic Railway. The wheels of the carriages of the Big Dipper rattled overhead as we waited in the queue. After our ride I took aim but the mouths of the clowns didn't swallow the balls I threw at them, even with Ray's help.

I sat upon my steed as the merry-go-round made a slow turn around and around. I caught my reflection in the large, gold framed mirror. I saw a shining face full of happiness and pleasure. I also caught a reflection of my sister on her steed. I saw a face unmoved by the day's fun. Why? We were with Susan and Ray.

The next morning I heard Susan and Ray talking in bed. Good. I'd been lying there for ages waiting for them to wake up so I could have a cuddle in bed with them. Hearing my knocking on the door Susan said, "come in". I jumped on them giving them big kisses and hugs. They pretended not to like it and said, "stop" but they were laughing, pulling the covers back at the same time so my sister and I could climb in. While I was waiting for them to wake up, I'd already chosen the book I wanted them to read, 'Snow White and The Seven Dwarfs'. I handed it to Ray. He was so good at reading stories. We snuggled in.

After the story was over Susan said, "Time to get up. What do you want for breakfast?"

No, I didn't want to. More cuddles and stories was what I wanted.

"Where are we going today Susan?" I squealed with delight when she told me.

We drove to the Ford Motor Company picnic in Ray's blue Falcon. Susan made a picnic lunch which she'd packed into her cane basket. We all shared lunch sitting on a tartan rug Ray spread out on the ground for us in the middle of the football oval. He offered my sister and I the sandwiches first then poured us a drink of lemonade. Ray was such a gentleman. Susan had made a fruit cake for later on. Her parent's had brought some watermelon.

"For energy", her Dad said. Paddy knew I liked to run in the races and her Mum liked to cheer me on with him.

Ray and I went in the sack race first, then Susan and I in the egg and spoon race relay. The race I liked best at the picnic was the 440-yard; my race, the last of the day though I competed in all of the running races. Each year I got a place, including first sometimes. I really wanted to come first today because Paddy and Mags were there too.

Waiting for the starting gun to go off I dug my bare toes into the grass, arms bent ready to pump hard when I ran around the track. "Bang"! Already puffed from the start, it wasn't long before I had a stitch in my side, my legs feeling heavy. Then I saw Susan, Ray, Paddy, Mags and my sister on the bend. Except for my sister, their waving, clapping and yelling "go Julie go" as I ran past pushed me from behind towards the finishing line. My sister just stood there, not watching the race at all. I could see the tape. Wanting to break it with my chest first I ran even faster. Before I knew it I was over the line. A marshal came up to me, tapped me on the shoulder and said, "First". I looked for Susan and the others. They rushed up to me giving me a great big hug all together. My sister dawdled behind them. My lungs were hurting, my legs aching but their hug gave me the strength to step up on the dais to receive my ribbon. All the people clapped but my family clapped loudest of all, even my sister who joined in even if she didn't really know why.

I didn't want the weekend to be over even though I knew there would be a next time. I wanted the happiness to last and last.

Julie's broken child clung to its life giving juice, desperate to store it somewhere inside to sustain her until the next time she visited Susan and Ray. Suburb by suburb she succumbed to the chewing, clawing, scratching inevitability of going home. Susan and Ray ushered the two sisters to the door of uncertainty. The front door was opened by their mother with a long face. Julie was home.

Snuggled down in bed after my weekend at Susan and Ray's, I drifted off to Mum's voice reading 'The Far Away Tree' my favourite Enid Blyton book, a quiet time shared as we both loved to read. With a kiss on the cheek Mum was gone, the door closed behind her. But there was the night ahead. I looked over at my sister. She was asleep.

Mum and I must have heard the car pull up at the same time as we both rushed to the front door. Dad was pounding on it like Fred Flintstone did when he locked himself out while putting Dino outside for the night, yelling at his wife Wilma to let him in. Dad and I loved that show. That was our favourite part. We'd laugh and laugh. I didn't think it was funny when Dad did it.

"Go back to bed!" I took a step back as Mum took a step forward and opened the front door. The locked fly-wire screen preventing his entry fuelled his anger. He shook the handle with trembling hands stumbling back over the front door mat.

"Let me in!", he yelled.

"No!" Mum flung open the screen door and threw the evening newspaper at him. It fell open as he tried to catch it, most of it landing at his feet. "You're not coming in here you bastard. You can sleep out there".

"Let me in!".

"No!" Mum slammed the door shut, the glass panels shaking in their wooden frame.

He walked away and Mum went to bed, the door shut on her fury. I looked out the lounge room window. There were lights on next door and across the road but the neighbours never came to see what was going on. Dad fell onto the red and blue painted stripes of the garden bench outside on the front lawn near my willow tree. He tried to pull a few sheets of the newspaper over himself but he was already snoring. The fallen sheets of newspaper lay in a pile around his feet.

I was glad that was over. At least there would be no more fighting tonight. At last I could go to sleep. I stood at my sister's bed. She turned over on her side snuggled up with the teddy bear she'd turned over with her, her face to the lavender wall. She must be far, far, away. Maybe the Faraway Tree held my sister in its branches each night, keeping her safe. And in them, she danced with the fairies. I hopped into bed, snuggled into Tabs and tried to go to sleep.

Mum came into our room pulling the covers from my warm back. I wedged myself against the wall to make room for her as she slid in beside me. I put my arm around her. Her tears ran in the spaces between the buttons of my pyjama top, wetting my skin.

"I hate him", she sobbed. I stroked her hair and held her tight.

I lay there unable to move, the knot wound another notch firmer in my gut. With each sob that escaped from Mum's body it shook in mine. I looked over at my sister. I called her name asking if she was okay. She didn't stir, her breath even. I closed my eyes. We slid into an uneasy sleep. I wished that was the last time Mum came to my bed but I knew it wouldn't be. I wanted the morning to come so I could get up and go to school. When it did, there in amongst the bird song, sunshine and the frost under his feet, lay the sleeping, hungover hobo I called Dad. He was still there when I walked by him on the way to school.

The seeds of Julie's femininity she wished to plant in her garden so her inner beauty may grow withered in the heat of the continual arguments between her parents. They withered in the rocky ride of rejection; the game she played on her father's knee. They withered further in a token gesture of love given on the night of a ballet concert he promised to be at while she was sleeping; a gesture that didn't fill her empty heart. An empty chair in the lounge room, the empty side of a marital bed, the empty space in the carport, the house filled with a longing for a father never home even when he was there. Her traumatised mother only saw the endless and repetitive chores of domesticity that went with the responsibility of raising children with a husband preoccupied with his job and drinking, who often wasn't home.

Though it was the mother's task to plant and tend the garden, it was the father's to water it with love so Julie's seeds would take root and blossom. In the loving embrace of family life with Susan and Ray the seeds stirred, spilling from her basket wishing to be planted in her garden.

Mrs Jones recognised and fostered the desire of her friend's daughter to nurture her seeds of femininity lived within daily family life. She also recognised her friend was unable to provide that sustained experience for her daughter within their own family. Mr and Mrs Jones worked in their manicured garden on the weekend; snipping, pruning and planting their flowers and trees.

Their garden was well watered and fertilized, the grass lush and green. Gardening was a pleasure they both enjoyed. In turn so did their children. Mrs Jones was a true gardener because in the simple every day chores of domesticity she tended the sprouting seeds of femininity in each of her daughters with loving care and provided a garden for them to grow in. Mr Jones watered them with love so the seeds would blossom and grow with his patience and constancy. Mrs Jones knew that with her guiding hand and loving heart; sewing, baking and knitting connected herself and her daughters to all the women who came before them, not in drudgery but in communion. For in the teaching of those skills she and her daughters shared much more than the satisfaction of mastering the steps to make a cake, or make clothing. They shared what was on their minds and in their hearts while they did these things together. In that communion I, The Temple Woman dwelt.

This hotchpotch garden of Julie's was one that couldn't be maintained. Through the patient and loving guidance of Mrs Jones more seeds opened waiting to be planted in Julie's garden. It was Ray who watered all her seeds with patience and constancy. Her own father unable to do so as he wasn't present enough in her life to know that it was his job to water them so they would flourish. And it was Susan who provided the warmth of love for them to take root and grow, Julie's own mother too traumatised to be able to provide a garden for them to grow in. These people outside her family who loved Julie could only hope to plant the seeds in tiny pots, watering them each time they visited until the time came for them to be planted in Julie's garden.

... scene 7 ...

the family argument

In another empty bottle that lay in the broken child's picnic basket was a sad story and full of loss that belonged to Julie's father's family. Like her mother's sad and loss filled story, it spawned many more whose origins were in generations past and handed down to her.

I took the beer bottle now emptied of its story adding it to the pyramid in the cave. Dad was sitting at the table with his family pouring himself another drink, now tired of Grandad's war stories. Reluctantly, I took another bottle from my basket and stood it on its end. A woman with brown eyes and a severe perm dragged on a cigarette as she rode out of the bottle on the spiral of smoke with her story. Her brunch coat was faded and stained, her slippers sporting two worn bumps, housing each big toe. She shuffled over and sat down at the kitchen table.

I reached into my basket for an old black and white photo I'd found wedged between a couple of the bottles. I looked at the woman at the table then back at the photo. A woman in a smart coat with a severe perm and a determined look in her eye stared back at me from the photo. She'd been snapped walking between her two children, a tall young man in a suit with dark hair and eyes with a big smile, and a grumpy little mousey haired girl dressed in a smart coat who'd given me the photo not so long ago. Dad had refused to give me any photos of her when I asked to know what my grandmother looked like. I could relate to that look in her eye and the no nonsense expression on her face because I shared that look and expression with her.

I stared at the photo and back at my grandmother sitting at the table. I thought she and Auntie Win were very alike with their glasses, short permed hair and brown eyes. Summoning up my courage, I walked over and stood behind my grandmother. Pa reached for the beer bottle, poured himself a beer and one for Dad. They clinked glasses both taking a long draught. Auntie Win topped up my grandmother's beer and offered her a cigarette. My grandmother pulled a box of matches from the pocket of her apron. They both lit up, staring at the clock on the wall, its second hand keeping up a constant ticking that filled the lull in the conversation. My grandmother shuffled to the fridge, took out a couple more bottles and put them on the table. While she was up, she gave the stew on the wood stove a stir with a large wooden spoon then put the lid back on at an angle to stop it drying. The sound of the lid going back on the pot stirred Auntie Win out of her thoughts. She wriggled in her chair and looked at me. She sipped the head of her beer leaning back in her chair. She took a puff of her cigarette, expelling it with force.

I tapped my grandmother on the shoulder, handed her the photo. "Your son looked so happy to be with you but your daughter looked so sad".

"That was because your father knew me better. She hardly knew me at all. She was sent away to live with her grandmother because I couldn't look after her. I might have been a drunk but at least your father had a relationship with me, even if it wasn't a very good one".

"That's all I know about you; that you were an alcoholic who died not long before I was born".

"I drank myself to death and there was nothing anyone could do to stop me. I was too far gone, totally dependent on the bottle. Your grandfather and I drank together. That was the only way we could communicate, that and fighting. He was very frustrated about my lack of care for myself, for him and the children".

Both women took another long drag on their cigarettes before grinding them into the metal ashtray alongside the other ones. I liked Auntie Win. Dad hated her. No-one would tell me why.

He flared, banging his glass on the table and growled, "You moll!"

His mother pushed her chair back looking to caution him but her hand dropped in her lap. No words were said. She had another sip of her beer, resigned. His clenched fists and jaw asked to fight another round. Pa shook his head and had another draught of beer.

"I didn't blame your grandfather for finding another woman after what he went through in the war. I could never understand why your father resented him having Win. She and your grandfather looked after me and cared for my children out of respect to us as a family until I died".

Auntie Win glared at my father and added, "You can't blame me for taking your mother away. The drink did that and you know it. We all know it". She couldn't help having the last say because it was the truth.

Dad threw back his chair and the rest of his drink then stormed off from the table. Auntie Win raised her glass to his back. My grandmother pulled the top off another beer while Pa drained his glass.

Opening another bottle Pa offered Auntie Win and my grandmother a top up. They lifted their glasses towards the bottle. He obliged. Not only did they share a beer, they shared a weariness that sat on their slumped shoulders. I inched in bit by bit between my grandmother and Auntie Win, sliding onto Auntie Win's knee. I stared into Pa's blue eyes. He looked even shorter than he was beside these two women. I asked him, "Why did you drink so much? I hated all the arguing. It was the same every time I came to stay at your place".

He put down his glass. "That was how our family bonded; through drink. There was so much to forget; the war, failed relationships, hopes and dreams, the harsh reality of everyday life and raising children in those circumstances. It was a very difficult job working with the mentally ill. I saw a lot of human suffering. The drinking dulled it but at the same time it was fascinating work and I had my sense of humour to get me through. Win and I understood about the nature of our work and the stress of it, the need to let off steam by sharing a drink with our work mates".

Auntie Win put her arm around me, taking another long drag on her cigarette before butting it out. "I did love your grandfather but the drink got to the both of us. We didn't always fight like we did when you knew me. There was love and care there but it died. All the family fought and drank, that was the only way we could communicate".

I slid off Auntie Win's knee and walked back to my basket. I picked up the empty bottles beside it and put them in it. The basket was heavy. I waddled to the slippery pyramid, adding all the empties to the other ones already stacked up against the wall of the cave, suddenly startled by the sound of high pitched cackles. I turned in the direction of the sound coming from where Mum and her sister were doing the washing and mending. I followed it.

I was led to a big pile of dirty washing on the cave floor near a rusted boiler tipped over on its side beside some of the washing machines, all the washing a dirty beige color. Dirty socks and underwear were poking out of work shifts and cardigans. I shuddered as the women in their beige shifts, muttered and fought over the washing, some trying to count it others trying to put it in the large industrial washing machine. They lived in the loony bin. That's what Dad called it.

... scene 8 ...

the loony bin

Visiting Pa's place meant visiting the hospital first where he worked as a nurse - a stop on the way to his place I would have been happy to miss not because I didn't want to see him but because of the sort of hospital he worked at.

Dad and Mum went to find him while the two of us waited in the car. He told us to lock the doors and wind the windows up "just in case". The times Mum went with him, they told us to lock the doors and not to get out for any reason, they would be back soon. There were a lot of scary, creepy people living there.

Monroe knew our car. He liked Dad. I hoped he wouldn't come up to the car while Mum and Dad were away. He got upset if Dad wasn't there. I saw him shuffling down the covered walkway in his wide brimmed gardener's hat all bent out of shape like himself. I pushed my sister down the seat sliding down after her.

His face appeared at the window. He started banging on it. He had a smile on his face Pa called a grimace. When he smiled like that he started to jerk his head from side to side. Then he rolled his head around in circles stopping to yell, "Monroe". Then he'd do it again then again. I couldn't watch it. I clasped my sister close shutting my eyes, hoping he would go away. The car started to shake. I opened my eyes.

Others had joined him and circled the car, pushing on it, making it rock. They were yelling, muttering and laughing. What if they smashed the windows? What if they tipped the car over? Now they were banging on the windows. Where were Mum and Dad? *"Come back!"* I screamed inside myself because I was too scared to shout it out loud. I heard Dad's voice. The rocking stopped. I felt dizzy. I wanted to throw up.

My sister wriggled back to her side of the seat, gripping the door handle. Mum and Dad were laughing, chatting away to the men still gathered at the car. Dad unlocked the driver's door and hopped in. Couldn't they see how scared we were?

Mum called in through the door for us to come out, we were going to find Auntie Win. Dad waited in the car, still chatting to Monroe and his friends through the open window. I opened the car door with unwilling fingers and followed Mum and my sister over to the women's wing. I saw Auntie Win and called out to her. She smiled when she saw me.

The women followed us down the breezeway. They started to touch me, giggling like I did with my friends. As we approached the wide open doors of their wing they circled in on me, stroking my hair, pulling on my long pony tail. Mum kept walking in front with my sister's hand clenched in hers. The women's fingers loosened the pink bow from my pony tail. They tried in turns to take me by the arm, pulling me to them. They cackled and muttered in my ear, their sour breath wilting my shaky smile. I stepped back. They stepped forward circling me in a closed bunch, taking my breath away. They poked me with their fingers, grabbed my hands, all wanting me to themselves. One kissed me, then the others copied. I turned my face away looking for help. Another tried to grab my hands to pull me out of the circle, then they all tried.

Mum and Auntie Win were busy talking at the other end of the dayroom while my sister stood by them waiting. I ducked through a hole in the circle of women and ran to them free of their pawing and poking. They disbanded, confused, wondering where I'd gone.

An old lady, her grey hair twisted in a bun with a grey shawl draped on her shoulders, sat in a rocking chair by the window. Her eyes were locked on something outside as she rocked back and forth. Auntie Win led me over to her by my arm and introduced me to her.

"This is Julie".

The old lady looked at me then dragged me on to her icy knee. She continued to rock back and forth, her eyes fixed out the window. I was uncomfortable but kept smiling. I didn't want to upset her as I didn't know what she might do. She was a loony, that's why she was here in this loony bin.

I tried to slide off her knee but she'd handcuffed me with icy fingers. I wanted to be rescued but Mum and Auntie Win had walked over to the far end of the room with my sister to speak to another patient. I wriggled out of her grip with a push and rushed over to them, glad to be by their side. I was even gladder when we returned to the car and Dad drove Mum, my siter and I to Pa's place.

After tea, my sister and I went to the bedroom that Pa used for his study. Mum opened our suitcase on the chair between the beds. I closed the door and started to unpack so we could get ready for bed.

Hanging on the back of the door was a map of the human body with its bones, muscles and blood. All Pa's books with cold, hard medical facts filled the wooden bookshelf. The white sheets on the spare bed were starched crisp with cold. The thick, heavy grey blankets failed to keep the damp air off me. There was plenty of heat in the lounge room though, fuelled by another round of rum or whisky and beer, the bottles all lined up in a row on the coffee table.

Voices were rising like the damp in Pa's room, the shouts of laughter fighting the shouts of argument. No-one noticed I'd opened the door and crept across the hall to see what was going on. Work colleagues from the hospital and some of Dad's drinking mates, friends since school, joined in, swaying to the tune of this drunken chorus; one I knew off by heart.

Auntie Win filled her glass with the rest of the beer and stood the empty on the table with the others. She picked up another record and put it on the player, a Tom Jones hit, 'Delilah', then turned up the volume. She yelled over it to her friend who lurched at her, cigarette in one hand, glass of rum in the other, "Julie was on old grandma murderer's knee today". She nodded, laughed then took another drag on her cigarette and a swig of rum. I wished I'd never heard that but that was the risk I took when I went to check if everything was all right.

Mum left them to it, the evening cabaret in the tiny lounge room not for her. I looked over to her closed door but I knew she would just get angry and tell me to go back to bed if I tried to find refuge in her bedroom. I checked my sister before closing the door. She was still sleeping. I wished they'd stop drinking soon and go to bed. Dad and Auntie Win's voices rose, vying for top pitch, as I hopped into bed, Auntie Bev adding her voice, the swearing sounding meaner and dirtier. Male voices cut in with dirty jokes trying to stop the nastiness with some humour but it didn't work. Other voices shouted for Dad and Auntie Win to stop arguing and another one told Auntie Bev she was drunk and to go home. The loonies' mutterings still buzzed in my ear and the chill of the icy knee of a murderer went deep into my bones. I pulled the pillow tight over my ears, closing my eyes, wondering how long before sleep would come and take me away from the arguing in the lounge room.

There was work tomorrow no matter how hungover the people were after drinking at Pa and Auntie Win's place till late the night before. Auntie Win decided I was old enough to earn some pocket money so asked if I'd like to go to work with her. I liked the idea of earning some money of my own, just not at the loony bin.

She insisted I wear a skirt to work even though I hadn't packed one. She picked a cream woollen one out of her wardrobe that was way too big for me. I pulled it up over my check slacks, tightening it around my waist with safety pins, the hem at my ankles. She decided it would do, I could go to work with her that afternoon and Dad could pick me up later. It was impossible to argue with a head nurse. I looked ridiculous in this borrowed skirt with my own stockings, paisley shirt and navy sneakers, embarrassed to be walking in them to work with her. Auntie Win introduced me to some of the nurses.

"We have a new worker today". I smiled, hitching up my skirt, my legs already starting to itch. She turned to me, "I'm going to put you in the laundry".

We walked out the back of the ward to a big room full of dirty washing with boilers hissing and steaming. A group of women stood there waiting, stained grey aprons tied around their beige shifts, wearing bobby socks like I wore to school.

"I want you to help these women count the laundry and put it into piles ready to be washed. Write it on this form". Auntie Win handed me a blue clipboard and pen. She swept out of the room to her next job. The huge bunch of keys she carried in her pocket to open and close all the doors jangled at her hip like my tambourine with the gypsy woman on it. Though I didn't want to be left with these women I tried to be confident.

"Now let's do this basket first", I said in my best teacher's voice.

They started fighting with each other, tugging washing out of each other's tall baskets and dropping it on the floor.

One of the women started counting, "One, four, five, seven", as she removed the socks, underpants, towels and the shirts, then dropped them in a pile on the ground. The others started giggling copying her counting and dropping their dirty washing on the ground too.

"No. One, two, three". I started picking up the washing and counting it. "Socks in one pile, towels in another". They followed, stopping when I did. I became very flustered. How was I going to get the job done? My skirt kept dropping from my waist. I needed to hold it up with one hand while trying to pick up and count the washing in the other. I was also trying not to cry. I wished someone would come and rescue me. They were closing in on me making me very nervous.

"How are you going there?" Auntie Win appeared in the doorway.

"Not very well". I climbed out of the pile of washing and stood next to her. "They can't count properly".

"Come with me then. You can help sweep a couple of the wards".

After work, I was quick to get out of my uniform, relieved to have shed the silly image it represented and freed from the madness always there enclosed in the walls of the hospital each time I visited.

The cave of sorrows where the broken child dwelt encouraged the rotting seeds of hurt to fester, filling the cave with the odour of stagnation that unhealed trauma and pain breeds with its constant argument that is never resolved.

This putrid garden fertilised with angry words and the stench of beer and stale cigarette butts had the same type of gardener tend it generation after generation. Their well-worn story of lost hopes and dreams with its attendant despair was passed down in their basket from mother to child. This basket of hurts is woven with loss, the sorrow wrapped around the shoulders of the child of the next generation in a sorry embrace. Blood is its lacquer carried with a thick gnarled handle of a well-worn story that tie families together that is hard to break.

With each generation the weight of the story and its legacy of loss and damage grew heavier in their baskets as it continued to be passed down unresolved, its origins lost in time and with that little hope of understanding it. The bare bones of the story continued to rattle each generation, its source in another time and place but still felt in the dark recesses of the broken child's realm; the cave.

... scene 9 ...

we were a footy family

I scooped the football out of my picnic basket and tried to bounce it on the cave floor but it landed with a dull thud, the laces worn and the bladder torn.
"I would have come home to boys".
I spun around at the sound of Dad's voice. Even though I had no brothers, we were still a footy family.

Sitting in Julie's mother's basket of hurts was an unripened seed that would never bear fruit. Christopher Mark was the boy Julie's parents wanted and never had.
There is an unspoken direction where the energy of a girl and a boy must go to fulfil the mothers' and fathers' dreams for a child in each generation of families.

I mightn't have been a boy but I knew how to play football. I liked to go down to the bottom oval at lunchtime and play kick to kick with the boys. We practised hand passing the ball to each other, then running towards the goal and giving the ball a big kick to see if we could get it through the posts. I could kick as many goals as the boys and I was just as fast. I was the only girl who joined in with training at lunchtime. The boys would let me because we played tag and British Bulldog with some of the other girls in my class at playtimes. The girls liked netball better but I liked footy.

Dad scooped the football up off the cave floor. He held it in his hands and looked down readying to kick it though it was deflated. He looked up at me as I went to get it to put it back in my basket. "Imagine the good times your mother and I would have had with boys. I would have coached them and we would have cheered them on each Saturday, and pie nights and club meetings to go to with them. I could have been the president of the club or the coach, your mother on the committee. When they grew up they would have been league footballers too". The short, sharp stab kick flew off my father's boot and hit me in the centre of my heart. The leathery assault winded me as the ball dropped back to my feet and lay there rocking back and forth. I picked it up and hand passed it back to Dad to kick through the goalposts of his broken dreams.

The last year of primary school brought Dad to the school. I'd have liked to say it was because of me but it wasn't, it was my teacher. He was a major league footballer like Dad had been, Dad's matches played in the reserves. He had a team of boys to coach for inter-school matches and needed an assistant coach, a position Dad was eager to fill.

Now the boys preferred to kick the football with Dad and my teacher on the gravel playing field, rather than with me. I walked past their training on my way home, the school yard not mine anymore. Dad bought me a mitt, softball and bat and told me to practice. I did, with the kids in my street.

At half time on inter-school match days, I handed out the oranges to the boys on the bottom oval I'd helped cut up in the staffroom at lunchtime. Dad was in a huddle with the boys yelling instructions, while my teacher listened ready with further tactics to use to beat their opponents. I returned to my softball match, now the captain. As I stood on fourth base waiting to make a home run I looked down to the bottom oval. Dad was pacing up and down the boundary line, engrossed in the game of football.

My footy mates were now my Dad's footy boys. While they were doing laps of the school ground at lunchtime training for the school sports I'd found two of them with Leanne and Wendy at the large slatted wooden door that led under the school. I'd stopped and watched them giggle and kiss before but this time they caught me out. The boys ran over to me and asked me to play kiss chasey with them even though they knew I'd say no. Craig grabbed me and tried to give me a kiss. I pulled my face away and kicked out at him. Andy stood close and blocked my escape and tried to kiss me too. They were both cross I wouldn't play the game. I kicked Andy hard in the shin and ran.

They started to follow me in the playground at lunchtime and waited for me after school, calling me names. They made me cry. They weren't my footy mates any more. I kept telling Mum they were teasing me and calling me names. She told me to go and play somewhere else or tell a teacher. That didn't stop them. They waited for me after school. Craig would push me over onto the asphalt my bag landing on top of me. I'd get up, my knee often scraped and bleeding, grab my bag and run home as fast as I could, sobbing the whole way. Through my tears I'd tell Mum what had happened. At last Mum did something about it.

After school she was waiting at the classroom door. She pulled those two boys to one side and told them to leave me alone or else they would be in big trouble. Their eyes grew big and their faces turned red as our classmates filed out around them looking at them wondering what was going on.

Their name calling didn't end with Mum turning up at the school and telling them off. "Teacher's pet, teacher's pet" followed me across the playground because I didn't get into trouble like some of the others did in my class. I'd get a bit silly and giggle sometimes, often when the teacher read a story. He'd hold up a finger and tell me, "laugh at that" and I'd giggle even more. I couldn't help it. It was all the laughter escaping out of me I couldn't let out at home. The kids in my class knew he visited my place after school sometimes.

While the lounge room was the ladies' salon, the kitchen was the barber shop. My father had cut the hair of the wealthy husband's at the salon, my mother had done the hair of their wives. A battered cardboard box of clippers and razors, combs and scissors sat on the kitchen stool on the small table beside Dad. He tied on the plastic sheet borrowed from the ladies' salon over one of the police boys who dropped in for a few beers and a short back and sides after a nightshift. Though he didn't need an apprentice, I'd watch when I wasn't shooed away. Dad dipped the comb in a glass of water and wet his work colleague's hair with quick, smooth strokes. He sucked on a cigarette and sipped on his beer as he snipped, combed and razored the back of their necks.

Dad did my teacher's hair too. After school he'd come to our house and sip on a cup of tea while he was given his short back and sides. I'd never met a man who didn't drink even on special occasions. I was so relieved he didn't. He didn't smoke either. I hung around in the kitchen to watch and listen to what they were talking about before I was told to go outside and play.

The last year of primary school brought my mother the hope she could go to weekly footy matches again and barrack without being distracted by a restless child by her side. While other children may have wished for a fairy godmother, I had a footy godmother. It was Auntie Helen's job to take me sometimes to major league matches, educate me on the rules of the game and train me to be a good supporter like Mum. She bought me a flogger; a black stick with black and white satin ribbons tied to a small black ball at the top. I liked waving it and yelling when our team scored a goal.

Mum was surprised and delighted when Auntie Helen told her how good I was at sitting and concentrating on the game. That meant it wouldn't be long before we'd be going to a game together on a Saturday afternoon. Until then she had to be content with listening to the match on the radio at home.

Mum shut the kitchen door when Dad was asleep after a nightshift. She'd say, "He's asleep now. Don't disturb him. Play quietly".

The heavy winter rain hit the window. I draped the grey blanket over the kitchen table and crawled under it into my cubby. The clattering of baking tins and the whir of beaters fought the commentary on the radio that sat on the bench, the man shouting out a goal for Mum's team. Mum would be happy if they won today. I was happy when Mum was happy because that meant peace and quiet in the house for a little while.

She brought me afternoon tea, a welcome intrusion for a change. I tried to tune out the man's voice while I read a Secret Seven adventure, crumbs of warm cupcake dropping into my lap. I didn't know how Dad slept through the noise even with the door closed.

"Your father will be awake soon. Pack up. We need the table to have tea". I closed my book in mid-sentence and sighed.

Mum had many years of barracking experience which began when she was a teenager standing on the sidelines watching a local match in the country town she lived with her family. When we visited Pa in wintertime, she grabbed the opportunity to barrack for the local side at a match Pa was in attendance as the head trainer. Pa ran onto the field with his bag and flipped it open beside the injured player, rubbed his knee with liniment and helped him stand. As he ran off to join the game, Pa sprinted to the boundary line and waited on a wooden seat near the coach's box until needed again. Dad was recruited from this team. He sat in the coach's box joining Pa each quarter while the coach barked instructions to his players that carried across the field.

Our car was parked behind the goal posts for a better view of the game. I sat on the bonnet of the car, my sister in the back seat, staring out the side window. Mum stood at the white railing on the boundary yelling encouragement as the goal umpire leaned over ready as the ball came off a player's boot toward the middle posts. I jumped off the bonnet, ready to chase it and throw it back to the field umpire. Mum shouted it through the middle posts then jumped up and down clapping as the goal umpire raised the flags for a goal. The field umpire put his hand up to catch the ball amidst the huffing and puffing of players gathered near the goalposts and blew his whistle. I threw the ball hard and it bounced at his feet. He waved at me and ran off with it under his arm to the centre circle. He blew his whistle and bounced the ball high up in the air.

The last year of primary school I was asked to go and stand beside my teacher at the school assembly. I walked past my classmates and stood beside him wondering what this was all about; calling me out the front and all the school looking at me. It was okay because I was standing beside him so there was no need to be nervous.

"Good, better, best, never let it rest until your good becomes your better and your better, best. Julie is a fine example of this. She practices and practices her long jump. She practices and practices her running at lunchtime and after school. Because of all that training, she gets better jumps and better running times. That is how she became the open long jump champion for the whole district, a hard thing to do with short legs. That is how she won the sprint at the inter-school sports. This is how guts and determination is rewarded. Give her a big clap".

It wasn't the children's applause that rang in my ears, it was my teacher's words of praise. I mightn't have been allowed to play footy matches with the boys but my teacher knew I had what it took to be a sportsperson just like a league footballer too.

... scene 10 ...

the last day of primary school

setting
under the budding child's willow tree of dreams

I sat in my well-worn school desk, my childhood treasures strewn round it in a happy playful way after being enjoyed once again under my willow tree of dreams. On my last day of primary school I didn't want to slide out of my desk, walk out the door of my classroom and have to say goodbye to my teacher.

I dressed with a lot of thought that day. I went to the wardrobe and took out the sleeveless yellow dress with a lime and brown paisley print. It was worn just above the knee as was the fashion, with a yoked neck in the same style as the dress my footy godmother Auntie Helen brought back from Carnaby Street in London. I popped it over my head. I took out a pair of white lace tights from the chest of drawers and pulled them up over my underpants with the pink spots and bow. I'd already laid my shoes at the end of the bed, black patents with a slight heel and a cloth bow. I asked Mum to do my hair in a bun like when I was Susan's flower girl. She brushed it and pulled it up to the top of my head, wove it through the ring and then placed a wide, white band over it. I wanted to look my best for my teacher.

We'd been cleaning up all week. He asked me if he could keep one of my books as a reminder of me. I blushed and passed him my Social Studies book filled with the pictures and words about the different countries we visited during the year. He said he did it every year with his special students. He also said I looked very nice. I blushed even more and smiled, pleased the extra care I'd taken was noticed.

I swung between the desks in the aisle, mine two down from his desk at the back of the room where I could turn around to talk to him. I watched him walk by to the front of the room keeping him in my sight all day. He was removing papers from his desk and putting them in the bin. Some of my ex-footy mates were sweeping the floors and some of the girls were going through the cupboards under the chalkboard, throwing torn paper and worn pencils out. I went outside and banged the dusters after I'd wiped the blackboard clean with wet rags, fighting back tears as the spelling champion of the week box was erased where my name was written many times. My classmates and I went back and forth to our school bags emptying the contents of our desks into them cramming them full. Hawaiian hula music played from a tape our sister class sent us during the year.

Just before lunch we were allowed to sit on our desks as my teacher did when he read to us and we sang together one last time. He led us in to 'Shenandoah' my favourite song to learn of all the ones he sang to us during the year. I loved to hear him sing. He had a better voice than the singers on the weekly school broadcast. The party food made by the mothers was laid out across the front desks on paper plates and washed down with frozen Sunny Boys the mothers at the canteen had provided as a special treat. I loved that orange cordial. Frozen on a hot day was the best way to drink it sucking on the hole to get the thawing icy cold cordial out drop by drop.

... scene 11 ...

the last day of primary school

setting
in the broken child's cave of sorrows

I sat on my picnic basket, the deflated football I'd handpassed to Dad to kick through the goalposts of his broken dreams, at my feet. Using it as a foot rest I gazed into the darkness, shadowy figures appearing as my eyes strained to see who it was. I could just make out my father dressed in his football guernsey, shorts and boots his hand in the air signalling for the ball to be kicked to him. I heard its thud as it landed on his chest. He stepped back and booted it high up into the cave in the direction of the goalposts of his broken dreams. One of his footy boys marked it and kicked it through the centre posts.

The last day of primary school brought Dad to the school. I bet he didn't want to say goodbye either.

I went outside to play with my classmates for the last time but once I was there I didn't want to. I walked to the shelter sheds and stood at the steps that led down to the bottom oval and watched the boys kicking the footy up and down yelling to pass it to each other. I looked over to the empty long jump pit, the sawdust spilled over on to the grass. The sports shed full of balls, netball vests and softball equipment was being packed up ready to be locked up at the end of lunchtime. I moved away and sat on a bench in the shelter shed out of the hot sun trying not to cry.

Dad waited outside the door for the bell to ring for the last time. I looked around the room at all my classmates, some going to high school with me and others to technical college knowing this was the last time we would all be together ever. It didn't feel possible that it was about to end though it would when the bell rang. As it did my heart thundered in my chest as I watched my classmates file to the door and go out to collect their bags. I didn't move as my teacher stood at the door and said goodbye to them one by one until I was the last one to get their bag. Dad collected it off the hook in the corridor and told me to come and say goodbye. I couldn't bring myself to do it. Dad gave me a gentle push towards the door. I burst into tears. My teacher placed his hand on my shoulder as I sobbed. We promised to write to each other. It was a long walk home that day even with Dad carrying my school bag. We walked in silence.

Before tea I wandered outside. Standing tall in the front garden the wattle tree's many thick, black arms reached out to me. There was no need to test them. They were my friends who were there to support my arms and legs each time I climbed to the top and sat down. I picked an orange coated sap lolly, licking its sweet stickiness while I stared out over the high school and its sports fields beyond the busy main road. What was it going to be like there? It will be so different changing classrooms and doing all those new subjects. Will my old friends still want to play with me when we were in different forms? I tucked my legs under and fell back pushing my body back and forward until I was swinging. The colors of the sky and ground whirled and blurred into one.

The pleasure was pierced by Mum's voice. "Get down from there. You'll hurt yourself".

I swung myself back up on to the branch. "I'm not swinging".

"Get down! If you hurt yourself you won't be able to do ballet".

The front door slammed. I liked to think it was the wind.

I stared at the blackbirds sitting in my tree. They whistled to each other and were called away too. They were free. I did as I was told. I ran over to my willow tree, knelt down and parted the branches, the long strands of green leaves caressing my back as I crawled in and lay down on the ground in its veil of quiet and closed my eyes.

"Where are you? Come inside right away".

I didn't answer. She would have to find me.

I, the Temple Woman, watched the two children who lived inside Julie grapple with their conflicting emotions on the last day of school that signalled the ending of their childhood.

The broken child didn't want to leave the protective walls of her classroom or the playing fields of her sporting achievements; both a refuge from the boxing ring called home. The budding child didn't want to leave the support, encouragement and befriending of a teacher who with his care, education and love, watered the seeds she'd plucked from her flower girl basket, putting them into little pots Julie hoped one day she could plant in her garden. These precious seedlings grown in beauty and tended with respect and care, were added to the other pots in her hotchpotch garden alongside her beloved Susan's and the cheerful Mrs Jones. The budding child, knowing she couldn't entrust any of these seedlings to her mother and father's care, gathered all the pots together and placed them under her willow tree for safekeeping.

ACT 2

awkward adolescence

... scene 1 ...

first kiss

setting
under the budding child's willow tree of dreams

I looked in the small round mirror with the pretty pink swirls, dappled sunlight spreading through the branches of my tree reflected in it. As I turned my head from side to side I caught Susan watching me with a smile, dressed in her going away outfit she wore on her wedding day, a small suitcase in her gloved hand. She put the suitcase down, removed her hat and gloves and placed them on the desk, kicking off her shoes with a laugh. She knelt on the ground beside the record player and looked through a stack of my 45's. I joined her delighted when Susan pulled out 'Julie Do Ya Love Me' by Bobby Sherman and put it on. We smiled knowingly at each other. She knew all about Mark. Mum didn't. I could tell Susan anything.

Mark's friend Rob had tried to talk me into a kiss with Mark over many lunchtimes sitting on the long wooden bench in the quadrangle. Just one kiss. It was all arranged. Mark would walk me home from school as he did most nights, holding hands and our schoolbags. This time we'd go down to the vacant block in the court around the corner first and kiss. I so wanted to kiss him but I was too scared to. I didn't want to get into trouble off Mum.

We sat in class holding hands under the desk while our form teacher Mrs Gates patrolled the aisles making sure we were taking notes from the blackboard. It was convenient because I was left handed. We could still hold hands and take notes, plus put up our hands to answer questions. Mrs Gates wouldn't know we were holding hands. I could see my classmates tapping the classmate in front and pointing at us. They were the ones who alerted Mrs Gates.

"Hands above the desk", Mrs Gates said in a firm voice as she stood beside our desk.

Red faced, we pulled our hands apart and folded them in front of us. The giggles and looks weren't enough to stop us doing it again in another class even though we knew we would be asked to stop. You shouldn't hold boy's hands in class. What if Mum found out?

The desire for a kiss triumphed over my fear of being found out by Mum. All shaky and warm, our school bags at our feet for ballast, I swayed about in his strong arms uncertain on the footpath in front of the vacant block in the court. He lowered his head, his mouth finding mine and we kissed. I hoped the kiss was worth it. It must have been because we ended up on the footpath down the court other nights after school.

"You've been kissing boys!" Mum turned from her pill bottles lined up on the kitchen bench, her eyes frosty. The accusation in that sentence hovering in the air between us. I shrank inside as something beautiful I'd held in my heart was torn from it and shredded to bits. I knew I shouldn't have given in. I knew Mum would find out. That's why I'd said no in the first place. But I liked Mark. He was kind to me so I thought I wasn't doing anything wrong. I shook, matching Mum's stare.

"Answer me! You've been kissing Mark after school. I saw you. Keep away from boys. You are too young to kiss boys. You can when you're old enough".

"When's old enough? I'm in high school now".

Mum turned away from me stirring the casserole on the stove with a wooden spoon. I turned on my heel slamming my bedroom door on the argument, kicking off my sweaty school shoes and tossing my long grey socks on the floor. Flopping back on the bed I played with the zipper on the front of my school shift knowing I hadn't done anything wrong but feeling like I had.

Reaching across in front of Susan I put the needle back to the beginning of the record again that Mark bought for me after our first kiss, not tiring of hearing my song. Susan and I sang the chorus out loud together our hands over our hearts Susan pretending she was Mark, me fluttering my lashes at her. He sang the chorus to me in class. He sang it in the school ground and on the way home together after school past the court where we had our first kiss. He sang it while we walked up Thompsons Road together on the morning of my first bleeding.

I'd walked into the toilets where the incinerator the girls put their used sanitary pads in was smoking. The girls stood at the sink in front of the long mirror combing their hair, others sneaking a cigarette taking advantage of the smoke from the incinerator to disguise their rebellion. I'd run out of clean underwear so had to wear my white tennis pants with the wide layer of lacy frills at the bottom to school that day. I closed the toilet door and pulled my pants down to find them stained with fresh, bright red blood. I looked at the blood in disbelief, shaking. I needed to go home and get cleaned up. It wasn't a sports day so I didn't have my red bloomers in my bag that went under my sport shift that would hide the stain. Swallowing hard, I knocked on the headmistress's door and told her what happened. She called Mum.

As the car pulled up in the driveway Dad walked out the front door and waited at the top of the steps. As I approached him with my head down, I heard him say as I walked past, "You're a woman now". I burst into tears.

Mum opened her wardrobe and found the spare elastic with the metal clips and showed me how to attach the pad to it. I went to my chest of drawers, found some fresh pants and fiddled with this contraption that would sit over them every month from then on for a very long time. I put my bloodstained underpants in the dirty wash basket. After having something to eat Mum drove me back to school with some clean pads folded in a brown paper bag. I walked down the corridor to the library with the extra weight I carried in my underwear feeling like it was obvious to everyone that passed me they knew what I knew; I now had my period.

I slid the record back in its sleeve and looked in my mirror with the pretty pink swirls. Susan took the ring off my flower girl's bun then removed the bobby pins out of the donut my hair was wrapped in. She picked up a brush and untangled my long brown hair with gentle strokes. As she brushed my hair I opened my ballet case. I sifted through my Barbie doll clothes with one hand until I felt what I wanted out of it. Pouting my lips, I ran an empty case of lipstick over them Mum had used then blotted the pretend excess off with a tissue as I'd seen her do many times. Now mine, I got out the half wig that was once kept in the drawer in Mum's dressing table for adding to her hair on special occasions. Susan put the hairbrush and my mirror in her lap. I twisted my long hair up on top of my head and pushed the short haired wig over it tucking in the loose ends creating a new look as I'd done for Barbie with her assortment of wigs many times. I picked up the mirror turning my head from side to side looking at myself with short hair. I liked my long hair much better. I'll have short hair when I'm grown up. I slipped off the wig tossing my head from side to side feeling my long hair swishing across my face like a curtain blowing in the wind. Susan pulled my hair up high, took a tie out of the ballet case and put it in place. I found my pink headband and placed it over my hair. Susan twisted my hair pinning it into a more grown up version of the bun I wore on the day I was her flower girl. She held the mirror up behind my head so I could see her handiwork and patted the loose bun. We both smiled at the result.

Susan picked up a daisy that poked out of the grass of the floor of my willow tree retreat and poked it into the hair tie, the finishing touch to my new hairdo. A pale blue daisy sat between the white cups of my first bra. I'd seen the bra under the wig going through my ballet case each cup stained with sweat, the straps worn. I hadn't wanted to wear it. It cut into me making a red rash under my breasts and red marks on my shoulders that itched from the thin straps. Wearing it made my breasts stick out more. It was so embarrassing. I'd pushed on my breasts, angry at them for appearing. Now I couldn't run so fast, they got in the way and hurt. Why couldn't I be a boy? I wanted my flat chest back.

Picking up the empty lip gloss pot that Leanne had given me from my ballet case, I undid the lid digging my finger into it hoping to find enough lipstick to smear a little across my lips but there was none left. Mum's empty lipstick cases in my ballet case belonged with dress ups and ballet concerts where make-up was allowed. I wanted to wear real lipstick to look pretty for boys like Leanne was allowed to. Leanne liked boys and her mother let her pursue her interest in them within reason. She was allowed to wear make-up now she was at high school. Mum said I could wear make-up when I was older but she never told me how old older was. If I wasn't allowed to wear it I could watch Leanne use hers. I'd stood at Leanne's dressing table, her beige beauty case open on the glass top. Leanne pulled the bottle of foundation from behind its strap and a thick cotton ball. She shook some onto it and dabbed it across her cheeks then applied more to the rest of her face. Next she undid the mascara and stroked it onto her lashes then blinked to make sure it had set. The lip gloss pots were all lined up in their straps. She chose one, a pale pink and spread it on her lips, rubbing them together. She asked me if I wanted to try some. I said no, because I knew I wasn't allowed.

I put the mirror down smoothing the creases in my flower girl's dress as I returned the empty pot to my ballet case, closing the lid. Lipstick or not, I'd tasted my first kiss. Other boys wanted to kiss me too but I wasn't quite sure I wanted to in case Mum found out again and there'd be another argument. I didn't want that. Leanne kissed boys and her mother didn't get upset with her when she did. Going to the caravan park where Mr and Mrs Jones had a permanent site with their own van presented many opportunities to kiss boys. Geoff wanted to kiss me and he tried hard to. Though she was everyone's friend, Leanne liked one boy in particular and wanted me to like his friend just as much. I didn't like Brian's friend Geoff in the way Leanne liked Brian but Geoff liked me in the way Brian and Leanne liked each other. Even if I did, it wouldn't make any difference as I wasn't allowed to have a boyfriend. Geoff was as persistent for a kiss as Mark had been. I didn't want to kiss him. He, Leanne and Brian had other ideas.

Blackberry bushes lined the dirt road that ran along two sides of the caravan park. Old fibro beach shacks that could have done with a good coat of paint and the garden with a good prune sat next door to vacant blocks. Mrs Jones gave the four of us some plastic bags and a large bowl to put the blackberries in.

Once out of sight of her Mum, Leanne and Brian had locked lips leaving Geoff and I standing there. I stuck my head into a section of the bushes where I could see some blackberries and started picking them. Geoff was at my side at once. My white T-shirt with the large red apple and bands of black around the arms was soon stained with berry juice as were my lips from eating the ripest ones. Geoff held the bowl while I dropped some berries into it. He found some too. Keeping close, his thick black hair streaked with dead ends from the canes of the bushes he'd buried his face into, he added more berries to the bowl. His body smelled of a strong odour I found unpleasant, that came from eating herbs and spices in food from another culture that was alien to me. He did have a big, happy smile, kind eyes and plenty of chatter for a boy. But it was still not enough for me to want to kiss him and have him as my boyfriend.

Leanne and Brian brought over their plastic bags tipping their pickings into the bowl that was soon full. They held hands as they strolled back to the caravan. Geoff put his hand out to take mine but I stepped ahead of him. He fell in step with me and tried to put his arm around me. I shrugged it off. I didn't want to hurt his feelings but I didn't want to lead him on. I'd tasted my first kiss and many more with Mark. That was enough for me for now.

... scene 2 ...

first date

Tipping the jewellery box upside down bangles and necklaces fell onto my lap as the wind swirled through the branches of my willow tree. Tangled in the plastic pink and purple beaded bracelets was a silver necklace with a pewter heart attached to it. I removed it from the bracelets with patience and held it in my hands stroking the small dimples in the heart that held the bittersweet memories about the boy, my first date, who had given it to me. I lay the heart against my heart as I held the chain around my neck. Susan closed the clasp for me and gave me a kiss on the cheek. I'd hoped for a kiss on the lips from the boy who gave it to me on the way home after my first date three weeks before my fifteenth birthday.

I'd begged Mum to let me got but she said no. I'd begged Dad to let me go out with Gary. He didn't say no but he wasn't sure about it either. Not because of my age but because of the movie I wanted to see. He called it 'Carnival of Knowledge' but it was 'Carnal Knowledge' that was showing at the cinema that Saturday night. It wasn't about the movie, it was about being allowed to go on a date with a boy I liked. Dad relented in the afternoon and let me go. I didn't have a clue what the movie was about. We walked over to the theatre, hand in hand under the stars, rugged up against a chilly spring night. Gary and I sat holding hands during the movie viewing graphic sex scenes between consenting adults, my heart soft and warm being close to a boy I liked who wanted to go out with me, hoping he'd kiss me on the lips on the way home. I felt uncomfortable and awkward seeing what was happening on the screen and I didn't like all the swearing but I was interested in being with Gary more than what we were watching.

As he escorted me to the front door, I saw Dad sitting in his big, gold, comfy chair in his pyjamas and dressing gown. He came to the door and waited while we said goodnight so there was no kiss that night.

Sometimes Gary's class finished before mine. He'd walk past my classroom with a straight back, books under his arm, eyes ahead like a soldier while the rest of the students pushed him along on to the next class. He had tinges of copper in his hair like mine, a smile that was grown up and a broad chest I wanted to lay my head on. Kim kept an eye out for him too and gave me a nudge if she spotted him first. She had a vested interest in doing so because her boyfriend Dennis was his best friend and wouldn't be far behind. Kim and I, two high school best friends, wanted to go on double dates so we could still see lots of each other as we liked to do.

Now we were dating Gary gave me a gift for my birthday. It lay nestled in a black velvet heart shape in a silver box. He gave it to me after school as we walked down Thompson's Road past the jewellery shop where he'd bought it. After I'd opened it he took the pewter heart out of its case and put it around my neck. It stayed there except for when I showered. I hid it under my school uniform so it wouldn't be confiscated by the head mistress. I sat in class feeling its heat against my chest, keen for the class to end so I could look for Gary in the corridor hoping we would meet.

It was his eighteenth birthday two days after my mine so now he had a licence and could borrow his parent's car to take me out. I felt so grown up having a boyfriend that age. We drove to the beach and stood on the sand dunes, the blowing sand stinging our faces and feet. Gary drew me in close to his chest and kissed me, my long hair lashing at his face. I felt his heart beating against my chest and the wanting in his kisses. My face flushed. We drove to the drive-in and while the movie played on the big screen, we kissed. We drove to the Joe Cocker concert in the city in the back of a panel van with a group of Gary's friends and stood in the front row kissing while Joe sang 'Feeling Alright'.

I drifted, locked in a silent bubble when I was with him. My normal self-confidence evaporated when I found myself in the presence of a handsome boy who thought enough of me to buy me a pewter heart. I clung to his hand saying little and to his lips, too uptight to loosen up when we kissed even with his gentle perseverance.

Three months after my birthday Kim and I caught a train to the city to go to the movies, Kim quieter than usual.

As we stopped at a station many stops from where we got on, she blurted out, "Gary doesn't want to go out with you anymore. He's dropped you".

"Dropped me? How do you know that?"

"Dennis. Gary told him he doesn't want to go out with you anymore. He told Dennis to tell me to tell you".

Kim didn't know where to look as the tears poured down my cheeks. My pewter heart burnt my chest and the chain dug into my neck. I wasn't going to take it off though. It must be a mistake. It would be sorted out at school on Monday. I couldn't believe Gary didn't have the guts to tell me himself.

It was soon evident that it was true. Gary avoided me for days. Dennis wouldn't tell me where he was and Kim wasn't helpful either, her loyalties divided between us both. I saw him in the quadrangle at lunchtimes with another girl in my year sitting on the long wooden bench where I'd been talked into my first kiss with Mark. Kim told me they were dating. Not long after, they both left school. Kim told me Gary got her pregnant and they were married and he was a truck driver in the army. Later in the year I saw him walk through the double doors towards the sixth form common room dressed in his army uniform to spend some time with Dennis and their other mates. My heart lurched, the feelings for him still there but he had made an enforced new life for himself now with my former classmate so I had to get over him.

I put the silver box the pewter heart came in back in my jewellery box, the ballerina turning in a jerk, jerk, jerk three-four time waltz, threatening to wobble off her ageing pivot. The match making and pairing of youth had continued in a circle like a turn of the ballerina in my jewellery box within the friendship groups formed in the classrooms, corridors and the quadrangles of my large suburban high school. Gary's friendship group Kim belonged to kept the match making and pairing turning for me. As I was shy with Gary, Gary's friend Paul was shy with me. As I was too quiet for Gary, Paul was too quiet for me but I liked him because he was gentle. His mother had us married off after an invitation for dinner with the family, which was far too presumptuous of her. Though there was never going to be an engagement ring, walking me home from school his cheeks flushed as he fumbled in his blazer pocket and took out a rectangular silver box which he handed to me. Inside was a chunky silver bracelet.

Though he didn't have my heart like Gary he had given me something that opened my heart. I asked him to put it on my wrist and we kissed. I wore the bracelet long after the short time we went out together. I picked up the bracelet out of my jewellery box and tried to put it round my wrist. Susan saw me struggling and took it so I offered my wrist to her. I jiggled it as I liked to see it turn on my arm its weight against my wrist.

As I looked around under my tree I noticed frills of blue lace peeking out from behind my ballet case. I thought it was one of my Barbie's outfits at first but it belonged to a doll with a pouting red mouth that a boy would buy his sweetheart at a sideshow. It went with a track from an album another boy had given me along with the doll that expressed to me how he felt. As he wasn't very good with words he sang the song 'You're Sixteen', by Ringo Starr to me over and over in his broad Scottish accent. I sifted through the 33's and put it on the turntable, the needle bobbing up and down on the warped vinyl. Tad was the builder's apprentice who'd come to build a new bedroom for me on the back of the house. He had no taste in gifts but a lot of love in his heart for me. I sat the gaudy doll on my desk as the song finished. I took the needle off the record staring with a smile at the doll.

... scene 3 ...

my cheesecloth dress

Susan picked a dress out of the small suitcase that lay beside the record player and held it up in front of me, a cheesecloth dress with a wide bow that tied at the back. I looked in the suitcase to see if the white leather shoes with the high cork heels were there too. I took them out and dusted them off, the leather now cracked, as I slipped off my flower girl shoes and slipped my cork platforms on.

Not wanting to ruin my hairdo I stood and pulled my flower girl's dress up over my head a bit at a time and laid it on the desk. I took my cheesecloth dress from Susan, pulled it over my head turning around for Susan to tie the bow at the back. She obliged liked Mum had when I asked her before I went out somewhere special. Though I wanted to go clothes shopping with Mum, instead Mum, my sister and I went clothes shopping with Dad.

We used to meet him at the factory in an inner city suburb where he was stationed. He arranged with the owner for us to go there sometimes as he let Mum and I choose some clothes. We walked by the women at their sewing machines running colorful fabrics of various shapes and sizes through them at a great rate.

The owner met us in the reception area and we followed him up to his office where we looked down on the workers through a large window. A lady came in with a rack of clothes. I chose a cheesecloth dress with a patterned bodice and a wide bow at the back and a pair of paisley hot pants with a matching sleeveless long jacket. Mum chose an orange linen mini with a big floppy navy bow and a spotted skirt with matching navy jacket to wear to Ladies Day at the races.

Dad had the same arrangement at the shoe factory, our next stop. I chose a pair of white leather shoes with high cork platforms to go with my cheesecloth dress and a pair of white leather clogs to wear with my hot pants. Mum chose a pair of navy high heels and a pair of white wedge shoes for herself. My sister had to wait until she was old enough to fit into these clothes and shoes.

My cheesecloth dress hung in the wardrobe in the front bedroom of Susan and Ray's old period home waiting for an occasion to wear it while my sister and I stayed for the school holidays. This time it was different as Susan was pregnant with their first child, something she and Ray never thought would happen but were delighted it had.

"Oh to be sixteen again!", Susan's friend who'd called in to see her said as she stood at the wardrobe door holding the dress up against herself. "I'd never get into that". Susan patted her growing belly, smiled and said, "Don't think it will fit me either!" We all laughed.

Susan covered her aching feet in some iced water then put them up on a footstool and lay back on the divan while I massaged them for her. After she'd had enough I got my sister and I a drink and sat by Susan. We watched TV while she dozed off in the heat.

When Ray came home from work, he told us to get dressed - we were going out for dinner. I rushed to the bedroom, put on my cheesecloth dress and asked my sister to tie the bow at the back.

I wore my cheesecloth dress with my high heeled shoes the day I visited Susan in hospital. She held her new born baby daughter out to me. I sat up on the bed beside her as she passed her to me. I cradled her in my arms her face all squashed up, content. My sister stood back until Susan patted the bed beside her. She leaned in against her and watched the sleeping baby. Ray leaned over the bed and held their longed for baby girl's hand.

My cheesecloth dress was my favourite dress to go dancing in. My boyfriend Chris drove me in his parent's station wagon to the old weatherboard hall half way between both our homes where the dance class was held every Friday night.

My friend Debbie from primary school who had danced en pointe like Dame Margot Fonteyn had swapped her ballet shoes for a pair of ballroom dancing shoes with a heel and sparkling straps. They enabled her to sashay across the dance floor with style and precision with her dance partner. Other members of my old dance troupe donned similar shoes and were emulating Debbie's style.

Chris took my hand. We stepped onto the floor with the rest of the dancers who wanted to have a dance before the class started. Joining in a waltz, dipping and swaying his lead firm, my body light and free, we glided over the dance floor.

There were many more boys lining its perimeter watching than on it dancing. They had a different agenda, to meet and make out with willing girls. Quite a few of them were already outside with them having a smoke or locked in passionate embraces. My friends, Leanne, Wendy and the boys they used to play kiss chasey with were out there more than on the dance floor. Kim and I just went outside to get some fresh air during a break. Kim's boyfriend Dennis and his friends thought ballroom dancing wasn't cool, preferring to spend their Friday nights at a teacher's place. They had an open house invitation there to party as long and as hard as they liked with others from the high school.

Our dancing teacher Ron stepped up onto the stage and put on some cha-cha music. He asked the boys to find a partner as the class was about to begin. The other teacher Jill opened the doors calling the smooching couples and other stragglers inside closing them in, ensnaring them against their will.

Stiff and awkward boys tried to make their feet go where Ron and Jill showed them by their example and in time to the music. The girls tripped over their feet as they slid into the boys bumping toes and laughing with embarrassment. It gave Chris and I an opportunity to put into practice what we had learned in preparation for our Latin American medal exam that was coming up. Many hours were spent at the old weatherboard hall across the road from my old primary school where I'd already spent just as many hours learning and rehearsing dance steps with my dance troupe.

The lights were dimmed for the last dance of the evening 'The Crunch', the reason many of them came to dancing. Jill put on 'Happy Together', by The Turtles. The boys with their confidence lifted by the dim light approached the girls of their choice to get up close and steal a kiss full on the lips if the girls would let them. Chris led me onto the floor. I put my arms around his neck as he put his around my waist drawing me close, the smell of menthol cigarettes lingering on his breath as he leaned into my ear and nibbled on it.

As was the way of 'The Crunch', Chris and I changed partners. I made my way around the circle being held close by boys who would like to be closer but who I didn't want to get any closer to other than for a brief sway, relieved I could move on to the next one. A combination of their after shave and perspiration, the odour intensified by anticipation, thwarted any advances they may have wished to make, even if I hadn't been dating Chris. For many of the girls, it made no difference at all.

In my eyes Chris was as much a trophy as the ones we collected for the various dance categories we won together. Handsome and well-mannered, he treated me like a young lady. He opened doors and pushed my chair in at elegant places he took me to for dinner before we went dancing at various town halls where weekly dances were held. His practiced sophistication came from already having left school, studying engineering at university and supporting himself with a part-time job. This was dating that with time leads to the commitment of marriage if you let it. Chris was ready for it and I wasn't.

Susan stood up and stretched her fingers touching the top of my weeping willow tree. She folded my flower girl's dress over her arm and smoothed it into place in the suitcase with her fingertips. She handed me the turquoise gloves from the ballet case and matching headband that'd been removed when she'd done my hair in a grown up bun. The gold bangle she'd given me for being her flower girl was placed back on its maroon velvet pillow inside the matching box with the faded gold trim. She returned them to my flower girl's basket where they all belonged together then twisted the yellowed white satin bow straight on the basket. She stood it on the desk then arranged the stack of 33's into a neat pile beside it. After looking around my willow tree to make sure all was in order she put on her hat, gloves and shoes and kissed me goodbye with a long hug to go with it.

Susan walked out the doorway of the budding child's weeping green world leaving her to its sanctuary, knowing she had done all she could to nurture her to grow up into a young woman. Even though Susan loved her as if she was her own child and would continue to do so remaining a central figure in her life, it was a mother's job to tend her daughter's garden to help it flourish and grow.

Undoing the bow on the back of my cheesecloth dress I lifted it over my head. Taking off my high heeled shoes I placed them beside the dress then unfolded my flower girl dress stepping back into it not wanting to crease or tear it and put on my turquoise shoes. I picked up my flower girl basket, took out the maroon box and put it in my jewellery box. I laid the cheesecloth dress and platform shoes back in the suitcase with the turquoise gloves and matching top knot ring. I liked my new, more grown up hairdo and would keep my hair that way now but not the cheesecloth dress that went with it.

Through Susan's love and attention Julie's budding child gained the confidence to explore the seeds of her femininity as she grew into a young woman. With this growing confidence she was able to shed her flower girl's dress and shoes and clothe herself in a pure white dress and matching shoes that reflected her desire to express her new found femininity. However, something held her back though she wanted to be more grown up. This knowing was strong in her, stronger than her desire to express her femininity as a young woman. It was the pervasive fear of the broken child spreading across her heart entangling itself in the hotchpotch garden of her small pots of seedlings, strangling their growth. Her confidence shrivelled up as she negotiated the challenges of teen romance and so she shrank back down to a young child again happy to be dressed in the comfort of her flower girl's dress. Her desire was to keep her precious seedlings safe at all costs until the opportunity came to plant them in her garden and watch them flourish and grow.

... scene 4 ...

drinking

setting
in the broken child's cave of sorrows

The tears slid down my face. Wiping my eyes I stood up and wandered through the cave. I tripped over some bottles causing me to fall flat on my face. I knelt up holding my side, winded. I picked up one of the culprits responsible, a Cinzano bottle. There were others, as well as empty gin, vodka and brandy bottles. Different colored swizzle sticks their tips cracked and broken were strewn in amongst them.

> This family debris littered the cave, each bottle responsible for the perpetuation of a family story filled with pain and grief, it's only resolution to be found in a drained glass of alcohol.

Jutting out of a pile of dead leaves, was the top of what I thought looked like a large packing crate. I swept the leaves away with my hands, revealing a bar built of cane that in places had peeled away from the frame. On the top of it was my parents record player. I looked behind it for my records and found a stack of them on a ledge underneath in amongst theirs. I dragged over the speakers and chose a record, 'Sgt. Pepper's Lonely Heart Club Band' by the Beatles and put it on, the music bringing some of my high school friends out of the shadows.

Mum hurried up to the bar, led there by the blaring music bouncing off the cave walls, curious to know what was going on. She smiled when she saw Tammy, Louise and Vicki giving out hugs and kisses to my high school friends. They ranged in size; tall sophisticated Tammy with the long hair and legs, medium sized Vicki with a cheeky smile that matched her sharp wit, and pint sized Louise who had energy to burn though quiet like tall and dark haired Carolyn until they got a few drinks into them.

Laughing, tea towel in hand, Dad wiped the glasses shiny clean between taking orders with a red wine in his hand and a bottle on the counter, happy to run the bar. My friends and I liked flavoured soft drinks; coke and rum, lemon squash and gin, dry ginger and brandy. We liked juice drinks too, orange and vodka my juice drink of choice. I bent down and picked up a couple of the swizzle sticks. I turned them over in my hands. One of them had stirred my first drink when I was twelve. I'd taken the yellow swizzle stick Mum offered me stirring the drink round so fast the ice bobbed up and down crashing against the sides of the small glass with a thick, bubble bottom. The slice of lemon tossed about as the dry ginger frothed and fizzed daring to spill over but I stopped stirring just in time.

We sat down on the couch clinked glasses and said cheers. The bubbles went up my nose as I sipped on my first glass of grown up drink and giggled. I didn't like the taste of Cinzano and dry. It was bitter. I'd had sips before. I drank it because Mum did before tea when Dad was home to keep her company. I'd asked for my own glass before but she'd said no. Since I was in high school now, she'd changed her mind saying I could on the condition it was a weak one and only on weekends. I'd felt a very grown up and sophisticated twelve year old burping and giggling some more until I drank it all while watching the TV; all warm, tingly and a little light headed. Now the flavoured soft drinks became a party starter at my place on weekends.

I heard a familiar voice singing a familiar ditty coming from the direction of the bar in the cave.

"Every little boy would like to be, a fairy under the Christmas tree". It wasn't Christmas and it wasn't Santa, though he had a rotund belly the size of his. Light on his feet for his height and girth my history teacher danced and sang in front of the bar, a glass of white wine in his hand. He was egged on by my girlfriends who were also part of his class and get-togethers at my place. We all laughed as Macca did a twirl on his tippy toes like the ballerina in my jewellery box. We were allowed to call him that when we weren't at school. We were also allowed to know he was gay.

He clinked glasses with the members of his history class and did a twirl on his toes up to the bar to top up his wine where he passed around his packet of cigarettes. Carolyn and Tammy took one each and lit up. Louise looked through the records as the music had stopped. More was needed to keep the party going. She put on some Led Zeppelin.

My friends grabbed Macca shaking themselves up close to him to the heavy beat. He moved his huge girth towards them threatening to bump against them making them squeal with laughter.

Not to be left out of the fun, Dad whipped out his top set of false teeth. He plonked them on the bar top pounding his fists to the beat. They jumped and rattled along the counter threatening to leap off the end to our screams of laughter. He juggled them in his hands like a slippery creature popping them back in his mouth with a grin. Mum laughed along at the high jinks.

Like Mum, my sister was drawn to the blaring music. She stood there with her bag of lollies, her teddy bear tucked up under her arm watching. Large glossy posters with bits out of them of pop stars flapped on the front of the bar catching her attention. She put down her teddy and bag of lollies tearing a poster off taking it away from the revelry and laying it on the ground nearby. She knelt down on it placing small rocks on each corner to flatten it out not wanting to tear it any further. This group's music wasn't played at these get-togethers as my friends and I didn't like it. Gone were the days sitting up close to the TV eating lollies bought from the money left in her fairy ring, eyes locked on the screen watching cartoons in silence. She satisfied her sweet tooth now she was older with the pop group Sweet. Sitting in the same position in front of the TV she had as a child she screamed and cried at the group when they appeared on a pop show singing their latest hit, their posters plastered all over her bedroom wall.

My sister put her teddy and lollies down on the bar top and took a small, sweet flavoured drink with a dash of alcohol Dad offered her. Though her music wasn't played at these get-togethers she joined in and partied too. I grabbed her for a dance, her long waves of thick, brown hair swishing across her waist as we jumped from side to side holding hands singing along to 'Venus' by Shocking Blue.

Dad stopped pouring drinks for a moment and tapped me on the shoulder. He bounced the football at his feet he'd taken from my basket yelling to me to catch it as I kept dancing with my sister and friends. I spun round until I was dizzy crashing into Macca. I fell to the ground and kicked out at the football in hysterical laughter grateful for Dad's presence at the bar, hopeful it might mean he wanted to spend time with me.

As he poured more drinks for us all, our drunken revelry rivalled that of his family sitting at the kitchen table near the slippery pyramid of beer bottles. He bobbed down and like in a Punch and Judy show let his fingers dance along the bar top. My friends squealed with laughter. They made the peace sign at him chanting 'Top Cop', their name for him. He made the peace sign back.

My closest friend Kim didn't join us. Coming from a family of teetotallers, she didn't drink. She knew how to have fun without any in her. Her big, grey eyes twinkled without it matching her mischievous smile. We'd meet on the other side of the horse paddock every morning.

She'd watch as I climbed under the barbed wire fence throwing my school bag over the top dodging galloping horses and their mounds of poo to get to the end of the gravel laneway where she waited for me. We giggled and gossiped all the way to school about boys, teachers and the other girls, past the shops up Thompsons Road then again on the way home. I ducked under the fence throwing my school bag full of books over it, a couple of horses galloping in hot pursuit.

Though absent from my primary school years until the final year, Dad was at the high school often in his capacity as a detective.

The siren went off and we were told over the loudspeaker to go to the assembly area and line up in our forms. Another bomb scare. That meant Dad would arrive soon. I saw the squad car pull up and him get out with the other police boys whose voices I knew from a 'quiet drink' late at night at our place after a shift; voices that kept me awake. I put my head down squeezing up against some of my friends who called out 'Top Cop', making the peace sign at him. He ignored them as he was at school on official business. After he gave the police boys instructions, they searched under the school and in the toilets. Dad went inside the school building in the direction of the Principal's office.

I was very uneasy when he came up to the school in the police car as many of the students knew he was my Dad. A couple of older boys recognised him too, ones he'd charged with shoplifting, doing drugs and stealing cars. Those were things I knew about, even if my parents and Macca thought I didn't. Knowing those things caused me trouble. It started with being followed after school.

As I walked down past the court where I shared my first kiss with Mark I heard a car start up. Humming to myself to keep my nerves at bay I hurried home with the car following me. It turned in to my street and came up beside me. Boys I didn't recognise wound down the windows and stared at me. I looked away and ran the last bit until I was inside yelling for Mum.

"These guys followed me home. Come and look". Mum looked at me not sure what I was saying. I tugged at her arm. "Come outside with me". Mum followed me to the gate and looked down our street. They saw us coming. The driver started to reverse slowly to the street corner, the passengers still staring at us.

"Did you get the rego?" Mum asked.

"No. I didn't want to look at them in case they did something". They were still parked at the corner watching us.

"Let's go inside and ring your father".

Now I was worried having to walk the last part home from school by myself. What if they came back? Why were they trying to scare me?

When I asked Dad all these questions when he got home, he said gruffly, "It's a police matter. It's taken care of".

I wanted to believe it was true and it wouldn't happen again but it did. They waited at the bottom of the street. When they saw me coming, they drove off. I hastened my pace looking back just in case they came back and drove up my street. I was relieved when they finally stopped turning up at the bottom of the street after school.

Then the phone calls started. I picked up the phone. There was heavy breathing at the other end. I spoke and the line went dead. Then they got up the courage to speak. I hung up when a different young male voice started to talk. He was just one of the many boys at school I passed in the corridor going to the next class. He might have known me but I wasn't aware I knew him at all. It wasn't just the students knowing my father was a policeman that was a problem, it was also my English teacher.

"Pig's daughter". I turned my back pretending I hadn't heard. Some of their friends joined in, chanting louder and louder, "Pig's daughter, pig's daughter, we're going to get you pig's daughter". One of the boys pushed me to the ground. I jumped straight back up pushing myself into the thick of the assembly not caring if I wasn't with my form any more as I was supposed to be so the teachers could do a head count.

Pig was a word he was fond of using in class.

"Julie. Stand up!" he shouted as he glared at me. I was only half listening, as I didn't like him. Like his students, he had a uniform too; jeans, dirty sneakers and a faun blazer with patches on the sleeves. When he passed by to correct our work his clothes smelled musty and he stunk of body odour. There were whispers at the school he was a left wing radical socialist. By the way others said those words, I gathered that wasn't a good thing to be. I refused to stand up, continuing to watch him. He stood at the front of the class holding a magazine in his hand.

"Julie, stand up!" All eyes were on me. Kim held my arm as I stood up on shaky legs. She looked worried. So did the rest of the class. He pointed at me and said, "Your father is a fascist pig. You are a pig. This is a police state. Our freedom is being taken from us every day". He walked up the aisle to where I stood thrusting the magazine in my face. I could see his angry face and his mouth moving but I couldn't hear a word he was saying. The tears fell down my cheeks. He must have seen them but he didn't stop ranting. That was all he cared about, exhausting his anger. Why did I have to be a policeman's daughter? I felt Kim's arm around me as I sat back down beside her, still shaking, my mouth dry.

I wanted a drink of water and the bell to ring for the end of the period. After, with Tammy, Kim and Carolyn in a huddle around me, some of my classmates came up to me and said, "We're going to get him. He's an idiot. He's not going to get away with it". He's a madman I thought, as I blew my nose on a tissue Kim handed to me and tried to stop my tears.

After school I told Mum what'd happened. She said if he ever did something like that again to tell her. It didn't but he had the last word by marking each of my assignments down. Before my marks were high. If I questioned him, he started to raise his voice at me so I walked away.

Dad's side of the family were oblivious to the revelry at the bar in the cave but Nana must have been disturbed by it. She approached my party with a black duffle coat over her arm. She tapped Dad on the shoulder and pointed at it. He took it off her and put it on me, the football tucked under his arm. The coat was very dusty the material worn thin at the elbows but the white number 40 was still intact on the back. Lengths of black and white crepe paper all matted, the colors bled into one another from the rain, trailed from the ends of the coat. Nana tore them off the coat to add to the pile of wrappers and bits of driftwood she'd collected, ready for another fire to make tea when she needed a rest from cleaning up the cave. It was that coat that brought Dad and I to the men's department store on Thompsons Road.

We'd looked through the rack of coats together. The salesman helped with the size and I left the store wearing my new coat. Though he would never have the pleasure of buying a son his football gear to wear at a game, he had the small one of buying his daughter a duffle coat to wear to one.

It was a home game so the family sat in our usual spot in the grandstand. Dad joined us when he got off work, missing the start of the match. I spotted him at the top of the steps first scouting the crowd looking for us, wearing his beige woollen coat with the paisley scarf tucked into it. I stood up, waved and called out to him. We moved along and he sat down taking his flask of whisky from his coat pocket and taking a long swig 'to keep him warm'. We all booed the umpire when a decision didn't go our team's way - screamed and clapped when we scored a goal, just like my footy godmother had taught me. My sister and I waved our floggers we'd made out of crepe paper on the lounge room floor with Mum's help. Mum was the most vocal of us all.

At half time small goalposts were erected fast, creating a mini oval for the Little League. The young boys ran onto the oval the crowd clapping as their game got underway. There was one boy who played for our team in that league, the son of a local publican whose establishment Dad frequented amongst others on his beat. The weeks he played we picked him up and drove him to his match, Dad escorting him to and from the change rooms. Our footy family sat eating a warm pie with sauce each as we watched the game. My parents cheered and clapped when he touched the ball and shouted encouragement as he kicked it to another player or sometimes through the goals. We returned to the publican's son's home after the match joining the publican and his family for a drink to drown a loss or celebrate a win, the first round on him. When my parent's footy son stayed for the weekend, we sat in front of the TV watching the replay, cheering and clapping with a hot meal on a TV tray in front of us.

The noise of drunken revelry had died down in the cave. My girlfriends and I flopped into bean bags. The sides had split, the filling escaping as we wriggled to get comfortable. We sang the chorus of the last song played at the party over and over, giggling. Dad was putting the lids back on the bottles of spirits. As he lined them back up in the glass cabinet Macca stood at the bar watching him as he finished his drink and smoke. Mum was back with her sister at the clothesline bringing another load of washing in, my sister nowhere to be seen. Dad's family had gone quiet at the kitchen table, their drinking and argument spent for the time being, the table covered in empty bottles, the ash trays full of butts.

After Pa's funeral a crowd of people jammed into the house in amongst tables covered in empty bottles, ash trays full of butts, platters of sandwiches and plates of cakes. Auntie Win stood there in amongst the group in the kitchen making a half-hearted attempt to be hostess at her husband's wake, half drunk and half merry. Auntie Bev wandered between the groups of family friends and relatives, half drunk and half sad, both women incapable of expressing the extent of their grief at their loss. Dad was totally drunk and totally obnoxious, lurching in and out amongst the mourners, unable to cope with the death of his father. The person Dad looked up to and respected all his life was gone; a massive heart attack while assisting with first aid at a large bushfire some kilometres from his home, taking his life. It wasn't the first one, other heart attacks seeing him admitted to hospital while staying at our place. Those times standing by the hospital bed with Dad I glimpsed moments of the kind of tenderness between father and son I longed for between Dad and I. Dad kissed Pa's forehead and stroked it, pushing his hair back off it with a gentle touch. Pa's face was grey and he looked tired. I gave him a kiss on the cheek and stood there not knowing what to say. At these times there was no drunken banter to hide behind and the laughter and jokes that went with it, which I had joined in now with a drink in my hand.

The day of Pa's funeral I didn't have a drink. I stood by the kitchen table and drifted off thinking of the times Pa came to stay at our place in an attempt to distance myself from the noise that filled the house.

Pa rose very early each morning before sunrise. He woke me with the grunting and slapping of his sides as he did his star jumps and knee bends then running on the spot in the kitchen making the floorboards creak and groan. The clattering of cups and plates and the kettle whistling told me his breakfast was just about ready. I turned over trying to go back to sleep, giggling. It sounded like we had a giant mouse in the house.

He waited for the morning paper to be delivered. By the time the family were ready to read it he'd managed to fold and crumple it into such a badly made piece of origami that even with slow unfolding of the pages back in place made it impossible to read. It made us laugh.

One year a man Pa visited in the city drilled holes in his head each time he came to stay with us. The man filled them with strands of his hair he'd taken from the long bits he'd let grow down his neck. The hair was supposed to grow and fill up the top of his bald head. It looked like a shower head full of fine spray holes. I thought it looked hilarious. I giggled as he sat my sister on his knee at the kitchen table tugging on her pony tail while we waited for the roast to cook. "Did you 'ice-cream' your pants today?" My sister nodded her head. He bumped her on his knee tugging her pony tail again taking a swig of whisky from his cut crystal glass swimming with ice cubes.

"Argh", he said. My sister half smiled not sure if she was in trouble or not. She looked at Mum. She got angry when she 'ice creamed' her pants or worse, the bed. Mum had to strip it down and change it in the middle of the night. She put a change of pants in her school bag just in case. The first thing Mum did when my sister arrived home from school was look in her school bag to see if there was a wet pair in there.

"She should have grown out of it by now. Better take her to a doctor and see if there's something wrong with her bladder", Pa told Mum and Dad but they didn't answer.

Dad got up, pouring another whiskey for himself and Pa. Mum took the roast out of the oven asking Dad to carve. He went to the junk drawer and rummaged through the odd knives. He grabbed the bone handled one worn uneven down both sides. He sharpened it first, attacking the roast with it just like some man had attacked another's flesh; one of the perks of being a policeman was being given knives to take home that were exhibits in a murder trial, he said.

Pa filled the house with the noise of his life. After we returned him to the railway station in the city, his head full of new holes filled with fresh little hairs, the house was as quiet as the inside of an empty church until Mum and Dad's next argument.

I saw my grandmother sitting at the kitchen table in the cave all alone, a single trail of smoke curling in the air from the cigarette in her ash tray. The beer in the bottom of her glass was flat, as were her eyes. I walked up to her wanting to say something to her but not knowing what, my grandmother being in drunken oblivion. She got up from the kitchen table and shuffled off, staggering and stumbling, weaving in and around the empty bottles near the bar. I watched her until the cave's darkness swallowed her stooped figure whole.

The broken child's transition from childhood to adolescence was not an easy one as she was no longer ensconced in the protective walls of a classroom with a teacher she loved and for whom she had great respect. Her father who visited her high school in his capacity as a policeman was unable to protect her from the bullying of the students he convicted for crimes, or the teacher who thought that being a policeman was a reprehensible profession not worthy of his respect so neither was a policeman's daughter. The spectre of the bully grew in size and influence without that protection, continuing to cast a murky light over her life. Julie began to adopt the family story and believe it was her own as she began to drink alcohol too; the reward a relationship with her father for the first time in her life, which she craved as much as the alcohol she consumed to deaden the pain she carried, as all her father's family had learned to do.

I, the Temple Woman watched the broken child sink further into despair and further into the family story, the one that was not her own, waiting for the time she was ready to meet and befriend the budding child who would lead her to me.

... scene 5 ...

looking for love

Laying in our beanbags the party now over, my girlfriends and I stopped singing. I hadn't noticed the large fan shaped chair, its back coming apart, upside down against the peeling cane bar. Hauling myself out of the bean bag I turned it over and sat on the sagging base, the bar now deserted and watched my girlfriends wander off after my father and Macca.

> That large fan shaped cane chair was used for boys to sit on and wait when they came by to pick Julie up to take her out. It sat outside her bedroom door across from her father's bar in the small family room.
> Her mother was kept busy coming in and hissing at her to hurry up, '*he*' was waiting. The budding child had often been up until the early hours at her desk trying to finish an essay that was due and was tired so slow to get ready. The broken child kept the same hours, drinking with her friends.
> There was one boy with a gentle heart and a short, strong body who sat waiting on the cane chair outside Julie's bedroom door for her. He started out of the chair when she appeared pale faced with black rings under her eyes, her long hair lank and greasy despite her washing it, dressed in her cheesecloth dress and white platform shoes. Grim faced, his young brow knotted with worry seeing the state his girlfriend was in.

Glen guided me by the arm to his old blue Morris and I jumped in exhaling a deep sigh relieved I was escaping this madhouse I lived in, even if it was for a few hours. After a movie and dinner with a group of friends we sat parked outside my house, the mist fogging up the windows as we kissed, his hand on my breast.
He whispered, "I love you".
"No, you don't".
"I love you", he insisted.
I couldn't let him love me. What if Mum found out what we'd been doing? I'd get into trouble. I mustn't get pregnant to anyone ever. I

pulled myself away and opened the car door. Glen held my shaking hand and walked me to the door. Even though I allowed him to touch my breast as I trusted and cared for him so much it was something I'd never let another boy do. I couldn't let it lead any further. Though I had deep feelings of love for him I wouldn't dare express them with the expectations it would awaken in him.

On the night's Glen and I went out the key was left in the front door and the light on. Now Mum waited for me as well as for Dad though I was the one often home first. I must have been dozing as the slamming of the car door woke me. He was in, muttering and cursing. He opened the kitchen door. He was close. The talking was getting louder. Who was he talking to? I opened my sliding door a crack to see what he was doing. He was talking, muttering, then laughing with the man in his painting on an easel in the family room beside my bedroom door, a German man with a monocle over one eye. Dad picked up his paintbrush and mixed colors on his palette. He dabbed at the German man's cheekbones and then his eyes, returning to the palette for more paint. He knocked the easel causing the man in the painting to crash onto the floor face down. He cursed some more fumbling about until he threw the painting of the man back onto the easel. He stood back, looked at the man in the painting and laughed. He mumbled some more at him before losing interest in doing any more. He closed the kitchen door cursing again as the hall table banged against the wall. The thumps were dulled through their closed bedroom door. He went quiet.

I walked into the kitchen to turn the light off then stopped to look at the painting. I didn't like the man. His eyes looked mean. I wondered why Dad wanted to paint him and why he wanted to talk to him during his late night painting sessions. He was out of control. It just wasn't right how he behaved. Was he a loony too? I closed my sliding door and climbed back into bed. Thump! What was that? I clutched the blankets in my fingers, my heart pounding. Was he all right? I hoped Mum would come and have a look. She must have heard it too. I crept to the sliding door of my room and peeked out the kitchen. The light on again stung my sore and tired eyes. He was on his knees on the kitchen floor vomiting, his hacking cough turning me cold. I wasn't cleaning that up. I hated the smell of vomit. It made me gag. Mum opened the kitchen door and saw him, noticing me too.

"Come and help me get him up".

"*No*", I wanted to say, "*I don't want to touch him*". Without saying a word, I did as I was told, my feet getting cold standing on the tiles. I just wanted it all to be done with so I could get some sleep.

I sat in the sagging cane chair in the cave, swinging my legs back and forth. I kicked the empty pill bottles that kept gathering at my feet amongst the dead leaves, the empty liquor bottles and torn posters poking through them, another old argument ringing in my ears.

"I can't put up with much more of your behaviour. It's driving me mad". Mum banged about in the cupboard looking for a saucepan to start dinner to have it ready to heat up when we got home from the doctor's appointment.

"I don't want to go. There's nothing wrong with me. I just need to be left alone to study so I'm ready for the exams".

"You're going and that's it. You're impossible to live with at the moment. You need some help to calm and relax you".

"No, I don't. I'm sick of taking pills. They don't work anyway. They haven't done a thing to help you".

"Don't talk to me like that. You know you have to take antibiotics for your tonsillitis. You keep getting it all the time. You've got your exams to get through. If you need the help, you have to take them. You have to get through your exams and then you can relax".

I gave in. I didn't have any choice. When I left home I could do what I liked. I won't be taking any more pills that's for sure. I hate taking pills. They make me feel sick in the stomach and nauseated, dry in the mouth and they put me off my food. I loved to eat despite Mum's efforts to get me to cut back on what I ate. The family doctor prescribed a sedative.

"Just half of one a day to start with. If you need to, you can bump it up to one a day".

"I don't want to take them".

"They will calm you down. Take the edge of your nerves. You are going through a very stressful time preparing for your final exams", the doctor said.

"She wants to be a teacher. If she doesn't get good grades she won't get in to college, so she has to work hard. She can't afford to get sick now. The exams are just a few weeks away", Mum said.

"I can't think when I take tablets".

"Well just try, see how you go. If you have any problems, make another appointment to come and see me". Mum got up and followed me out. I'd have to take them. She would never get off my back if I didn't.

I wriggled in the sagging cane chair in the cave, leant down and begrudgingly put an empty pill bottle in my basket, baulking at the inescapable inevitability of it finding its way into my basket, no matter how I tried for it to be otherwise.

I stared at the bottles of spirits lined up on the dilapidated bar. Dad's love was tied to the alcohol I consumed from that now empty gin bottle that lay in my basket. I needed to drink to assure the continuance of his love. I wasn't going to jeopardise losing it when I'd spent so long trying to find and keep it. I took the gin bottle out of my basket and stood it on its end, an empty and silent witness to my pastime of drinking, now that I had become a fully-fledged member of the new generation of family drinker's.

Eddying around and around inside my empty bottle was my lament, "There has got to be more to life than this" and the story of quiet desperation that went with it. I kicked the football away from my feet in the direction of Dad busy handing out fresh drinks at the bar in the cave. He had Louise and Carolyn with him who were training to be teachers with me and new friends I invited home from my college group after a boozy night out.

I'd scurried down the patio steps, car keys in hand, waving my parent's goodbye, with my sister in tow with some bottles of gin. We were on our way to another union night at college and friends to pick up on the way.

"See she's turning into an alcoholic just like your mother", Mum shouted at Dad and to my back. I'd loved to have yelled back, '*Like my father!*' but I knew that would fall on deaf ears so I didn't waste my breath. I was out of there. I hopped into my blue Mini, my sister beside me. We reversed out the driveway to a night of dancing and drinking with Louise, Carolyn and our new college friends until we were ready to come home.

"Everyone back to my place. Let's keep partying'. I rounded up those I knew as the union night wound down and told them to follow me home. A convoy of cars rolled up outside the house. With bottles clinking, voices raised in fun my guests spilled into the family room outside my bedroom door congregating at the bar. Neil found the records and put on a Beach Boys LP, while I got glasses for those who were making mixers. I opened the kitchen cupboard to get out some bowls and serviettes putting dips and chips into them. We all had the late night hungries. "What's going on in here?" My parents bleary eyed and angry burst into the kitchen.

"Just asked a few back for a drink".

"It's 2 am!"

"I know". I danced past them with a bowl of chips.

"Well, keep it down then". I fell down onto the fan shaped chair by my bedroom door and took a big gulp of gin squash. My friends spun around in circles bumping into each other doing a surfie dance. My head spun as I tried to focus on their whirling bodies.

Sitting in the cafeteria nursing a hangover having a break between lectures with some of last night's drinking friends, I looked out the large windows at the traffic lights at the top of the hill. A constant stream of traffic was stopping and starting at the intersection then moving on, just like I had with Glen. Now that he was at university and I was at teacher's college we had new interests with new found friends that were incompatible. Neil was sitting at the table chatting to Louise. In a moment of mind drift his face flashed in front of my eyes and I saw us by an open fire our feet covered in thick socks, resting on a large footstool. We were married. I didn't know Neil well even though he was in my group. What about the man I kept seeing sometimes out of the corner of my eye when I sat and drifted like now, short and dark with brown eyes and a moustache, sometimes a beard and European. Neil was tall, clean shaven and Australian so I hadn't mixed them up. The European man's face flashed before my eyes again to let me know he was still there. I freed this scene from my mind with a shake of my shoulders turning my back on the traffic. I picked up my gym bag as the others at my table did the same and we headed to the change rooms.

Our group of physical education sub-majors dressed in our tracksuits and runners dodged and wove through an obstacle course of witches hats. We were barked encouragement by our teacher to keep up our speed and agility. Dressed in shorts, a polo shirt and runners, he was timing us with a stop watch. Louise and I were in the corner of the gym waiting for our team's turn, giggling and eyeing off the boy she liked who looked like our favourite Beatle.

"If you're going to muck around like that get out!", he shouted at Louise and I. We stopped laughing and tried to concentrate but we were lost to our silliness and Louise to her romantic notions about Ben. Neil was doing running jumps up the wall then bench presses with Ben and some other good looking boys in his team, one of whom Carolyn fancied. Some of them were league footballers like my former Grade 6 teacher who was taking this unit, now a sports lecturer at the college. I couldn't control myself, so out of respect to him I ran out the door with Louise to the cafeteria to get a drink of water and try to calm down.

He didn't see me as a child any more, the one he'd held a finger up to, to laugh at when he read a story in class. He didn't see the giggly teenager who babysat his children while he and his wife attended a football function. He only saw a footballer in a team training exercise showing lack of discipline, something a league footballer couldn't abide. I did however still possess the qualities he'd pointed out to the school assembly that day when he was my primary school teacher. I was the captain of the college girl's football team.

My team lined up on the bottom oval in the college grounds with some witches' hats and footballs, hand passing and stab passing the footballs to each other in small groups, training for an inter-college match. We had a home game the following week.

On the day of the game the ground was deep in water. My jumper and shorts were soaked, my football boots caked in mud as I stood near the goals yelling encouragement to my team mates. Carolyn ran down the field with the ball and did a passable drop kick that landed at the feet of one of the girls from the opposing team. She fumbled with it while trying to hand pass it to one of her team. Louise grabbed it off her and ran with it, bouncing it all over the place as she tried to keep the rhythm and kicked it to me. Taking a chest mark proved difficult with my big breasts but I was willing to endure the pain it caused for the good of the game.

Few goals were scored by either side and it was just on three quarter time. We got in a huddle all yelling instructions to each other as there was no coach, the girls on the other team doing the same. I wanted to kick a goal so much because I wanted to know if it was as exciting as it looked when I cheered the ones scored at the football each week.

Half way through the last quarter I got my chance. I grabbed the ball and kicked it as hard as I could. It rolled through the goals. The umpire raised up the two flags. Seeing those two white flags go up had me running up the oval with my hands in the air my mouth wide open with joy just like the footballers I cheered every Saturday. It didn't matter that we'd lost. I'd kicked a goal.

I picked up the football and booted it across the cave in Dad's direction where he stood in the small circle of men, listening to more of Grandad's war stories. It fell short of them, just as I'd fallen short of my father's expectations for the boy he never had. A chant started in my head like the ones we chorused after a goal was scored for our footy family's team.

"Footballers, football, drinking. Footballers, football, drinking. Find them, find love".

I looked over at Dad and the other men in the small circle with Grandad, the chant getting louder in my head, wondering how to make it stop.

I found a footballer. The party at the share house had been going for hours. Cigarette butts overflowed in ashtrays, empty bottles littered the tables in the kitchen and the lounge room, the thumping music beat through my thumping head, my body dehydrated from way too much gin. We staggered into his bedroom but not to the bed. I fell back on to his large wooden desk my head spinning, out of it. The lower half of my body felt cold then it felt warm but there was this weird wet sensation. Had I wet myself? I raised my head. One of the footballers from college had his head between my legs his friend in the door way watching, his lips curled in pleasure. He backed away and left the room with his friend as I groaned and groped around for my briefs dragging them up over my legs. I needed to get home. How was I going to face them knowing what had happened?

Easy. Pretend it never happened.

I found another footballer. He had led me well away from the union building down to the football oval. We fell down on the grass his weight on top of me and his rough hands grabbing at me wanting more than I was prepared to give him when I first heard my sister and Carolyn calling my name. They were standing at the top of the embankment looking down on us holding the string bag between them with a near empty bottle of gin in it.

"Get away. What are you doing with him? He has a girlfriend. You know he's no good. Come with us". Wobbling to our feet we swayed about a breath's distance from each other, eyes closed trying to keep our balance.

My sister stumbled down the embankment grabbed my hand and tried to pull me away.

"I don't care". I pushed her away.

"Come on. What if his girlfriend finds out?"

"I don't care".

"Come on. Let's go". Carolyn and my sister took an arm each and dragged me up the embankment. My sister picked up the string bag and we headed back to the lights of the union building. How was I going to face seeing him and his girlfriend again?

Easy. Pretend it never happened.

I found another footballer. It was an away match for our football team. We were in the student union building of another teaching campus across town celebrating our win with some of the boys from the home campus football team. Louise, Carolyn and I had consumed most of the gin out of our bottle. I was sitting on a drunk footballers knee, kissing this stranger with intoxicated abandon while the music blared from the speakers set up on some tables at the back of the room. How was I going to face seeing him again when he and members of his team played a round of the fixture at our campus?

Easy. Pretend it never happened.

The game of football the broken child played was to handpass herself from one drunken footballer to the next in the misguided belief she would find her father's love now that she drank like him and sought the company of footballers as he once did before she was born. Her misguided belief created new stories of her own encouraging more rotting seeds of hurt to fester in the putrid garden of her father's family, when it was her desire to shed the seeds from her basket for good.

Her contribution to the continuance of her father's family story she participated in through footballers, football and drinking allowed its power to take hold within the broken child's life adding more unhealed trauma and pain to it from a new generation's basket.

... scene 6 ...

teaching

setting
under the budding child's willow tree of dreams

I rolled a piece of chalk back and forth across the desk under my willow tree. I put my head in my hands swinging my legs under the desk trying to contain the disappointment the dreams I had of being a teacher didn't bring me the happiness I'd found playing school after school with my sister. I leaned over and dragged my blackboard towards me, the duster wobbling on the ledge. Learning to be a teacher hadn't matched my childhood expectations. I was disheartened. In comparison to lectures and tutorials that taught the theory of teaching, teaching rounds where I could practice and learn the skills to teach were few. I picked up the chalk and made patterns, the same as the children in my teaching round class had copied to loosen up their fingers before they formed the new letter they were to learn to write. I banged the duster on the board splatting the patterns, the dust from the chalk making me sneeze.

Seeing me struggling Mum and Dad enlisted the help of my former Grade 6 teacher to see if he could offer the same support he'd given me in my last year of primary school, and to a lesser degree through my high school years, to help me stay focused on achieving my dream. I flew interstate to stay with him and his family where he was studying at a university and playing for a league team there. I came home afterwards and returned to my teacher training feeling just the same as I had before the trip, though happier after spending some time with him and his family.

Not only was there the work needed to complete my teacher training, there was work to do to supplement the small income I received from the studentship I'd been granted.

My father found me a job in the last two summer holidays of teacher training through a friend, the first a manager of a homewares store. I was assigned to training with the floor manager, a woman with years of experience in the trade. She soon had me making sales in the small appliances section. The manager prowled the store keeping his eye on the staff and his eye on the sales they were making to ensure they were achieving their quota. And it became apparent also keeping his eye on me.

On my morning break heading to the tea room up the back of the large store I was intercepted by my father's friend, the manager. I said hello and in one swift move he had me up against the back of a wall of carpet samples his hand on my breast, his mouth on my lips. I slid out from under him. He didn't try to stop me as he straightened his tie and walked back on to the floor stopping to speak to a customer. How was I going to face seeing him again?

Easy. Pretend it never happened and hope it never happened again.

My father found me another job in the next summer holidays through another friend who owned a furniture store. A pool party was organised on the weekend at the home of one of the staff members for all of us who worked there. I hopped in the pool splashing about with the rest of the staff and their families. I dived under the water in the deep end and came up in the middle of the pool where I could stand. One of the men I worked with swam under the water just near me. He threw me off balance as he took an opportunistic lunge inside my bikini bottoms with his hand, inserting his fingers inside me hard. He came up out of the water smoothed back his wet hair out of his eyes in one swift motion, turned his back making easy strokes to the pool edge, waving to his wife and children who were happily entangled in a large pool ring. How was I going to face seeing him again?

Easy. Pretend it never happened and hope it never happened again.

Then my father found me a position at a school closer to home through someone he knew in the Education Department. My assigned posting to a school on the other side of town consisted mainly of a migrant community. The parents and children had little grasp of the English language and all the problems associated with their low socio-economic status.

Shown over the school by the vice-principal he told me there was no class for me at that stage so I would be a 'floater', filling in and helping the other teachers. His tour confirmed exactly what I'd felt at college that I was ill-equipped to become a teacher, and in particular at this school as I had no experience with migrant teaching, which required different skills that I didn't have. It didn't matter if I was disheartened, part of the terms of my studentship required me to teach for three years after attaining my diploma.

On the first day of my new posting I was escorted by the Principal down the steps to the end of the corridor with empty rooms across and beside my classroom, given a box of chalk and told to teach 'them'. 'Them', were a small class of seven and eight year old's with learning and behavioural problems. An experienced teacher's nerves had crumbled trying to teach them. They were well behaved for me and eager to learn despite their troubled home lives, even those living in the boy's home who liked to drink alcohol and smoke cigarettes after school. The children didn't know how to spell basic words or recite the easiest tables. So I started with exercises children in their first year of school learned hoping they'd pick up on what they'd missed.

We created our own little world down there at the end of the corridor. No-one seemed to mind what we did there as long as the children were quiet and kept out of trouble. However, my inexperience and the lack of support from the teacher's in my department and the principal, despite my fondness for my class, placed undue pressure on me, a teacher in her first year out of college.

At team meetings for my children's year level I was cautioned I needed to keep to the curriculum appropriate for their age. I argued I was giving these children basic skills they'd missed out on so they could catch up and gain confidence in their learning abilities. I was reminded I wasn't teaching a remedial class as the children were already included in remedial programs. When I gave lessons more suited to their age level their self-confidence plummeted and their behavioural problems started to return.

One lunchtime in the storeroom while getting some more pencils and paper for my afternoon class wondering what I was going to do with my limited resources, I felt a presence behind me. I jumped in fright and spun around. The Principal backed me into the corner pressing me up against the shelves leaving me nowhere to go. He started fondling my breasts and tried to kiss me as I turned my face away.

"Don't turn away. You are so beautiful".

"Get off me!" I pushed hard at his shoulders, trying to prise him off me. That broke the trance he seemed to be in and he backed away quick smart. He straightened his tie, smoothed back his hair and adjusted his glasses in one swift movement. He then walked out to the corridor as if nothing happened. My knees gave way and I slid to the floor. I pulled my dress over my knees and pulled my cardigan tight across my breasts, shaking. What on earth made him do that? I hadn't spoken to him much in the few weeks I'd been there and when I had, he'd been pleasant and polite. I heard the bell ring. In a minute these children who needed me would be lined up ready to come in. I stood up on wobbly legs, gathered up the pencils and paper and went to greet them with a dry mouth and a pounding heart. How was I going to face seeing him again?

Easy. Pretend it never happened and hope it never happened again.

This time I couldn't. I wasn't going back to that school again. I made an appointment with the family doctor for the next day.

"Have you been taking your tablets?" he asked.

"Yes but they don't help me. They make my brain fuzzy. It's fuzzy enough already because I don't get much sleep. They make my mouth dry and that makes me want to eat and when I do I can't stop". The doctor wrote out a prescription for more of the sedatives and also for sick leave handing them to me. I took both, resigned and despondent.

Curled up on the couch in the lounge room watching some daytime TV with Mum and Dad I saw a large white Falcon, just like the patrol car Dad brought home from work sometimes inching up the street stopping outside my place. I couldn't believe it. It was the Principal. I flung the blanket off me and bolted for my room but Mum stopped me.

"Where are you going?"

"It's the Principal. I don't want to see him. I'm going to my room. Tell him I'm too sick to see him".

"Don't be silly. It's kind of him to visit and see how you are. Don't be so rude".

I couldn't escape now. He'd seen me through the lounge room window. He was smiling in at us; that nice kind smile he showed to everyone. I felt dizzy. I wanted to run. If only people knew what he was really like.

I made another appointment with the family doctor and told him, "I can't cope with teaching my class".

"I'll write you some more sick leave and I'll write a letter to the Education Department advising that for health reasons, you need to be moved to another school and a normal classroom environment". I breathed easy for the first time in weeks. I'd never have to see that Principal again, the real reason for not coping.

> I, the Temple Woman watched the two children who lived inside Julie grapple with their conflicting emotions about finding love as their adolescence drew to a close. The menace of assault had touched both of them entering the realms where they dwelt. The budding child's willow tree shook and shivered with sharp blasts of air that lifted the branches and tossed the leaves about exposing her to the harsh reality that daydreams aren't always the same when you grow up and you get the chance to live them. This unexpected and continual assault on the seeds of her femininity, left her as wounded and in despair as the broken child who had allowed herself to be handpassed from one drunken footballer to the next in the misguided belief she would find her father's love through them. It scattered the budding child's pots from her

hotchpotch garden all over the floor of her willow tree. She scrambled about to retrieve them and bring them back under her tree. She gathered them at her feet trying to stop them blowing over. She pushed the seedlings back into the pots rescuing all the soil she could to cover them with in the hope they wouldn't die. She put her arms around them and kept them close with one hand, pushing away the swaying branches with the other that threatened to tip them over again. The festering seeds of hurt from the broken child's putrid garden began to entwine around the tender shoots in the budding child's hotchpotch garden she tried so hard to protect, threatening to stunt their growth. The pervasive fear of the broken child once again spread across her heart.

Both the budding child and the broken child were stymied in their efforts to grow up. Though now both adolescents, neither of them had been able to fulfil their heartfelt desires that both remained unchanged; the budding child's to plant the seeds in her flower girl's basket in a garden where they could bloom and grow, the broken child's to shed the rotting seeds of hurt from her picnic basket. So there they both remained in their childhood realms though they were on the brink of adulthood.

… scene 7 …

love found

setting
in the broken child's cave of sorrows

I flopped back down in the sagging cane chair, years of living in argument and now the menace of assault casting long, dark shadows over the walls of the cave. I picked up the empty pill bottle that had found its way into my basket of hurts, no matter how I tried for it to be otherwise and rolled it between my hands. My head started to spin off and away to my bedroom where the white flowers on the aqua wallpaper were opening and closing, hypnotising me as I stared at them sprawled on my back on the bed.

I could still feel the agitation running through my veins a bottle of gin hadn't quieted. My energy was spinning with the flowers like I was about to fly off and that was what I wanted to do. I'd had enough of this constant pressure. Whatever I tried to do to make it go away or to live with it, didn't change a thing. I wanted it all to go away. If it wouldn't, then I would. I groped around on the bedside table, nearly falling out of bed hearing the pills rattle in their bottle. Got them. I grabbed at them and the bottle fell to the floor. I leaned over the bed and picked it up, fumbling with the lid as they rattled some more, stuffing pills in my mouth. Good old sedatives. They've really helped me, I don't think. Now they would. Off in the distance I heard the bottle rolling on the floor. Must have dropped it. Don't care. Don't care about anyone or anything. Out of here, get me out of here … mouth dry. Heavy. Sick. Going. Going. Stop those bloody flowers opening, closing. Sleep. Where's sleep? I never wanted to wake up again. I was cold. I could hear a voice somewhere shouting at me. Where am I? God my head hurt. I wanted to wake up but I couldn't. I kept drifting off in this thick fog. This was some hangover. Never had one so bad. I could hear moaning. Oh that was me. There's that voice again. I know that voice. Mum's. What does she want now?

"Time to get up". I could feel her shaking my shoulders. I tried to sit up but the room spun. I fell back on my pillows.

"Water", I moaned through a thick mouth. I reached out for the glass I kept on my bedside table at night but it wasn't there.

"Get up. It's past lunchtime".

"I can't. I feel too sick. Get me some water. Please". I could feel myself drifting off again. I'd never been so grateful to drink a glass of water in my whole life. The cold liquid hit my burning insides waking them up. I burped. I noticed my pill bottle on the floor by the bed. What was it doing there? I leaned over and picked up the bottle, empty. I wish I hadn't done that. The room was spinning again. Then I remembered. Didn't take enough of them. I'm still here. What am I going to do? I am all alone.

I walked up to the bar in the cave as I'd noticed Neil there, a rum and coke in his hand and Dad with his now customary glass of red wine. They didn't see me approach as they were bonding over a drink, Dad's favourite pastime. I listened unable to understand their conversation as Neil's tongue loosened and his words slurred. His smile broadened, his normal reserve gone with each round of drinks.

Carolyn, and Louise with her new boyfriend Greg she'd also met at teacher's college, walked up to the bar and were offered a drink. They sat up on the rickety bar stools and sipped their drinks of choice made by Dad, joining in on the jokes and laughter.

Aside from the broken child partying with Neil until late into the night, he and the budding child shared lectures, tutorials and enjoyed outdoor activities together. On weekends away with college friends they enjoyed camping and hiking, going to the beach to body surf and playing games of golf or tennis. Through spending time pursuing these mutual interests, they became close.

Neil put on a Beach Boys record while Dad poured himself another wine. We all danced together beside the bar in the cave like we all did at a beach themed college ball all dressed in our surfie gear, me in a long skirt, a yellow and white Hawaiian shirt and at this late stage of the evening, bare footed. I'd snatched the stuffed seagull off the stage as the band belted out "Good Vibrations" by the Beach Boys, weaving through the dancers in front of the stage and cawing like one. A security guard approached me grabbing it from my hands and returning it to the stage. Snapping me out of my drink induced high, the noise, the lights and the late hour led me to go outside for fresh air by our car, Neil not far behind me. I was still dancing to the music coming from the venue when Neil took me in his arms to quiet me. I was still jigging about in his arms my tongue loosened by the alcohol I'd consumed and said what I'd want to say for a while, "let's get married". He grinned at me his tongue loosened by alcohol too.

"Why not?".

I didn't know if it was the drink and the night talking but sober and on a new day the decision held true. We kept it to ourselves until we felt it was the right time to announce our engagement.

In Neil, Julie found the handsome gentleman of her budding child's dreams and the footballer of her broken child's dreams. She had found love.

ACT 3

finding the temple woman within

... scene 1 ...

getting married

setting
in the broken child's cave of sorrows

Margaret's were the sharp eyes of a mother who had watched over a sickly child, intuiting danger, ready to strike in an effort to keep her son safe and well. She nursed him with an anxiety underpinned by the loss of her mother to cancer at a young age. A serious fall as a child left Neil with complications from internal injuries, requiring multiple surgeries. Though her son didn't dwell on this childhood mishap; robust enough to pursue his love of playing sport, his mother continued to fret about his health.

Though imprisoning them both with her worry to the point she had a nervous breakdown, Margaret had passed him to Julie's care with her blessing. She had chosen her for her son out of all the teenage girls from teacher's college who came to Neil's house one night for a party, nothing like the ones her son went to at Julie's house. This party was more fitting for a child's birthday; cupcakes, sandwiches, party pies and cocktail frankfurts were served with lemonade for the girls she wanted and never had, though she loved Neil and her older son Barry. Some of the guests had brought alcohol to drink which they were allowed to do with reservations, discomforting Neil's parents. Neil was eager to tell Julie that his mother told him after the party she thought her the prettiest and smartest one there. When she got to know Julie better she realised she was good with money, to her mind unlike her son who wasn't. Good money management was very important to Margaret and her husband.

As a symbol of her trust Margaret presented Julie with a large cane wash basket at the kitchen tea a couple of weeks before the wedding. Julie had earned that trust by her care of her son when a holiday had turned into a medical emergency; a severe chest infection leaving him interstate in hospital for days. Taking good care of a mother-in-law's son is a prized asset for any wife even though it will never be in the mother's eyes quite like hers. That Julie was able to care for a sickly son made her even more valuable. Even though the trust of his care had been given to the budding child, the wash basket belonged in the cave with all the others as it contained a mother's trauma that she would lose a son as she had lost a mother. This basket's appearance in the cave hadn't gone unnoticed by the broken child though she didn't know whose it was.

"Look after him, he's a very sick boy". The voice was coming from the direction of an upturned wash basket lying in this basket graveyard in the cave, feathers sticking through its weave. I turned the basket over picked out a couple of the feathers and examined them. Hawk feathers. I pushed them back into the upturned basket, suspicious. This was a brand new basket unlike the other ones in my cave. I jumped up as I felt someone behind me and turned around. A woman reached in front of me and righted the basket. What was she doing in my cave? She picked it up and strode back over to the clothesline, her chunky gold antique bracelet with a matching locket attached with a chain catching her basket. Annoyed, she put it down. She smoothed down the sleeves of her fine knit cashmere cardigan and well cut beige pants then took a child's football jumper from her basket and shook it. Bits of dried mud fell off it landing on her soft leather loafers with gold buckles. She dusted off her shoes and looked back in her basket finding a pair of white football shorts and a football whose gut had burst through the frayed black lacing. A pair of dusty football boots lay turned on their sides, a pair of football socks snaking out of them. She tipped them all out, banged the basket on the ground, then wiped the inside with a towel. Neil ran past in his football jumper and white shorts, kicking the ball as hard and as far as he could. It disappeared with a faint thud as it landed deeper in the cave. He threw his hands up in triumph and grinned.

Two voices called out to her as the football one of them had kicked dropped back at his feet. The man who wore the same jumper with the same number on his back during the football season as Neil, appeared in it with clean white shorts, his boots laced tight around his ankles, mouth guard in place, ready to take his place on the forward line. Neil's hero, my Grade 6 teacher, raised his hand to indicate to kick the ball back to him. Dad came out of the shadows in his team jumper dressed ready for play in the back pocket. Soon the three of them were having a kick to kick in the cave.

The two men took Neil aside offering him some coaching tips. They put these into practice with a circle of hand passes and short kicks.

Margaret put down her washing and watched, happy for her son to be kicking a footy with his hero but not with his future father-in-law. She and her husband Richard both teetotallers by choice had their fill of the drinkers in their respective families, witnessing the damage it could do. They'd raised their youngest son well and not to drink, alarmed to see him ripping into the drink, partying with Julie's family and their friends, not getting home until the early hours of the morning. What Margaret couldn't see was Julie's broken child numbing herself with alcohol as she'd been taught to do to take away the pain of the basket of hurts she carried.

The ball landed at this woman's feet who I now realised was Neil's mother. She picked it up, tossing it back in the footballers' direction. I intercepted it, running off with it. I kicked it to my soon to be husband; Dad and my former teacher cutting in front of him, jostling for the ball.

... scene 2 ...

wedding day

setting
leaving the budding child's willow tree of dreams

The memories, reawakened in Julie's budding child since we met that day at Pompeii, shone light on her seeds and helped to nourish them with a little awareness. The sunlight coming through the arbour of her weeping green world, the willow tree, shone light into her heart where she found the seeds of her life's promise that were planted there on the day she was born.

These were the seeds of her own story she was unable to inhabit within the family stories she was raised in. Re-entering her realm under the willow tree that day at Pompeii, she had found them again. Revisiting the daydreams she enjoyed under her tree allowed the seeds in little pots she had left there from her hotchpotch garden to awaken.

Unable to plant them in the garden her mother was supposed to provide for her, the budding child decided to plant these potted seedlings she'd left under her willow tree for safe keeping in a new garden, one she would fertilise and till with her husband in their married life together. Her mother encouraged and supported their planting as her daughter would marry up the social ladder to a young man with a private school education and wealthy parents. His father had retired in his early 50's after a lucrative career as an insurance broker. For an interest in his retirement, apart from travelling overseas most years with his wife, he restored then sold antique furniture.

A good reputation in society was very important to Julie's mother as was social standing. On that her mother and her soon to be in-law's agreed. Her father's tastes had changed as Julie grew up, more suited to those of a wealthy man. He loved classical music, fine food and wine provided by those he crossed paths with in the pursuit of criminals.

On her wedding day Julie's budding child stepped out of her weeping green world full of anticipation, her flower girl's basket she carried brimming with her potted seedlings. I, the Temple Woman walked with slow, measured steps behind her to help steady her feet.

Going to her side, I put her basket on the ground in a secluded clearing so she could take off her flower girl dress, which I folded putting it in my basket with the reverence in which she had worn it. I watched as she stepped into her long white wedding dress made of chiffon with a three quarter overlay featuring a small leaf pattern.

The budding child undid the bun at the top of her head shaking her waist length hair loose, placing a large white picture hat on her head. She picked up her basket but I took it from her as her sister as her bridesmaid passed her a white parasol. Reaching into my own basket I took out a white silk pouch embossed with stars with a drawstring top. Taking the crystal, feather and the pack of tarot cards out of her basket I placed them in the pouch, pulling the top tight then tied it round her waist with white silk thread under the overlay of her dress.

The broken child within Julie stood at the entrance to the cave trembling, wary of the change, her basket of hurts in her hands. She left it there, went back into the cave and brought out the budding child's brand new wash basket. She knew it was hers because she'd seen Margaret take it and place it beside her worn one. She also knew that she would need it in her married life.

I placed the budding child's potted seedlings in it, her flower girl basket now empty which I returned to my own basket. She carried her new wash basket laden with promise and walked towards her future as a married woman. I, the Temple Woman took the broken child's hand. We kept pace together behind the budding child watching her take confident steps forward to her future.

My sister and my oldest friend Leanne stood in low heeled sandals, both dressed in rose pink knee length dresses with a lace insert across the top. They held their cane baskets filled with rich red carnations, waiting for the photographer's directions.

I stood looking out the lounge room window, the light coming in through it like it had lit the aisle in the church the day I was my beloved Susan's flower girl. The photographer adjusted my hat and parasol then the bottom of my dress and asked me to smile. The shutter on the camera clicked rapidly as I posed. My mother in a sand colored dress with a slight sheen and matching high heels fluttered and fussed around us, waiting for the photographer to ask her to join the photo shoot. My father stood back dressed in his pale grey suit, watching as the photos were taken.

The family car was parked in the driveway with a big white bow tied to the bonnet. The driver, a neighbour and friend who joined my father for a drink when he was home, waited by the car. Few words were spoken on the long drive to the stately Victorian home, a short drive from Nana's house where I'd left from in my flower girl's dress the day my beloved Susan married Ray.

I watched the sky darken and felt the humidity build as we made our way to the venue, willing it not to rain until the ceremony was over. I'd told Mrs Jones it was a bad omen if it rained on your wedding day. She'd laughed.

We approached the entrance to the driveway. The gates hadn't been opened since the Queen visited many years ago but the manager had allowed them to be opened for me. As we drove up the drive Dad kissed me on the cheek and said, "Goodbye daughter". I waved at the children from my new class at my new school waiting there with their parents, who waved back with big smiles. As I stepped out of the car Jody approached me with her mother and gave me a white lace horseshoe to hang on my wrist, Susan right behind her. She gave me a kiss and a hug and told me I looked beautiful. Ray stood beside her beaming like a proud father. My footy godmother Auntie Helen came up to me and kissed me hello. I wore my hair in my usual style, parted in the middle and flowing down to my waist so there was no need for Auntie Helen to do my hair on my wedding day.

The guests were gathered on the lawn, Nana sitting on a chair in the garden close to the table and chairs where Neil and I would sign the certificate to make our union official. Grandad stood behind her in his best suit. Nana's eyes twinkled, smiling at me with pride as I walked toward her. Neil stood in front of the celebrant with a nervous grin on his face waiting for me to join him.

After the ceremony the children trailed through the garden after me smiling and waving. They watched the wedding party having photos taken and left as the guests made their way to the reception. Neil and I greeted them in the ballroom as they lined up to congratulate us and wish us well. Thunder clapped overhead and rain streamed down the windows. My girlfriends and their partners gave me kisses and hugs then moved on down the line to exchange greetings with my parents and new in-laws before accepting flutes of champagne from a waiter.

Mum's voice, loud and proud was telling each of her relatives as she greeted them with a big smile, "She was a virgin when she got married".

I thought I was hearing things but she said it again, then again. I kept smiling, greeting my guests as if I'd never heard a word of what she said. Inside I burned with rage, wondering why she had the need to tell them that. I hoped none of the other invited guests had heard. I asked the waiter for another glass of champagne. 'Make this night be over so I can get on and start my new life', I said to myself. I smiled and laughed with my guests with a feeling of unease closing in on my heart.

My former Grade 6 teacher, my new husband's hero, with a glass of lemon squash in his hand asked everyone to raise their glasses and toast us after making a speech about both our fine characters and our suitability to engage in the journey of married life together. With my heart still full of love for my former Grade 6 teacher my spirits lifted for a moment as the words, "To Julie - To Neil", resounded through the room.

... scene 3 ...

married life

setting
the budding child enters the broken child's cave of sorrows

With nowhere else to go, I stood at the entrance to the cave, reluctant to enter after what I saw and heard my mother's family doing, looking in that day before I returned to the sanctuary of my willow tree. I was as committed to protecting the seeds in my flower girl's basket as I was back then. Now a married woman, my desire and commitment was to plant my potted seedlings in a new garden with my husband and watch them grow. Removing my seedlings from my wash basket I bunched them together between two rocks so they wouldn't tip over allowing them continual exposure to the sunlight and rain.

    I peered in, curious to see if that child in the pyjamas with that odd assortment of objects she took from her picnic basket was there this time. As my eyes adjusted to the dim light the only thing I could make out was the area where the laundry was being done. I wasn't prepared to venture any further than that. There I spotted a pile of Neil's dirty washing. I tucked my basket under my arm and walked over to it. As I sorted it out a familiar scent wafted from the dirty clothes. I parted the washing and found a bottle of perfume the letters on it scratched and faded. I twisted the lid off and gagged; my mother-in-law's signature scent, a present from her. I tossed it over on to a pile of old toiletries to join an empty lipstick case. It landed by a rusted washing machine and an old boiler that had dirty washing lying around it.

    I folded Neil's football jumper in the colors of the local team he played for and his white shorts I'd just removed from the washing machine, catching his mother's expression of disapproval out of the corner of my eye. A sickly child can play footy with his friends or attend a match to watch his hero play and barrack with his mother, but a grown one shouldn't. It was too dangerous. I'd stood on the sidelines of an outer suburban football oval and barracked for Neil's team most Saturday afternoon's as Mum had once done at an inner city oval for Dad's.

"Look after him. He's a very sick boy". Those words of Margaret's rose out of my wash basket as I continued folding the washing. Margaret turned her back to the washing line, refolding her son's underwear still left on top of the washing machine. I heard those words after every headache, every virus and every upset stomach he had, then received detailed instructions of how to treat each ailment and told to have Neil call them when he was better. If he didn't, they called most days, until they knew he was. Though an adult, to his parents he was still their very sick boy. My job was to look after him to his mother's standards made evident the first time my in-laws came for tea after we were married. That brand new wash basket sat in the laundry full of folded clothes ready to be ironed. The table was set with our new Wedgewood dinner service and silver cutlery, a beef casserole cooking in the oven, our small unit cleaned to the highest standard, fresh flowers placed on the kitchen table. I was on show and I was nervous. Margaret and I stood in the kitchen, me checking on the casserole, she what was in my kitchen cupboards. She continued to do so while I stirred the rice on the stove. She laughed when she saw me looking at her in disbelief and asked if I minded. I wanted to say yes but didn't dare as I wanted the night to go well.

She followed me out of the kitchen as if to join Neil and his father in the lounge room but instead walked on ahead to our bedroom and turned on the light. I found her looking in our wardrobe going through our chest of drawers, opening them one by one picking through our underwear. I stood beside her outraged at such flagrant disrespect, my fists and jaw clenched.

She picked up a pair of her son's underpants, refolded them and said, "I always folded them this way. I hope you're remembering to iron them and his socks too". She refolded a pair of his socks.

"I won't be ironing his socks and jocks for him. He puts his own underwear away after I've washed it. We share the chores".

Margaret's mouth tightened. She strode out leaving the drawers and wardrobe cupboard wide open for me to close and to turn off the light. I returned to the lounge room with drinks after I tried to calm down in the kitchen busying myself with the meal. I found Margaret picking up our wedding gifts on the pine sideboard, turning them over. When she noticed me looking she kept turning them, rearranging them in a different spot to where I'd placed them. I bristled but kept quiet.

Neil sat down in a lounge chair beside his father, both watching, unperturbed by his mother's bad manners. She hopped on his knee kissing him all over the face and hugging him.

"Do you like my new perfume?, she giggled as she leaned her neck into his face. Her son looked uncomfortable but smiled.

"Look at my lipstick". She leaned back smiling at him. I noticed it was the same shade I wore, not Margaret's usual choice.

The meal was served and eaten in the kitchen on our new pine furniture with the cheery yellow padded seats. While my in-laws drank their fruit juice I served myself and Neil another wine from the cask in the fridge, their eyes flickering at each other in mutual disapproval for a moment before the bright conversation they led resumed.

In the cave, Margaret lifted the bottle out of her wash basket with shaking hands, undid the lid and tipped out some pills. I continued folding Neil's washing as my mother-in-law threw some pills down her throat and swallowed hard.

It was imperative Margaret maintained equilibrium at all costs for the family's sake as another breakdown with its repercussions wouldn't be tolerated. This rule was enforced by her husband Richard with rigour and adhered to by Neil, his brother Barry and his wife Carol, all well-conditioned to it, accepting it without question.

Margaret took a hand mirror out of her wash basket. She applied fresh lipstick and tucked the ends of her short, brown, bobbed hair under. She looked from side to side to see that she looked respectable.

She flicked me a look, her lips pursed. "You were nothing like I thought you would be after I got to know you. You had your own mind and ideas and weren't prepared to toe the line. The more the family tried to coerce you, the more you rebelled. I got so angry. So did Richard. And as for the drinking - you and your family led my son astray".

I continued folding the washing from my basket, not answering her. Margaret had underestimated the independence that went with my kindness and care. She had wanted another accomplice in the family to assist her in having her own needs met first, in her own way.

Richard appeared at Margaret's side as she started to cry. He adjusted his navy tie, pulled at the collar of his white shirt and pushed the sleeves of his cardigan back up a bit. Shoving his hands deep into the pockets of his tailored pants, he rattled the keys and loose change against his legs. He flicked an empty washing powder packet away with his foot, annoyed some had stayed on his shiny black shoes as he picked it off. Neil red faced, didn't speak. He and his father stared at me. Margaret dabbed at her eyes with a white lace handkerchief she found in her wash basket, the same one she'd used as tears were shed by her on a kitchen chair by the window in the lounge room of our new home.

Richard had laid his hand on his wife's shoulder and with the other, shook his finger at me and spat out, "You make the bullets for our son to fire!"

I leaned forward on the couch and glared at him. "I do not. Neil can think for himself you know!" I was angry too. I'd had enough of these people and their interference in our lives.

Neil took a step back towards the mantelpiece over the open fire, knocking against the screen.

"It's your fault she's having another nervous breakdown", Richard accused as his grip tightened on Margaret's shoulder and her sobs grew louder, his green eyes darkening with rage as they hunted me down, willing me to look away.

Holding his gaze I said, "What a load of rubbish. I won't let you put that on me. Just because we're family doesn't mean we have to do things your way all the time. Your son and I can think for ourselves. We have our own lives to lead. We have the right to do what we want without asking your permission".

"I'm older than you. I have more experience in life. You need to respect your elders", Richard shouted.

"Respect! You have to earn that. How can you expect me to have respect for you when you interfere in our lives, telling us what to do all the time then get upset if we don't do as you say?"

"Just remember who gave you the money!" Richard ran his hands through the tight curls of his silver hair, his broad face grey with temper.

"I didn't ask for it. I thought that money was supposed to be given to help us, not to tell us what we can and can't do with it. I never wanted your money. We can support ourselves just fine".

"Well son, it's time to choose. It's either her or your family". Richard stared Neil down, waiting for an answer.

I stared too, my heart in my throat. How could it all have come to this?

"I choose my family", Neil muttered.

His father looked at his mother and smiled in triumph. She sighed with relief and clutched his father's hand. Barry and Carol sat on the couch unmoved by Neil's declaration of loyalty to his family.

What about me? What about our marriage? I couldn't believe what I'd just heard. It was my turn to cry. I loved my husband and had made a life-long commitment to him, so I was determined to find a way to make it work.

This family, through exercising their unspoken rule to keep the peace for the sake of the matriarch at all costs, had shown great disrespect to me. It caused more hurt by asking their son to choose his family over me, his wife. That was a question that should never have been asked of him.

My fall from grace as the chosen carer of their sickly son just two years after we married was something I refused to accept. Though a choice was made it was important the family portrayed a united front as its reputation was at stake. What better way to show that than to have a family photo hanging on a wall in the lounge room in each of our homes.

I stood crying outside the photographer's studio with make-up on, in my best dress, already late. I'd told them right from the beginning I didn't want to be in the family photo but they wouldn't take no for an answer. They weren't interested in why I didn't want to be there. They were only interested in making sure the photo was taken.

"Please stop crying. You know how they are. It's better to go along with them, not cause a fuss. You know that by now. What's the harm in having the photo taken if it makes them happy? You put me in an awkward position with them", Neil sighed as he twiddled with his wedding band.

"No - they put *me* in an awkward position by neglecting my feelings then expecting me to go along with what they want. We wouldn't be having this conversation if things were different between us. We're not happy families, we're never going to be. I'm not asking for things to be all our way or what I want over what they want".

"We have all learned what works, what doesn't", Neil said.

"In other words, you've learned to do as your told. Well I won't be told what to do for the sake of peace".

Richard stormed out the studio door yelling at me to hurry up and come in, I was keeping everybody waiting. He yelled some more as the photographer snapped the photos that were never bought. They didn't want one of me crying in their happy family photo.

Margaret sent the family emissary with a pre-prepared speech ready to bend me to her will. I put Carol's mug of tea down on the side table in the lounge room and joined her. She sat in the same seat on the couch as the night she watched unmoved my being voted out of the family. This time her face looked friendly, her brown eyes showing concern.

She shoved her car keys in the front pocket of her jeans, unzipped her red windcheater, settling back. "I'm sorry about what happened the other night. Richard shouldn't have yelled at you like that in front of the photographer. He's always been very emotional, likes to do things his way. It's just the way he is. Don't take too much notice of it. Let it roll off you. You're taking it too personally". She picked up her mug of tea and had a sip. I'd hoped her visit was to offer me some support, understanding as a fellow outsider who married into this family. I should have known better.

"It is personal. You were there when I was accused of causing the latest breakdown. I'm supposed to let that wash over me, laugh it off as a bit of drama and get on with it? Have you ever been attacked that way by them?"

Carol hung her head and shook it. I leaned back in my chair, all the muscles in my body clenched nursing my mug of tea.

"All families have their problems. We have to live together, work them out as best we can. It's not easy".

She didn't tell me anything I didn't already know. "Well you can tell them an apology would help for the way they treated me. You know very well this isn't the only time it has happened. Remember, I'm not the one who starts these arguments, their interference in our lives does".

Carol looked uncomfortable. Her speech hadn't elicited the results our mother-in-law was seeking so she didn't waste time in leaving, her mug of tea unfinished. I poured it down the kitchen sink, rinsed our mugs, put them on the dish drainer, the tears hot on my cheeks.

Margaret took her washing off the line in the cave, while I put another load on. A breeze coming in through the cave entrance lifted the brim of my picture hat. I grabbed it with one hand and the overlay of my wedding dress with the other after it blew up over my face.

"I kept a thin veneer of acceptance and inclusion because you were his wife. I did have some manners and social graces", Margaret sneered at me as I smoothed the overlay down over my dress.

Adding the dirty clothes and some wash powder to the load I glared at my mother-in-law as she sauntered off with her basket of fresh clean clothes with Richard behind her. They sat on rickety kitchen chairs in the cave watching another load of Neil's dirty football clothes going around and around in Margaret's washing machine.

... scene 4 ...

louise

My attention was taken off my washing by Neil's parents talking to someone whose voice I knew well. I walked in its direction. Louise was standing at the peeling cane bar, a glass of gin and tonic sitting on a tattered coaster. Neil's brother Barry was also on his own near the bar but didn't come any closer, he and Carol now separated in ugly circumstances. Louise's ex-husband Greg, a beer in one hand and a smoke in the other kept his distance too. I had no time for him after what he'd done to her.

All our circle of friends from college Greg was a part of, were appalled he'd left Louise for another woman when she was not long pregnant with their child. We all knew he had a wandering eye well before he married Louise. Though we were all scandalized I was the one who'd supported Louise the most from the moment he left her. My heart went out to her for being put in such a position, knowing she loved him. I'd slept over at her place before Jason's birth and when she brought him home from the hospital until she settled in a routine with him. When she wanted company she'd walk Jason over in the stroller, bath him, stay for tea then I would drive them home. Neil helped too. He was a willing babysitter when we wanted to go out. We both liked having Jason stay when Louise wanted to visit a nightclub or go to dinner with friends. Neil was happy to do odd jobs around the house to help her too.

Louise had asked Neil and I to be Jason's godparents. I took that commitment seriously, knowing if something happened to Louise, Neil and I would raise Jason as our own, despite making it clear at the outset of my marriage I didn't want to have children.

Barry's separation from Carol led Margaret to undertake to find another suitable partner for their son, against his wishes as he still loved his wife and wanted her back. Margaret's choice was Louise. Though she'd been passed over at the party for me when we attended the party at Neil's place when we were at teacher's college, Margaret now reconsidered her for her other son. Barry and Carol hadn't produced a son much to Margaret and Richard's disappointment but Jason would want a sibling.

Encouraged and welcomed with polite chats and interest in her son, Jason, Louise engaged in conversation with Margaret and Richard when they met at social occasions Neil and I arranged at our place. This engagement was at odds with the history she shared with me about them. As best friends do, we shared our sorrows, fears and heartaches, our worries, our dreams. Louise knew a lot about the interference of my in-laws in my life and the stress it caused me. She listened to my gripes and grievances for hours on end, offering support and advice.

Margaret's matchmaking efforts proved futile, her son eventually reuniting with his wife and having another child, a girl.

... scene 5 ...

my sister's wedding

The broken child had taken herself and her basket well into the shadows of the cave where she couldn't be seen but could keep an eye on both sides of the family, oblivious to the budding child and her arguments with her in-laws just inside the entrance to her cave.

I heard Mum and Dad talking near the clothes line, wondering what would bring Dad away from his beer and circle of men. I crept closer, still out of sight but close enough to hear what they were saying. It was about what happened at my sister's wedding. Hearing enough, I ran off. No matter how far I ran, it would never be far enough away, the knifing hurt still burning in me from that day.

I picked up my picnic basket then attempted to step over a pile of old toiletries; the perfume bottles, empty lipstick cases and tins of talc all slippery under my feet. I hitched up the bottom of my pyjama's, hanging on to the rusted washing machine and old boiler from the asylum to get my balance, being careful not to slip on the empty washing powder packets. A pair of apricot shoes with their high heels snapped off sticking out of some of the dirty washing caught my eye. I bent down and picked up a shoe, put it in my picnic basket and kept walking, the sound of my father's voice bellowing at me in the foyer of the reception venue deep in my head from where I'd tried to lock it away. Myself and the other bridesmaid Rosie dressed in a pale shade of apricot from head to toe, were standing there waiting to be shown to our seats at the bridal table, while my sister and her new husband had some more photos taken upstairs. I was twiddling my bouquet of roses in my hands talking to Neil and Rosie.

Dad had appeared at the top of the grand old, wooden staircase in front of me, Mum scurrying along behind him trying to placate him as usual. His face was contorted in rage as he spied me and started yelling at me.

"You fucking bitch. Can't you shut that mouth of yours?" Many other harsh, slurred words rolled off his tongue as he weaved his way down the red-carpeted stairs, lost to me as I shut down.

Other guests had joined me in the foyer looking at Dad, then to me, mute. Wanting to move but I couldn't, wanting to speak but no words came, wanting comfort from somebody but there was none, clueless about what I'd done this time. I fled down the hallway. Seeing the doors to the kitchen open I rushed past the chef, his assistants and the waitresses all under pressure to serve the meal who looked up in surprise, flinging open the back door. I sat on the steps in the alleyway in my pretty dress. The tears came and the hurt, the wrenching, pulling, tearing hurt, the culmination of years and years of it I'd sat on hoping it would go away now that I was married and out of the firing line. How foolish to think that would change anything. Something was poking into my back. It was the flywire door, Neil trying to get outside. I couldn't move. He found another door, sat on the step beside me and passed me his big white hankie. Patches of black mascara covered it as I dabbed my eyes.

Mum's friend I couldn't stand came out and put her arm around me. "It wasn't fair to do that to you". My keening intensified with the truth of those words.

The chef came out to throw some rubbish in the skip. He looked uncomfortable knowing he was in the midst of something painful and awkward. I was trying so hard to pull myself together not wanting to spoil my sister's big day. All the guests must have been seated, the meal started by now. How was I going to get through this? I needed a drink, no, plenty of drink. If Mum had any sense she'd see Dad didn't come near me for the rest of the night. I needn't have worried. He was busy being the life of the party as usual, the guests happy to indulge him, Mum laughing and smiling along with him. I felt a smile on my face, lots of cheery words pouring out of my mouth but I wasn't there. I was deep in my wound, raw and gaping now, gouged out from years of harsh words directed at me with a force that defied logic or reason, fuelled by alcohol with its unquenchable thirst for destruction. At least I was a happy drunk.

Not long after the wedding Dad sat slouched in the chair in the lounge room looking contrite. Mum had rung and said he wanted to see me, could he come over. I didn't want to see him but I was curious to know what he had to say about his disgusting behaviour at the wedding. On the rare times we were left alone together, we had few words to say to each other. I didn't know my father very well. I only knew the angry drunk who on a good day could be fun to be around. Neil went out for a bike ride to leave us to it. Dad wasn't saying anything so I started the conversation.

"What do you want to tell me?" *At least an apology for all the years you've treated me like shit would be good*, I thought.

"I've decided that after what happened at the wedding I'm going to quit the force".

"Are you?"

"Your mother and I talked about it. We thought it was time I took it easy from now on".

So much for the big apology. I switched off. Now I needed to find something to talk about till Neil came back or Dad went home. Please make it quick. He was fidgeting in his chair. He wanted out of there as much as I wanted him to go.

I wedged the shoe in between some rocks in a corner of the cave and slid down them digging my bare toes into the filthy dirt, the same filthy dirt that had flown from my father's mouth on my sister's wedding day and over the years, that neither my mother nor I could censor. From that day on, my father was a father in name only.

I thought, 'there has to be more to life than this' as I wiped my nose on the sleeve of my pyjama top and dabbed my tears on my blood stained hankie that belonged in my picnic basket.

After putting my hankie back in my picnic basket and straightening my pyjama top, I paced the cave's interior with that weary thought still looping inside my head, *'there has to be more to life than this'*, trying not to trip on all the empty pill bottles lying on the ground. My pacing brought me back to where the laundry was done. I saw Margaret open the door of her washing machine take Neil's clean clothes out and place them in her wash basket. Richard watched her, tapping his foot, his hands turning the loose change over in his pockets.

I picked up some of the empty pill bottles to avoid tripping over them, unable to shake the fog from my brain and the taste the pills had left in my mouth, the only solution my doctor could offer for my frayed nerves and insomnia I'd had since a teenager. I heard a voice say out of one of them, "You haven't got a problem. They are the ones who have a problem not you". I shook the empty pill bottle hard. Dr Roberts our family doctor was standing beside me. He had the same warm smile and calm voice I'd found comforting since the first time he prescribed me sedatives as a teenager. He took the pill bottle from my hand and put it in his pocket. He said those words to me sitting in a suite at an inner city clinic where he was now a psychiatrist to whom I'd been referred. I introduced him to Neil. They shook hands and after we all took a soft black leather chair in his consulting room he asked me, "Well what seems to be the problem?" He nodded as I ranted about all the ongoing arguments and issues I'd had with my in-laws over the years.

When I was spent he said in a low voice, "You haven't got a problem". I was floored. I thought he hadn't been listening to me. What a waste of time that was. Angered, I'd got up to leave when he said, "They are the ones with the problem, not you". I sat back down and looked at Neil. He looked away, then back at the ground. At last someone understood what I already knew.

Julie's budding child and broken child had sensed the presence of each other in the cave as they encountered people familiar to both children. However the budding child's attention was focused on the new wash basket she had been given that contained the responsibility for her husband's care and the pots of seedlings from her hotchpotch garden she wished to plant in the marital garden.
The broken child teetered on the edge of her nerves, her legs wobbly, trying desperately to shield herself from more hurt as she tried to stand up to her father's disrespect for her feelings.
The budding child's wash basket and the broken child's picnic basket were both see-sawing up and down inside Julie's torn heart as she tried to balance the demands of both, unsuccessfully.
Julie's courage to stand up for herself and demand respect from her husband's family was the growing voice within the young married woman of the Temple Woman she was to become. Her efforts to fulfil the planting of the budding child's potted seedlings in her marital garden and watch them flourish at last were thwarted by the broken child's unmet needs within her family's story. They were still in control of Julie's life, the broken child's wailing louder than the growing voice within the young married woman.
Despondent, she walked out of the cave with her wash basket filled full with the responsibility for the care of her husband her mother-in-law had bestowed on her and the one sided care of their marriage.

... scene 6 ...

overseas

setting
in julie's tent of travels

I stood at the entrance to my weeping green world wishing I could re-enter its sanctuary with the unfulfilled dreams it contained but I knew I couldn't as I was a married woman now. I couldn't go back to the cave either. I'd had enough of the continual arguments with Neil and his family. I looked for my potted seedlings. They were still upright, bunched together between the two rocks at the entrance to the cave. I bent down and inspected them but they had grown very little. Tears pricked my eyes.

The wind lifted the branches of my willow tree scraping across the thick, grey walls of the cave dislodging the potted seedlings and flinging them onto the path near the river. I chased after them but the wind conspired to tumble them over just out of reach, the pots thankfully still intact. Exhausted and defeated I picked up the wash basket and walked down towards the river. A brown canvas three-man tent was pitched beside it, which I recognised straight away. As I ran towards it, Neil's football clothes bouncing up and down in my wash basket it slipped from my hip. I caught it and righted it again.

As Julie ran it loosened the ties of the pouch around her waist.

I banged my basket down and dropped to my knees in front of the tent.

The pouch fell to the ground, the contents I had put in there on her wedding day still tucked inside.

I unzipped the flap of the tent and crawled inside onto the mattress. My large brown backpack was open wedged up against the side of the mattress, my clothes and shoes scrunched up inside it. I picked out my red leggings, white windcheater with the map of Australia with a koala and kangaroo on it in bright colors and my white walking shoes. I took off my bridal attire, put it together in a neat pile against the tent wall and put on the clothes I'd chosen out of my pack. I sat cross legged in the middle of the blow-up mattress looking around my compact new home, eager to find out what was left in my backpack. I could smell the scent of sandalwood, so my elephant from the Ganesh festival was in it. I found its trunk sticking out of some socks. The plaques had to be wrapped up in one of my T-shirts. Lifting my red jumper I found them and unwrapped them placing the pair of dolphins moving through the waves of the Mediterranean side by side, fashioned in the ancient style of the Greeks with a crazed patina.

Feeling around the bottom of my pack the corner of one of my paintings caught my hand. I unpacked all my clothes to get to them and unwrapped them, the sharp black images of Parisian scenes softened with washes of pale water colors, each bordered with a gold frame were a delight to see again.

Unzipping the top half of my pack I found my red plastic bowl and mug, a knife, fork, spoon and the little kettle. Pushing my hand into the far end of the pack where I'd kept the tea bags there were a couple left with a box of matches. I put the tea bags in my mug and crawled outside. A few steps from the tent, I saw the small gas bottle with the burner lying on its side on the grass. Making some tea, I took it back to the tent with me, sat back down on the mattress leaving the flap open to air the tent. I picked up the plaques and stared into the blue waters of the Mediterranean, remembering my first morning in Greece.

I'd opened the shutters of the hotel room out onto a view of the Parthenon. Though in ruins it still commanded its position high on the hill in the pale golden dawn light, a light that brought a crispness and freshness to the day and my jaded spirit. An avenue of cypress trees stood erect like soldiers as I passed making my way up the path to the summit. The sun broke through the imposing pillars lighting up the grandeur and beauty of this worn stone structure that had stood as a talisman of ancient times through the Ages. I stood in the cool wind that rushed down the mountain to the city below, the sounds of the bells from the churches carried by it into the homes and the hearts of its citizens. As the tourists started to arrive in droves up the path I was on my descent from the temple carried by the warmth of the sun and the elation of being in its presence.

While the tourists gathered there Neil and I walked to the parliament building. The soldiers in their pleated white tunics with the flowing sleeves and pom-poms on their feet strutted up and down outside with guns over their shoulders. They moved with the same precision I was taught to bring to the routines my ballet teacher choreographed for our troupe to perform at an eisteddfod.

The next day after a long drive up to a mountain top I stood with Neil taking in a rocky terrain covered in short grass that stretched out in every direction to the valley below. Enjoying the warm sun and fresh air I sat on the greyed blocks of stone that formed tiers in the amphitheatre. There the Oracle of Delphi's words once reverberated through the seated crowd, the oracle and her audience lost in her words of prophecy.

Huddled in a sleeping bag on the deck of a ferry to escape an airless cabin below on an overnight crossing brought me to the Greek Island of Santorini. The laborious excavation of Akrotiri dug at my thoughts as I considered its age and the society that once dwelt on this volcanic crater as I stood watching men and women picking their way through the remains of this Bronze Age settlement. From the top of the island's bare rock cliffs I sought the horizon of the Mediterranean wondering what lay beyond there. In this unhurried place where the tinkle of the bells of the donkeys that carried wares over the island could be heard well in to the night, I found a new rhythm to my step that slowed my harried mind. This rhythm, established through centuries old traditions of harvesting and ritual, was one I became reluctant to step out of.

Now she had found it again, Julie slipped easily into its rhythm as she continued her travels made of her budding child's dreams. They led her to the ancient ruins of a temple in a place she had first seen in a magazine as a child. There Julie would find the slow, measured step of I, the Temple Woman, a part of her who walks the unhurried path of timelessness.

... scene 7 ...

pompeii

Standing in an area of the ruins of Pompeii only the floor, a bit of one pillar and the moat where the water once ran into the bath inside the temple informed me of its existence. Without me being made ready time stretched and crossed for a few moments and the area I was standing in became a garden; the temple fully built, complete with running water. People were going about their daily lives dressed in togas, some carrying urns with water they filled from the pool, others tending the garden and a large area of vegetables. A tall slender woman with a coil of black hair piled on the top of her head was giving orders to young boys tending the garden. I sensed preparation for a celebration was taking place.

The birds sang and the warmth of the sun fell across my shoulders. I was aware of the tourists walking past me taking photos of the ruins, oblivious to my crossing. The scene faded. I tried to recreate it. Now it was like a distant thought, not real as it was in every sense a few moments before. Nothing in the past had happened to pave the way for this experience, but it left its mark. This twist in time showed me the possibility there was more to life; a hope I'd clung onto since a child.

I stepped back on the worn stone path and spied between the people leaning forward to take photos the contorted faces of the people and animals frozen in time and fear I'd stared at in the photos of my magazine, as mesmerised by the images now as I'd been as a child. I waited until the people moved on and stepped forward for a closer look through the fence. Were any of these people with their contorted faces in the garden I'd seen through a twist of time going about their lives in a time long ago? A faint image appeared again in my mind of the woman with the coil of black hair piled on the top of her head. I felt I knew this woman and her purpose. She'd had a position of authority evident in the way she carried herself and how she gave orders to the young gardeners. There was a celebration about to take place she was overseeing so she knew what it involved. Another group of tourists arrived and crowded round the fence pushing me out and away from my thoughts and so the woman's image faded from my mind.

As Neil and I made our way up the ridge of black, ashy rock to the top of Mt Vesuvius, tourists coming down in their sturdy walking shoes pointed at my thongs, shaking their heads. Stopping from time to time to look down upon the ruins of Pompeii as I climbed higher I was still deep in thought about what I'd experienced amongst its ruins. At the top, looking down on the tiered houses crammed together along the winding coastal road, the waters of the Mediterranean sparkled like the flecks in the inlaid wood pattern of the small carved table Nana and Grandad brought back from Sorrento. Through the haze I could just make out the Isle of Capri. Nana and Grandad had visited there but I had to be content with seeing it from the top of a mountain that'd been until now a special place I'd only dreamed of visiting one day. Humming the tune of the song that came out when the lid was lifted on that small carved table I remembered some of the words. I missed Nana.

... scene 8 ...

nana

"*You're* a funny girl but I still love you", Nana used to say to me.
"Why am I a funny girl?"
"You're not like the others in the family, you see things in a different way to them. You ask lots of questions about life, always wanting to know the answers to things. Why, why, why. Questions we can't answer. Why a little girl would want to know why the sky is blue and the grass green I don't know", she'd say one time. Another time she'd pat my head and say, "Your head is filled with adventure while your sister and girls your age are only interested in playing with their dolls, dreaming of marriage and babies when they grow up".

"Why am I different Nana?" I asked her one day.

She smiled at me. "You're the black sheep of the family. They are the ones who are different from the others. All families have them. They are the ones who don't follow what the rest of the family do or think, they question things".

I loved staying at Nana's. In the morning I watched Nana sleeping beside Grandad in their bed at the far end of the large front room, staring at them hoping Nana would wake first. The cuckoo in the clock in the hallway they brought back from Austria popped out of its nest every quarter of an hour and called but still they didn't wake.

I'd had enough of flipping through the National Geographic magazines kept in a pile on the shelf above my bed even though I loved looking at the photos of all those far-away places on the other side of the world.

When the alarm clock rang at last I was straight to Nana's side with a "Good morning Nana" and a kiss on the cheek before her hand reached out from under the covers and found the button to turn it off. Nana smiled at me as she swung her legs over the side of the bed looking for her slippers with her feet. She always left them just under the bed. Her silver hair was all over the place, pillow creases across her face. She lifted her pink chenille dressing gown off the end of the bed and wrapped it around herself. Taking her large white comb with the tortoise shell pattern off the dressing table she looked in the mirror and swept her hair back. She pushed the waves into place around her face and put down the comb after each one sat to her liking. I loved watching Nana comb her hair. Grandad was still snoring. Good. I liked it when Nana and I made breakfast together.

We walked down the long hallway, the polished floorboards springing under our feet, going to the dining room first. Nana opened the curtains then we went into the kitchen. She guided my hand, hers over mine as I held the knife and sliced the wholemeal bread evenly from top to bottom. Then I tried all by myself, my slice uneven. I popped it in the toaster anyway, pushed the side shut while Nana opened the larder door and took out my favourite jam; raspberry. She showed me how to scrape a little butter off the block and spread it on the bread without digging holes in it.

After breakfast Nana scooped the froth off the top of the washing up water and blew on it. Rainbow colored bubbles danced in the air before they popped. I jigged at her side wanting to do it too. Nana told me to scoop up the suds and blow very gently but I didn't have her touch, ending up with froth all over my face. We laughed.

On one side of the kitchen table was newspaper, on the other a big bowl, in the middle a brown paper bag of pea pods. We stood together and took them out of the bag one pod at a time. Squeeze, pop, pull, the pod was open. Would it be full of juicy peas all in a row or would there be some that hadn't grown? Disappointed if they hadn't, I dropped them on the newspaper and tried again. Between us and before too long the bowl was full and so was I after chewing on many sweet, juicy peas. Nana put them in the fridge ready to cook for tea.

I followed Nana to the laundry. She lifted the lid off the copper and dropped blue dye into the boiling water stirring it with an old wooden stick. We stood at the wringer and squeezed Grandad's singlet through until it came out looking like the scone mixture she and I flattened thin with the rolling pin. We made rings in the mixture with a glass jar. Nana cut around each ring with a knife and I wiped the tops of them with a pastry brush dripping in milk before she placed them on a well-used tray and put them in the oven.

Nana put the singlet in the large cane wash basket with the other washing and lifted it to take out to the clothesline. I took the other side. It was heavy. It tipped onto my legs but Nana had the other side steady in her hands. She walked slowly, ready to catch it if it fell. We managed to take it through the laundry door at the back of her house placing it under the clothes line without dropping it. I took the wooden pegs out of a greyed bag, and the smaller things I could manage from the basket, while Nana strung the clothes along the rope between two timber poles. The white sheets flapped in the wind like the sails of a boat on a stormy sea. They flapped against her legs as she pegged more clothes on the line.

I ducked under them with more pegs ready to pass them to her. Pigeons sat on the pipes on the roof of the house across the back fence cooing in the sunshine. It was a perfect day to get clothes dry. Nana picked up the basket to take it in but I took it from her hands. I stretched my arms wide to take the handles, following her back to the laundry and put it beside the copper.

I still loved staying at Nana's like I'd done as a child even though her old body was thin, frail and jaundiced, ravaged by pancreatic cancer, her time near. I stood behind Nana in the bathroom, now a widow in her last home, watching her comb her hair at the mirror still loving watching her do it. Though I offered to help, Nana was happy to cook dinner for the two of us, often a simple meal of lamb chops, mashed potato and peas. I felt her loneliness as we sat at the table and ate our meal. There is a certain quietude when a person who'd shared a space with someone for decades had gone, a space no-one else can fill, no matter how much they're loved, as I was.

After tea, I sat on Nana's bed while she got ready for bed. She opened the wardrobe and lifted the sleeve of Grandad's favourite well-worn tweed jacket to her face with tenderness, inhaling his personal cologne of tobacco, beer and shaving cream. I looked away, feeling an intruder in such a personal moment. Her face told me the moments of memory his familiar smell evoked in her were a blend of comfort and longing.

"It brings him back. He's here again". Nana laughed like a child as she rubbed the sleeve all over her face with glee, sniffing it like a dog would a delicious scent.

I tucked her in, gave her a kiss goodnight, retiring to the small spare room across the narrow hall and closed the door. The smell of old wood and furniture polish coming from the bedhead, dressing table and wardrobe was claustrophobic. I snuggled down under the thick woollen blankets and tried to go to sleep but the smell was overpowering. The window was stuck so I couldn't open it to get some fresh air. I got up, opened the door a little instead and went back to bed. The floorboards creaked in the hallway. It must be Nana going to the toilet I reassured myself. I waited to hear the toilet flush and Nana go back to bed but nothing happened. I heard footsteps. They stopped by my bed. A chill descended on the room. My chest tightened as I felt a suffocating presence standing over me. I was petrified. With my heart pounding I switched on the light wanting to run to Nana's room and get into bed with her. I ventured as far as her door to see if she was safe, as a breeze and a swoosh of air hovered over me sending me back to bed. As I hid under the covers the claustrophobic smell of the wooden furniture came back into the room and the heaviness in the air disappeared. I pulled back the blankets and took big gulps of light, thin, cool air, not the icy air that filled the room moments ago. I could breathe again. In the morning I told Nana about my experience.

"Oh that. It's just Jack. He visits me every night. I hear him walking up the hallway. He comes into my room, sits on the bed and I have a chat to him". Nana continued to pour my tea quite unperturbed by what we'd just spoken about.

I slept over many times after Grandad died when Nana needed company and more often after she fell ill with cancer. A one-sided conversation on her own with the spirit of her adored husband who sat on her bed each night wasn't enough to curb her loneliness.

It wasn't long before Nana came home from hospital, the doctors not able to give her any more treatment. Next time she wouldn't come home. She wanted to stay at home as long as she could to feel close to her husband until she joined him again; any small comfort to help her through her last days.

As I sat on her bed late at night holding her hand Nana asked me, "Where do you think I am going to?"

"Where would you like to go to Nana?"

"A garden, a big beautiful garden".

"Ok. You're walking along a gravel path, the sun is shining, the lawns on either side are green".

"There are flower beds on either side. I can see yellow roses and pink carnations. My favourite violets, there are big clumps of them dotted amongst the roses and carnations. It's shady where I'm walking through an orchard. There are lemon trees, cumquat and apple. Now I can see tall flowering gums".

I kissed her goodnight and left her smiling as she continued walking through her garden.

The end was soon near, a final hospitalization filled with bedside visits from Mum and her siblings who didn't know what to say or do through the discomfort, grief and inevitability of it. Her life force streamed out of her, her body consuming itself while I watched, helpless.

She chronicled her life for me as I listened to what were ramblings to me but not to her. The memories filled her with smiles and laughter complete with gestures as she reminisced with no-one other than herself in a hoarse voice thick from drugs. She was present in the times she talked about, very real to her in every way. She conversed with many relations I'd never heard of so her words didn't stick with me. The times Mum and her siblings were present while she spoke elicited nods, smiles and the shaking of heads with, "How does she remember that?"

exclamations.

On the wall opposite Nana's hospital bed was a poster of a rainforest. She tried to focus on it talking again about all the flowers and trees in the garden she would see where she was going.

I stroked her face and said, "It will be so beautiful; the colors, the fragrance of the flowers, the juiciness of the fruit in the orchard, those tall gums providing shade when you need a rest after walking along the path. Your mother, your sisters and your husband are waiting there to meet you when you let go of life here. They will take it in turns to hold your hand and comfort you when those who you love here can't any longer".

As her grip on life loosened, she closed her eyes and rested while I described her garden to her, reminding her she would soon be there with those she loved who had gone before her. Despite the pleasure this garden gave her when I described it to her she'd whisper in a hoarse voice, "I don't want to leave". I squeezed her hand, the tears falling down my cheeks. When she became too tired to speak as the days passed by I talked, she squeezed my hand in reply.

Standing at the side of Nana's hospital bed, her once well-groomed waves of silver hair now long, thin greasy strands pushed back off her face with bobby pins, her mouth sucked in, her cheeks hollow, I grappled with the thought that the single white sheet covering her would soon be used to cover her dead body. I sat down and held her dried up hand, her breathing shallow and laboured, the tears rolling down my face.

"Nana, it's Julie. If you know it's me squeeze my hand". There was a faint squeeze. "I've come to say goodbye. Thank you for all you've done for me. I'm really going to miss you. You've been so good to me, showed me so much love. I am going to miss that so much. No one can take your place". She squeezed my hand again, lighter than before. Feeling how weak she was I stopped talking, sat still and closed my eyes. Though I didn't want to, I knew it was time to leave. Walking out the door I knew I would never see her again. I wasn't home more than five minutes when the phone rang; Mum telling me she'd died. I felt privileged I was the family member she had spent the last moments of her life with.

... scene 9 ...

paris

Sitting in my tent of travels I found a hankie in my backpack. I dabbed my eyes, blew my nose then had another sip of tea wishing Nana was still alive so I could share my travel experiences with her. I noticed a postcard I must have pulled out with the hankie. It was of a woman, her fleshy form poised over a clam shell, her features showing through the cracked and faded pigments of an earthy palette. I'd sat opposite her in a hollow on a marble bench worn smooth with time in a corner of the Uffizi Museum in Florence in front of the painting, 'The Birth of Venus' by Botticelli. Overcome at being in the presence of such beauty and seeing this woman in the painting come to life was the first stop on a pilgrimage along an art trail inspired by grainy slides thrown onto a grey wall in a dull room in the arts wing in my final year of high school. I picked up the pair of water colors and propped them on either side of the tent flap so I could get a better look at them.

From a vantage point of great height standing on the steps of Sacré Coeur cathedral, I'd first seen the city of Paris spread out before me. A piano accordionist squeezed out a tune, a guitarist and two singers cast their blend of sounds over the crowd of people on a sunny Sunday morning, competing with the ringing of the church bells from the cathedral.

After strolling through the nearby artists' quarter of Montmartre a love of art, its pigments and compositions drew me to the scraggly artists to watch them for a while, their easels set up throughout the square, dabbing at their canvases. Deep passion coupled with a deep sense of patriotism welled in me that was unexpected and that I didn't understand.

Continuing on my art trail I found pleasure in the beauty of the paintings of Monet and Manet hung in the galleries of Paris. The dots and dabs of a fresh pastel palette applied to canvases recreated French gardens I now enjoyed walking through, inhaling early springtime scents of flowers and trees bursting into bloom.

As Neil and I stopped to enjoy the tasteful window displays of artwork and fashion along the Champs-Elysées, elegant, coiffured women strolled by in warm coats and long boots. They sat at tables in cafés at intervals along it, their designer handbags taken up with a fluffy toy poodle or a sleek chihuahua - others leading proud Great Danes and standard poodles on their diamond studded leashes with matching collars.

Neil and I sat at a table at one of the cafés, the waiter taking our order of coffee and almond croissants. An elegantly dressed and coiffured older woman adorned with gold jewellery was feeding the black poodle sitting on her knee with small morsels of pastry from an éclair as she sipped on a short black and cooed to him.

After the day's sightseeing, we rugged up and sat outside our tent on stools in a camping ground by the Seine, looking down the river to the Eiffel Tower. Our next door neighbours, two fellow backpackers, Italians who didn't speak a word of English, had offered to cook us a meal. We'd befriended each other with smiles, nods and hand gestures. As we sipped on glasses of cheap red wine one of them stirred the spaghetti in a pot on their gas stove. The other prepared a tomato sauce with the intensity of a chef in a five-star restaurant. After these two men had filled our plates with food I poured them some of our wine. The sound of the river's steady flow by the fence provided the right music to eat good food by as we watched the Eiffel Tower fade in the evening light.

Neil and I stood at its base early the next morning watching the people promenade along the wide gravel paths, past gardens filled with tulips. A queue had formed of tourists waiting for their turn to take a trip to the top of the tower. With my fear of heights, I didn't join them and waved Neil goodbye. As I waited for him I felt joy bubble through my body because the candy striped dreams from a dress with black poodles walking round its rim I'd worn as a child had come true.

Getting too breezy in the tent, I zipped the flap shut. I took another sip of tea, the words "Let's separate" intruding on my happy memories. Another heated argument had ended in Neil saying that for the first time while standing on the balcony of a small apartment in Lyon looking over the grey stone churches and buildings streaked with rain, the river bulging with snow melt. Like Neil, I was sick of the years of arguing and tension but was us separating all he could think of as a solution to our problems? I looked at my husband's unhappy face his blue eyes dulled with pain, the wrinkles deepened further across his forehead, feeling our mutual despair. I asked him to try to find a way. Tears welled up in my eyes. I looked away as there was no answer to comfort me, to give me hope. I loved my husband. There had to be a way to make our marriage work.

The decision to travel overseas was driven by me and agreed to by Neil as we were both worn down by our respective parent's demands. I'd hoped that some time away on our own with a new day and new adventure to be had while travelling in our VW Beetle and camping in our tent through Europe and the United Kingdom would restore our troubled marriage. It wasn't working. Neil lost weight and became more withdrawn the more kilometres we travelled.

We wouldn't have the year to ourselves either. When we told our friends and family about our trip, not long afterwards our parents told us they were going to take a trip of their own around Europe, planning to meet us in London. Neil's parents had similar plans to my parents but theirs included shouting us a tour of Spain, Portugal and Morocco.

... scene 10 ...

the tour

Richard's demanding voice cut across Neil's and my conversation. "Come on let's have lunch". He pointed at the fast food restaurant across the road.

Now I'd lost my appetite. We were in Madrid. What about trying some Spanish food? There were plenty of cafés to choose from. We walked along the crowded pavement, patrons seated at small tables amid a flurry of waiters carrying large platters of food with tempting smells wafting from them. I looked back with longing as Neil, Margaret and I were herded into a crowded restaurant by Richard, an arsenal of cameras around his neck.

"What'll you have?" he asked.

"Just some chips and a Coke thanks", I said.

"You have to have a hamburger. It's a long time till tea".

"I don't want one thanks".

"Look, you have to have one". His voice climbed up a notch.

"I don't want one. If I'm hungry later, I'll buy myself something", my voice rising to match his.

He snorted at me, asked the others what they wanted, then marched off to order the food. He came back with a tray full and doled it out to us. He tossed a hamburger in my direction. "Eat it. I paid for it, so eat it!" The other two looked uncomfortable but said nothing. I held back the tears and for the sake of peace, did as he said. We had a long way to go before this tour was over.

We drove through a grove of eucalypts in a small seaside Portuguese village. Their familiar scent coming through the open windows of the bus late on a hot summer's afternoon provided a surprising tinge of home. It reminded me how far I was from there.

The bus stopped in front of a charming little hotel with its wrought iron balconies, bright pots of geraniums and white painted brick walls. Andrea our tour guide opened the solid wooden door with a huge iron knocker and hinges and went in to find the receptionist to do the paperwork. Carlos our bus driver opened the boot and started removing the luggage. Richard was there standing over him waiting for ours.

"Come on, come on", he called to Neil and I. Some of the group still on the bus, rolled their eyes, looking at us with pity. I sighed, left my seat, following behind Neil.

"There's your stuff. Go on Neil, get it out. Don't keep the others waiting". His father pushed Neil forward to get our things. I wanted to scream. We all gathered in the foyer at Andrea's request.

"I'm sorry folks. There's been a problem with the accommodation. We'll have to squeeze some of you in together for the night. There are still two rooms for a couple". Andrea held up the keys to those rooms. Richard stepped forward, swiping a set from her hands.

"Those are for Neil and Julie, Richard. They've been camping for months so I thought they'd like a room to themselves to spread out in for a change".

"Thanks Andrea. What a lovely surprise. It will be a real luxury", I said. Some privacy at last. Neil beaming, stepped forward to take the keys from his father. So, Andrea had noticed what was going on too. Richard stormed off with Margaret and their luggage to their cramped room. I wondered who their roommate would be. It was the single older American, Ralph. Poor guy.

With my thoughts filled with the sunny skies and comfortable beds I slept in in Portugal, I put my cup of tea down and lay back on the sagging air mattress in the tent. As I wriggled to get settled I noticed the corner of the prayer mat I'd bought in Morocco sticking out from under the mattress, the next stop on our tour. Andrea had said, "I suggest you stock up on some nuts and fruit like oranges from the store in the next town before we cross the Strait to Morocco. It will be very late when we get to our motel in Rabat and there is nowhere to stop for any decent supplies. You have to be careful what you eat in Morocco if you're not used to the food like I am. This food is safe to eat".

We pulled up near the ferry and headed for the store, the Rock of Gibraltar a hazy outcrop of indefinable size clouded by a heat shimmer. I bought a large mesh bag of nuts in shells, another of oranges, expensive for us on our tight budget but if Andrea said we needed this food, I was prepared to trust her judgement. Margaret and Richard were in the store too but they walked out empty handed, which surprised me.

The Rock peeked out of the haze from time to time, the terns guiding us across the rippling water. We came so close I felt I could touch it. I was glad of our supplies. This was lunch. No meals service on this ferry of questionable seaworthiness.

Our bus wound through the endless miles of the Atlas Mountains dry, hot and dusty terrain, the glare of the heat bouncing off the windows. Stone boxes popped up at random, home to women clad in long black robes with mesh across their faces. A few straggly goats and thin children followed them. The children waved at us, the men digging the soil with rusted tools, tending meagre crops. How did they exist here in this nothingness and endless heat? I reached for an orange from the bag on my knee.

Margaret leaned over from her seat behind me. "How about one for me? Richard, do you want one?"

I was furious. They had the wealth to travel overseas often, to shout Neil and I this tour but weren't prepared to spend what was little money for them, on some food for themselves? They knew we had a tight budget yet they had no qualms taking from us what little we had. I bit my tongue, turned around, passing the bags of food to them. Margaret was all smiles as she peeled her orange. Richard chose an orange and a handful of nuts. I hoped they wouldn't ask again. I looked out the window as I sucked on a slice of juicy orange, the landscape's stark beauty haunting and absorbing.

An array of food stuffs on display in the medina in Rabat included donkey hoofs tied to the stone walls with old rope beside stalls and outside tiny shops, a delicacy for the people and flies that were buzzing round them.

In a shady alleyway, a reprieve from the searing sun, children's voices could be heard chanting words after a woman's voice said them first. As I walked past, a group of children were squeezed inside a small room in desks, the teacher with a black head covering pointing with a beaten stick at an old blackboard. I caught a couple of cheeky grins from those children distracted from their learning. I smiled back.

Dazzled by the bright colors and textures of the various wares for sale as we ambled by, I was led through the medina by our tour guide to the tannery pits, full of reeking water, young boys walking in them, others working with the hides they drew up from the pits.

The sounds of the muezzin calling the people to prayer startled me. I walked out of the medina into the street. People were dotted about the square on their prayer mats, bent low. I'd bought mine from a vendor who lived at the ocean's edge in a crude shelter, needing to climb up on large boulders where the mats were laid out, choosing one woven in the colors of green grass and rich brown coffee.

... scene 11 ...

amsterdam

I unrolled the prayer mat admiring the handiwork, thinking about the hours that must have been spent creating it, as I lay there on my air mattress. Needing to stretch my legs I unzipped the tent, crawled out with the mat and laid it across the entrance. As I straightened it I noticed a white pouch on the ground embossed with silver stars with a drawstring top. I picked it up, opening the ties. Three cards fell out; tarot cards.

In a narrow cobblestone laneway in a district of Amsterdam I'd stepped inside the door of a tall, thin building for my last meal in Europe invited to the apartment of a new found Dutch friend, Libby. Lit by a small candle, a table was laid with tarot cards. Libby introduced Neil and I to her friend Rose. She turned the cards over one by one, the silver bracelets up her arms tinkling in time. She beckoned me closer, drawing up a wooden chair beside her.

"Would you like to see how to do a reading?" I nodded. Five cards were laid out in a formation. She explained, "The one in the middle is for the present. The ones on each side are for the past and future. This below the present for a reason, the one above for potential". Pushing her glasses back on her nose, she peered at the first card, pointing at it with a bright red fingernail. She tucked a long tight curl of black hair behind her ear and turned over the other cards. Her hand hovered over them, the gesture seeming to tie the information she gleaned from their combination into some satisfactory order in her mind. She swept the cards up, asking in her distinctive American accent if I would like a reading. I shuffled the cards.

Rose laid them out and said, "This is the Celtic Cross spread that is used for a life path reading. Mmm. The present has an immediate challenge over it; going home".

"That's for sure. I don't want to go home. This gypsy life suits me". Rose nodded, smiling in silent agreement.

"The immediate past, the immediate future show you will face a period of adjustment but there's still adventure in the time left overseas. The next card, the best outcome, says embrace it. The next three cards shows reasons why you don't want to go home. It's inside you, your hopes, fears, your external experiences of life". Rose picked up the last card. "This is the final outcome. Change. A lot of change. Inside you and in your life".

I thanked her as she swept up the cards, determined to make the most of the time left before I had to return home.

... scene 12 ...

india

Rose was right, there was more adventure to come; found in India. The expressionless man who seemed to be blind, maintained his unsettling stare at me on the three-hour train trip from Delhi to Agra until he spread out on the hard wooden bench and fell asleep. He sat up after a couple of hours as the train rattled along, smiled and said good morning, not blind, his meditation and repose complete.

After the train ride, a young man pedalled his rickshaw at an even pace taking Neil and I past a procession of women and children with silver pots on their heads, ornate candlesticks in their arms on the way to prepare for a wedding ceremony. Another procession of men walked by with a parcel bandaged in white cloth between them; a funeral procession, the fire already lit by the river, the acrid smoke telling us bodies had already been burned on the pyre. In the distance I could see our end destination; the Taj Mahal. The rickshaw driver dropped us at the entrance.

As we walked towards its marbled beauty, the four spires reaching up in to the cloudless blue sky, a gathering crowd of Indian men followed us. We sat on the edge of the large moat wanting a photo in front of the Taj Mahal. We asked one of our followers to take the photo. The other men took that as a signal to have a group photo with them all in it. Standing in the water leaning in close to us they chanted "Adonis, Adonis" as they patted Neil's curly hair, stroked his tanned arms and long legs jostling to lean on his muscled shoulders wanting to be in the photo with their Adonis. They also wanted us to take them to Australia to live, with promises to work hard. Their demands and insistent attention grew until a guard approached sending them on their way. We were left to enjoy the refreshing greenery of the ordered gardens and the luscious space of intricate tiled mosaic inside the sanctuary of the temple dedicated by the emperor to the woman he loved.

Wrapped around the poverty, filth and crowds, was warm sweet air, and vivid color. Mounds of saffron and garlands of scented yellow and orange flowers, women in saris and the aroma of spices filled the marketplaces of Mysore. With the sudden onset of nightfall the endless stream of time that permeated the air and the people bled into me.

Susan, Ray, and their two young children who were living there while Ray worked on an engineering project, squashed into an auto rickshaw with Neil and I. We were rattled about making us squeal with laughter as we dodged people, potholes and other drivers their horns blaring. We put-putted by the palace draped in a constellation of starry lights on the way to the plush hotel in town for my birthday celebration that coincided with the annual celebration of the Ganesh. We walked through a lobby filled with elephant statues strung with flowers and backlit by candles to a room where a banquet with full silver service and fragrant rose tea was served. Susan's children Hayley and Scott helped me blow out the candles on my sponge cake. Ray raised his glass of beer, the others their tea and wished me a happy birthday.

The next morning the Puja man's incantations and prayers were heard ahead of him calling me to the front door where the swirling, smoking sandalwood incense wafted out of a brass jar. He stood bare foot dressed in saffron robes, his face painted with symbols. He smiled at me then bowed his head in a surprising gesture of respect. Susan welcomed him into their rented house where he chanted and swirled the incense throughout it as I followed him from room to room. A Brahman cow grazing in the front yard looked up at him, returning to chew the overgrown grass by the front gate as the Puja man walked down the drive to the next house in this secured road where the upper caste lived.

Beyond the gate at the road's entrance where guards stood with guns was an ice cream factory. On a daily walk there with Hayley and Scott we chose our favourite ice cream pistachio nut, its creamy flavour cooling on a hot, humid day. The block of ice cream was wrapped in newspaper by a woman with a smile who stood behind the counter. We hurried home before it melted and took a chunk with a spoon straight from the block.

A walk to the other end of the road for a game of cricket on the lush front lawn of a neighbour's house followed by a pitcher of icy lemonade swimming in limes to share, was another daily pleasure.

Later in the week, on his invitation, the Lama greeted Neil and I at a monastery high in the mountains, a morning's drive in our chauffeured car from Mysore. He ushered us along with Susan and the children who he'd already met before, into his sanctuary to sit with him.

We joined the monks seated cross legged at low wooden tables, turning the pages of large, worn books as other monks at the altar turned gold prayer wheels. The belligerent sounds of the long horns mingling with the clashing of small cymbals overlaid the monk's chants, creating a resonance in the air and in me that felt both familiar and harmonious.

The Lama invited us to his room after the ceremony. Stuck to the walls of his office were postcards from all over the world. On his desk was a globe of the world. With a wooden pointer he explained where all these people were from who he'd met in his monastery, inviting us to do the same. I took the pointer he passed to me, happy to oblige. He asked Neil and I to send him a postcard when we returned home to add to his collection.

A monk entered the room with a tray, setting out some cups and a pot of tea which the Lama poured. He bowed as he passed us each a small pottery cup. We sat in front of the Lama's desk on beaten up chairs, the sounds of chanting of prayers continuing in the long hall as we sipped our tea.

The day dreams of childhood to visit faraway places on the other side of the world had been sown under the budding child's willow tree and planted in her hotchpotch garden. These seeds sprouted and flourished in the garden she fertilised and tilled with her husband in her one-sided marriage. The tendrils of ancient memory opened in their little clear crystal pots I had been tending until the perfect combination of Julie and time and place arose for them to bear fruit. Entwined around the seed of Julie's essence, the tendrils tugged it open a little more as it lay bathing in the crystal lining of my basket inviting the young married woman to grow toward the Temple Woman within.

I, The Temple Woman, lifted a pink lotus blossom impregnated with rose oil out of my basket and laid it on a rock close to the entrance of the tent, enticing the young married woman to remember that I was also a part of Julie. I left her to drop deeper into her dreaming in her place of rest at her camp near the river as it was in her dreaming she would find me.

... scene 13 ...

the tarot cards

Julie sat down on the grass beside the tent and turned over the three tarot cards that had fallen out of the pouch I had tied to her wedding dress. They were three of the cards from the Celtic Cross spread reading Rose had done for her in Amsterdam; The Tower, The Hanged Man and Death cards that were all indicators of tumultuous change. In that turmoil the seeds of Julie's life story would be tossed about and thrust out of their pots along the winding path towards me, the Temple Woman, as the family story she had lived within disintegrated.

I looked at The Tower with its stark images of crashing towers, storms and black skies, the words "let's separate" sharpened in my mind again. My insides flipped in fear. The Hanged Man was me, hung upside down in Neil's family, strangled by their unspoken rule. Looking at the Death card I shuddered. I swept up all the cards off the ground, putting them in a pile.

One of the first things I'd done when I'd got home was to buy the same pack of tarot cards as Rose used, creating a daily ritual with them. Sitting cross legged at the coffee table in the lounge room as I'd done as a child with my jigsaw of the map of Australia, I looked at solving a new puzzle; what made me, me? I had the book with the interpretation of the cards by my side as well as a journal and pen, the cards spread across the coffee table. I chose three cards, placing them side by side. Opening my journal, I wrote the date then the name of the cards under it leaving space to jot down what detail in each card jumped out at me. A color or a number, the suite, or a small detail in the picture on the card, like a flower catching my eye. This daily ritual helped me realise each card told its own story, the entry point into it different each time. In combination with other cards they told me more of my own story reflected in my daily life.

My friends showed a mixed response to my interest in the tarot when I told them about what I was doing with them once I had gained confidence in interpreting the cards for myself, having filled a large exercise book with my stories over a few months. The curious ones asked me if I'd interpret a spread for them after a meal and a few drinks at our place which I did gladly as I wanted to see how it worked with others. The readings I did impressed them enough to ask if I would do one for family members and friends who were curious too. They came to sit at the coffee table in the lounge room on a weekend, choosing cards for their own story to be told. Other friends weren't interested in my new found interest in the tarot at all. Nor was Neil.

A mutual desire for change prompted Neil to seek a different path that would satisfy his material aspirations in a way a teacher's salary would never fulfil. "I've made my mind up. I'm not going back to teaching. I've got a posting but my heart's not in it. Dad's right. Teaching doesn't earn enough to have the lifestyle we want. With insurance broking you have a chance to earn a lot more".

"But what about the hours you have to work to earn it. No more holidays to relax, to go away or do things to the house".

"We don't earn enough to do all these things anyway. What about the future?"

"This is your father talking. He's been at you since you started teaching about you going in to insurance broking. He's reminded you over and over that teaching has no future; that it's not a career for a man. You're a great teacher. I won't stand in your way if you want to do this but it makes me so angry you're just doing it to please your father. Why do you give in to him? He wears you down in the end until he gets his way no matter what it is. Can't you think for yourself? It's your life, it's *our* life, not his". At the end of this conversation, familiar feelings of resignation and dejection washed over me setting in my heart.

The family's preoccupation with acquiring and maintaining wealth and the constant conversations about it bored me. Compared to our friends we agreed we weren't getting anywhere and for Neil that needed remedying. I had a desire for the nice things in life too but it wasn't what drove me like it did my friends and family. As they continued to embrace their careers and children, I embraced the exploration of the tarot. Through it I began to understand that what was happening in my inner world became a reality in some form in my everyday life shaping my future. Despite his father's adamant assurances that a move to a career as an insurance broker was the right one for his son, Neil remained at his stop gap job in a factory.

Though our paths were diverging, there were moments where they crossed and met. A clairvoyant with a reputation for being very accurate amongst the workers in the factory, prompted Neil to go and see her, to reassure himself a move to the new career he was considering was the right one. Neil didn't tell me very much about what Colleen said when pressed, just that changes were coming and she knew a lot about him which he couldn't understand how she did. He looked uncomfortable as he had a large gulp of white wine from his glass and took some nuts from the bowl by his chair after telling me the little he was prepared to divulge. I made an appointment to see her not long after as it was time for me to know why I sought a different path to the rest of the people in my life.

I looked up from my tarot cards. White clouds gathered on the horizon beyond my camp site by the river near the cave and the willow tree. The sound of chooks startled me. I couldn't see them but I could hear a woman with an Irish lilt calling to them further down the path. I couldn't see her either but I knew who it was; Colleen.

You know how you have some days you remember so well you can still see it all over again in vivid detail when you think about it. The day I met Colleen was one of those. I was wearing my old blue jeans, new red shoes and shirt with large blue and red flowers on it I'd bought at a department store in London. I'd knocked on Colleen's door clutching a drooping pink fuchsia from my garden as she'd asked me to choose a flower to bring along. The door was opened by a short, broad, brown eyed woman, her brown hair peppered with grey. She invited me into her lounge room, shooing half a dozen chickens off the sofa in her thick Irish accent. She took my flower, plonking it into a glass of half-drunk water on the coffee table. Patting the sofa beside her she invited me to sit with her.

She held my hands, looked into my eyes and said, "You're not of this world my dear".

I blinked at her in disbelief then turned to watch in further disbelief as flapping, clucking chickens jumped in and out of her bathtub then rushed to the kitchen and back. Colleen got up shooing them out of the bathroom, quick to close the door behind them.

She returned to the sofa, lifted my flower with a soft touch and said, "Such pain, sadness in your flower my dear". Her face looked pained as if she might cry as she said it. "So much study, so much learning to do".

"But I have. I'm a primary school teacher".

She smiled at me, patted my hand repeating what she'd just said then added, "You are very psychic".

"I am?" That piqued my curiosity. It was the cue to ask her one of the many questions I had for her. "I wanted to talk to you to ask about what happened to me while I was overseas". When I'd finished telling her about my experience at Pompeii I asked, "What was that all about?"

"Past lives. You're an old, old soul. You have been here many, many times". She held my hands again. "Did you know you have healing hands?" I looked at them, feeling and seeing nothing in them that would indicate what Colleen was saying was true. "You are a very powerful healer".

I decided to change the subject. "There was another strange experience driving through the countryside where Mary Queen of Scots was beheaded. I dreamed of huge steel masts in a rolling green countryside many times before I went overseas. Why would I dream of something like that over and over? It doesn't make any sense. Then, as we rounded a corner, there were the masts all in a row. All the hairs on my body stood on end".

"Pah! Your dreams are full of visions about the future and what has happened in the past". Colleen fidgeted in her seat, waving her hands in the air at my strange experience, indicating to me I shouldn't be surprised after what she'd just told me about myself. "You have much work to do".

Now I had work to do as well as study. This was too much. "I had a tarot reading while I was away. I bought a pack of cards. I've been playing around with them".

"That's just the beginning. So many big changes for you. The problem with your life is that you don't know all these things about yourself yet. You won't be able to use your gifts until you begin to realize and accept you are all those things I told you".

Many other things were said about my life that day in-between shooing the chickens out of the house; like how I loved ducks and cats. What she said both frightened and excited me in equal measure. Even though I couldn't see myself being the things she said I was, I felt a sense of relief because she had provided me with some direction about where my life was heading.

After listening to what Colleen said in Neil's and my readings, Louise decided to visit the clairvoyant too. She returned from her reading unsettled. When I heard her tape, I understood why. Colleen said Louise and I would have a falling out and no longer be friends.

I stood up with the pile of tarot cards and walked back to the tent dropping the cards into the wash basket. A scent of rose oil wafted by near the tent. Following its trail, I found it was coming from a lotus blossom spread on a rock. I inhaled its sweet scent as my friends and family had done the day I'd returned home from my trip. Neil and I had taken our battered and filthy back packs out of Louise's car. Throwing them on the lounge room floor I unzipped them.

I said to my friends, "If you want to know what India is like, smell this". A potion of stale incense, smoky spices and sweet rose oil wafted into the air as I tossed the clothes out to wash later, releasing the scent throughout the house of our last adventure overseas.

Sitting cross legged outside the tent on my prayer mat I closed my eyes closed in meditation like the man had done opposite me on the train trip to Agra. Louise, Carolyn and Mum's faces appeared. We'd all gone together to yoga class at the local hall when I was a teenager. I re-joined the class with Louise not long after I returned home from my trip.

After our time in India, I hoped Neil might be open to the idea of joining us. He tried a beginner's class, not liking it but agreed to attend the meditation class. I was thrilled, having high hopes this shared experience would bring some peace to our troubled marriage. He soon lost interest. Louise and I continued going to both classes together. We were invited to attend the esoteric discussion group after the class. Its strange teachings and ceremonies left me uneasy with a fear of being possessed by something outside of myself that I wouldn't be able to control. The Ouija board flashed in front of my eyes. I felt a chill go through me, like the day I last played it with my sister. I breathed in and out until I felt my body calm like it did in the relaxation exercise at the end of a yoga class. Unlike the man who sat opposite me on the train trip to Agra I found meditating hard, my mind filling with thoughts I couldn't block out giving me a headache. Other times all I saw were vivid colors dancing in front my eyes burning them.

> As Julie sought opportunities to explore activities that opened the seeds of seeing and knowing within her further, her in-law's interference in her marriage worsened. As the parental interference escalated the ferocity of her desire to live her own life was heightened. An intruding family to the left and right of a marriage will destabilize it, especially if only one is fighting hard for it. In that desperate situation there's no support or ally from within the family circle, so it needs to be sought outside it.
>
> Julie found that support in an unexpected way. It was the broken child who would eventually provide the ally she badly needed. It was she who would help her begin to write herself out of her family's story and orient herself to where her own story lay waiting to be found within the temple where I resided.

... scene 14 ...

a doorkeeper and an astrologer

I noticed a middle aged woman with permed grey hair standing with her back to me by the river over near the cave. It was Lois. I'd met her through my friend Vicki whom I'd supported by buying some items weekly from her health food shop in a small suburban shopping strip, her new business venture.

"You've got to meet Lois, she's into all that spooky stuff like you and does something with numbers. I'll take you in, introduce you", Vicki said as she helped take my shopping bags to the car.

Lois owned the craft shop next door. She stood straight backed behind the counter, folding hand knitted baby clothes. She smiled when she saw Vicki who left me with her. She invited me to the back of her shop where we sat at a worn table wedged in by shelves of doilies, knitted dolls and balls of wool and shared a cup of tea.

"What is your birthdate?", she asked in her proper English voice, laying it out on a grid on the back of a shopping docket. She leaned back in her chair, looked at me and said, "It comes to an 11, a master number. People with that number are best equipped to guide others into the New Age because of their intuitive and clairvoyant abilities. These could take many forms such as healing". Lois then explained the nine year peaks and cycles between the numbers on the grid adding, "The Arrow of Determination cuts across your chart", which she drew in a long streak with a stubby lead pencil on the grid. Then she said something odd. "You will be a doorkeeper to other soul's awakening as I am to you". She took my hand. "Come back and talk to me if you have any questions. I suggest you buy a book on numerology".

Each week, after I visited the butcher and Vicki's shop, I stopped by Lois's to have all my questions answered over a cup of tea out the back.

"Here, read this", Lois would say as she pushed a book across the table at me to flip through while she served a customer. For a week or two I borrowed books from her library on a spare shelf in the storeroom in the back of the shop. Books on dreams and how to interpret them led me to a series of workshops run by the Edgar Cayce Foundation, motivating me to keep a dream diary, which was easy for me to do as I'd kept a diary of my everyday life since I was a child. Books by mediums like Doris Stokes, a personal favourite of this medium Lois, who was now my teacher and some of the theosophical teachings of Alice Bailey, her teachings way beyond my understanding. Books on numerology. Books on astrology.

I'd bought home a blackboard and a box of white chalk from my classroom for Lois to use. A small group of friends gathered in the lounge room close to the blackboard ready for a numerology lesson. They brought their prejudices based on religious faith and upbringing with them, applying them to her teaching. Their birth dates were laid on grids and short readings given and received with discomfort, disbelief, to curiosity, laced with a big dose of scepticism.

Lois lay Vicki's birthdate out on the grid and said, "You're a trans medium".

"No - I'm a medium to small", she quipped. She looked around the room for a laugh and got it, except from me. I loved her quick wit but this time I wasn't amused.

"You two were brother and sister in a past life. You pulled her pigtails".

My friend grinned at me. "Hi sis".

Lois turned to another friend. "You were a ballet dancer in a past life but this life you are uncoordinated". Dave's wife Sandy laughed as it was true he had no groove on the dance floor. We'd all seen it.

He squirmed in his chair at being reminded huffing, "It had nothing to do with a past life".

This wasn't the response I was hoping for but I'd expected it. At least they'd been willing to come out, of all my friends I'd invited, eager to share my new found knowledge and experiences with them. Joking about it hurt my feelings as this path was leading me in a direction that was fulfilling and enriching in a way their materialistic path was for them. I didn't see how there being different ways to fulfilment should affect our friendship with each other. I thought that if I was happier in myself Neil would be happier too and that would help to strengthen our marriage in the years ahead.

I watched Lois walk along the rocky path by the river leaving her be as she looked deep in thought. A woman walked towards her with fair hair and complexion, also short like Lois. She looked familiar. When she got closer I could see she had a blue folder under her arm. She waved at me so I waited. She came up to me, smiled, handing me the folder. When I looked inside I remembered who she was; Marie the astrologer.

While Neil had worked and attended classes to gain the qualifications needed to perform the profession of his father's choice, I worked and attended classes in astrology. After completing the second level of the course, I was prompted by the teacher to have my own chart cast. As Marie walked off, I stood on the path and flipped through her interpretation of my chart. I stopped when I came to the part where it told of a transit coming up for me which could have a profound effect on my life; the transit of Pluto to Venus and the North Node. It said I would feel the transit's influence before the conjunction and for a couple of years after. It also said it was a time in my life when I would be evaluating my relationships and what love meant to me.

... scene 15 ...

the marriage breakup

A thunderstorm had been brewing, the sky rumbling with the threat of rain now starting to fall in big drops. Lightning lit up the sky and the rocky path along the river. I ran for the shelter of my tent, grabbing my wash basket on the way. I threw it in, zipping the tent up tight. I held onto the pole as the wind pulled on the corners of the tent encouraging them to let fly. Holding the pole tighter in my grip I hung on hoping the storm would soon pass. I heard Mum's voice before the next thunder clap shook the tent.

"Watch out for Louise, she's making a play for Neil". That's what she'd said to me as I sat at the kitchen table having lunch on my way home from shopping.

"How could you say that about my best friend?" I had angrily replied.

Words from your mother have a sharp edge that bite in a way no other woman's words can. I'd glared at Mum, dropping the half eaten egg and lettuce sandwich she'd made for me onto the plate, my appetite evaporated with her knowing smile.

At first, Neil walked over to Louise's place. I wanted to go too but he said he wanted to go on his own so I walked him to our front door waving him goodbye. Later, he cycled to Louise's place. He put on his bike gear, strapped on his wristwatch, training for another road race. He cycled to her place first then on to the city or the hills and the streets of our neighbourhood for hours on end. When his body hurt too much, he drove instead to Louise's place.

Neil was at the kitchen sink having a glass of water after returning from another bike ride.

I remarked casually, "You've been gone a long time. You've been at Louise's". We looked at each other. I could tell by the look on his face he had. "You have haven't you?"

"Well I have to have someone to talk to about all our problems. She knows both of us well so she can help".

He went to the bedroom to get changed. I stood in the kitchen wishing I hadn't asked knowing what the answer would be, but I needed to hear it anyway. Mixed relief filled me. At least he'd been talking to someone at last; someone I could trust. Louise would never hurt me. But why didn't he want to tell me he was at her place?

The rain lashed the tent, the sides sucking in on me. I pushed them back to stop the rain dripping on me while I tried to keep the tent pole steady. As I shut my eyes to keep the drips from getting in, I could see them kissing.

Neil had pushed Louise up against the kitchen cupboards, their lips and bodies pressed to one another in a passionate embrace, obedient to the moment. Our guests witnessed this long embrace with the drunken indifference of another New Year's Eve where these things happen. I knew things they didn't. No more pretence. It was obvious to me what was going on. Panic gouged a hole in my gut. Too much champagne giddied me, spinning me out and away from what I saw and wanted to forget by the morning.

Sobered by what I saw and what I was going to do about it, a couple of days later I blurted out, "I saw you kissing Louise on New Year's Eve. What's going on with you two?" The tears came but I stopped them filling my lids with a sharp intake of breath as I kept staring at the TV.

I turned to face Neil as he said, "Louise has been a good friend. She's helped me a lot with our problems".

"You've already told me that before. It looks like you're more than good friends".

"No we're not".

"Come off it. I'm not stupid. You'd better decide what you want. What does she have that I don't?" I asked as I held his gaze.

He muttered, "She's not too esoteric. She's nice and slim". I couldn't believe what I'd just heard. Its shallowness didn't warrant a reply. "She wants a family". I could understand that as a motivation, though I didn't want to hear it. "My parents like her and Jason". That stung, and the matter of fact way he'd made the comparison between Louise and I without regard for my feelings. That showed me he'd had a lot of time to think about it.

I said, "I'm going down the coast to stay with Susan for a few days to give you a chance to think. When I get back I want an answer". The program started again. I snuggled down in bed, watching it flicker in front of my eyes. Neil got out of bed. I heard him opening cupboards in the kitchen. I'd said it now. It was out. No turning back.

As the storm continued to rage outside the tent I whimpered. Not only had Neil chosen his family over me, now he'd chosen my best friend over me. The thunder crashed overhead, lightning flashes lit up the tent, the wind roared up the valley like a fighter jet whizzing overhead dropping bombs. My beloved Susan tried to make it all okay.

After a week of fitful sleep, worry and tears, Susan came into my room of the rented beach house with a thermos of peppermint tea and a mug putting it on the bedside table.

As I dried my eyes she sat on the bed and held my hand. "Thought you might like this in the night for when you can't sleep. The warmth will help you relax".

"Thanks. I'm like a lamb to the slaughter going home. It's not going to be good. I feel it".

"Try not to think about it too much. You need to build up your energy to cope with whatever happens. You will know soon enough". Susan gave me a kiss on the cheek, turning off the light and closing the door on my dark thoughts.

I stopped in our driveway late in the afternoon sitting there shaking, summoning up the courage to enter the house, the sunlight hurting my swollen, red eyes. I got out of the car and with jelly legs walked towards the front door. Neil rushed down the steps past me tears running down his cheeks he blurted out, "I can't go on in this marriage. I'm sorry".

He was in the car before it registered what he'd said. I ran inside blinded by shock, collapsing onto a kitchen chair. Then I saw the note. Snatching it up I read it. Instant amnesia set in to protect myself from the finality those words written in the note spelt out. Only hearing the repetition of Neil's voice in my head saying *"I can't go on in this marriage"* I screamed and screamed on the top of my voice and ran out the door, my legs unable to keep up with the speed my flight was taking me. Stumbling and falling against the next-door neighbour's front door I bashed it with my fists, sobbing. Dave opened the door.

I fell to my knees on the floor of his lounge room shrieking, "Neil's left me".

Dave crouched down and put an arm around me. I felt an object thrust to my numb lips. I took the glass and a gulp. Brandy. It burned my insides. I took another gulp and felt its warmth spread down my legs.

"I'll ring your mother".

"The animals…"

"Don't worry, we'll look after them". Dave looked to Sandy. She nodded.

I sat on the lounge room floor in front of the blank TV of my childhood home. The phone rang. Mum came in to say Richard had rung to see if I'd arrived safely and if I was okay. Ignoring her, I stared at my wedding and engagement rings, rocking back and forth in a rhythm that brought no comfort, saying over and over, "What am I going to do?" until Mum opened the heavy curtains on a new day.

Another gust of strong wind tipped the wash basket over inside the tent. The Death card landed at my feet. I turned it over so I didn't have to look at the skeleton's face, still hanging onto the pole wondering how much longer it would be before the storm passed.

Where were my friends? Mum had rung them to tell them what happened. Kim arrived first. We sat at the kitchen table. She held my hand saying nothing, her hands and face offering comfort. I stared at her wedding and engagement rings. She was still married. She had a husband. I'd lost mine. More tears came.

Carolyn arrived next. Pregnant with her first child she hugged me, the tears rolling down her cheeks. "I don't believe it. Louise has done the wrong thing. It's not fair. Michael says she's a slut". I held her and sobbed.

Mandy swept in with a food hamper and the reassurance, "You'll be friends again one day in the future. I know it will take a long time but you will".

Mum made them cups of tea to keep herself busy and her disappointment at bay. Neil was the son she never had and she loved him as one.

Susan rang. "I'm so sorry. He hasn't done the right thing by you. Maybe it's not all over yet. Wait and see".

It was. I wasn't going to try and force him to come back to me. If that was who he wanted to be with I wouldn't stand in his way. Because I loved him I would let him go. No more power struggles, no more fighting. I'd gone a long way down that road and I was spent.

Wave after wave of wind hit my tent and the rain poured down. I put my head down pushing the sides of the tent away from me again, droplets of water running down my fingers.

Louise. My mother was right.

I'd marched over to her house and pounded on the door. She'd greeted me in tears and hugged me hard. I pushed her away, barged into the loungeroom and yelled at her, "How could you do this to me? Why? I saw you and Neil kissing. After all I've done for you. How could you? How could you?" I heard my voice getting higher and higher, the sobbing louder, out there, far away.

As quiet tears rolled down Louise's face, all she could say was, "I'm sorry. I'm sorry". She tried to hug me for comfort as I'd done for her so many times before but I pushed her away. "I have to think of myself. Neil will make a great father for Jason".

"That's all you have to say? I have to think of myself! Neil will make a great father for Jason! How can you be so selfish?"

"I realized through my own marriage break up I have to look after my own needs first. You will find a strength you never knew you had from this and it will enrich your life".

I didn't want to hear such wisdom, not from her and not at this time. I shouted at her, "You of all people should know what it's like to be left for another woman and the hurt it causes. You're prepared to let that happen to me? We are best friends. Doesn't that mean anything to you? Don't you care what happens to me?"

Hysteria rose in me lit by a flame of disbelief. I needed to get away from Louise and the hysteria. Running for home I rushed out the door slamming it on her standing in the lounge room crying. Stopping at the gate I hunched over gasping for air my whole body pounding with adrenaline. Exhausted I plodded up our driveway knowing it was Louise's driveway Neil's car would pull up in that night.

The Death card blew into my face. I flicked it away as I tried to ride out this storm that was becoming harder to find protection from as the rain dripped into the tent. Lightning lit up Neil's football clothes in my basket. Louise and Neil were seeing each other. My friends had said it was official, going to their homes for tea as a couple and being invited over to Louise's where Neil had been staying more nights than not.

"We are just friends". I shook my head at his answer when I asked him if it was true when he came around to pick up some of his things. I'd heard Neil's car pull up in the driveway. I opened the front door and walked out to greet him. Once he stepped out of the car, I saw he'd lost more weight. He looked very thin, his face tense and pale. I wanted to kiss him hello, give him a hug. Tonia our dog who we both loved I'd hoped would be the patch over the deep wound in our marriage rather than a baby bounded up to greet him in excitement. He smiled as she licked his hand and stood all over his feet. She threw herself on the carpet in the hallway for a tummy rub. Tonia missed him as much as I did.

I asked him, "Would you like a cuppa?"

"No. I need some linen, towels and some things for the kitchen. I need my clothes".

The tears came but I fought them back, tired of crying as it brought me no relief. I followed him into the bedroom. He opened the wardrobe and started emptying his clothes on the bed while Tonia and I stood watching, unable to believe this was happening. He ferried them in batches to his car followed by the linen, towels, some pots and pans until the car was full. He wound the window down, stared at me and burst into tears.

I leaned in, took his hand and stroked it saying, "There, there. It will be all right". His sobs got louder. I gave him my hankie. "You'd better go".

He looked like a lost little boy. I gave him a kiss on the cheek and stroked his hair. He continued to stare at me. I wondered what he was thinking, why he wouldn't leave. I'm the one who should be crying. He'd got what he wanted. I wasn't standing in his way of having it. He should be happy. I'm the one who was missing out. He put his key in the ignition. I stepped back, waving him goodbye as he drove off.

I walked inside to the bedroom staring at the empty space where his clothes used to be, closed the wardrobe door, sat on the bed and hugged Tonia. The tears fell unbidden onto the top of her big, black head. I was tired of this procession back and forth to get his things, each trip tearing at my broken heart.

Where had my friends gone?

I let go of the tent pole unable to hold onto it any more. I unzipped one side of the tent, peeping out hoping to see signs of the storm passing. Kim appeared in front of the tent, then Vicki, Carolyn and Leanne. I shouted out the tent flap, "How could you keep seeing Neil and Louise after what they did to me? We were friends first, what about me?" I rushed out. They stepped back.

Mandy appeared then another group of friends Neil and I had made while we were married. They formed a circle around the tent while my inner circle of friends looked on.

The outer circle said one after the other;
"I never liked her".
"She's trailer trash".
"We don't like Louise".
"She played you".
"After all you've done for her, how could she?"
"What she did wasn't right".

Those sentiments flew around the circle with each clap of thunder convincing me they were as scandalized as I was at what Louise had done, offering me a measure of comfort. Their continued loyalty and friendship was the stability I'd sought through this time of intense bereavement. I fell back into the tent, found my raincoat and zipped it up putting the hood over my head as I stumbled outside dragging the wash basket after me.

After hearing the outer circle voice their disapproval my inner circle of friends rose to Louise's defence. They chorused huffily, "We have every right to see them, you can't tell us what to do".

I pushed past them outraged these friends had no problem seeing Louise despite their protestations her behaviour towards me was abhorrent.

Mandy kept her upbeat tone, "Just give it time. You will be friends again. It will be like it used to be".

"That will never happen!" I roared as I broke through the outer circle.

I heard others from that circle call out, "It's not the same without you".

"He was our friend first before you came along".

"We didn't like her even before what she did to you. That's the end of it for us".

I wedged the wash basket Margaret had given me against my hip and ran towards the cave, flung from being the central figure of a lifelong friendship circle to a solitary and isolated one out in its nether regions, a journey I didn't take willingly but was one I made. I raced inside the cave, hurling the wash basket into it as far as I could and ran out again under the pouring rain.

That day at the beginning of the year when her marriage ended, the conjunction of the transit of Pluto to Venus and the North Node in Julie's astrology chart was exact; the one the astrologer had told her would have a profound effect on her life. The realisation her marriage and her friendship circle had collapsed beyond repair left Julie, for the first time, a step outside and away from the story that she had inhabited all her life that was not her own.

Julie held the misguided belief that if she could find her way into my realm, the temple, as she was doing, it would save her marriage. What Julie would realise with time was that by doing so, she would save herself.

A clairvoyant, a door keeper to a soul's awakening and an astrologer, provided Julie with a potted history of the timeless path that I, the Temple Woman walked unhurried inside Julie. Colleen's reading provided a rediscovery of the lost temple arts that lay within her, who she was and where she was from. The numerology chart Lois laid out on a grid showed her life purpose through the master number 11 that her birthdate added to. Marie's casting of her astrology chart led her to studying astrology and the realisation that at the moment of her birth a snapshot in time had been taken that created a life map for her to follow and if she studied it, the co-ordinates on her map would give her directions to the Lost Temple of Julie.

I took the shiny gold number 11 out of my basket inlaid with mother of pearl. I attached it to the word beauty at the top of the golden triangle I had placed in the broken child's basket.

... scene 16 ...

the school in the bush

Julie stood outside the tent watching the storm pass. The rain had lessened to a drizzle and tiny patches of blue sky appeared between the clouds. An eagle was circling over her tent; a sign she was readying to enter the temple as I, the Temple Woman possessed the inner sight that would enable Julie to see life from a higher perspective. Julie would need to find ways to connect to hers to lift her out of the tumult her life was in, and rise above it in order to keep to the path that would lead her to me and her temple. I took the eagle feather from my tiara out of her pouch and let it flutter to the ground near the tent knowing when her seeing eyes became sharper she would find it and understand its significance in her life.

I looked up into the sky, cheered to see blue appearing out of the dark clouds, a sign the raging storm was over. A dark speck trailed across the blue patches. Unsure of what I was seeing I followed its path. An eagle. I watched it turn on the thermals it rode with ease. It was an eagle that had lifted me out of the tears I'd cried all the way to school. I'd wiped them from my eyes as I slipped behind the class I was to teach that day. The Principal waved hello and smiled while addressing the school assembly. He knew what I was going through trying to come to terms with my marriage breakup. He told me to take my time getting there when he called to say there was a day's work for me. It was so hard to rouse myself after another sleepless night. I was grateful for the work and his understanding of my delicate emotional state. Though my tears no longer showed on the outside, they continued to wash through me as I watched the gum trees sway on top of the ridge.

The eagle was riding the thermals over the quadrangle. With each round, she pulled me into her easy circle. My heart flew to her perspective of height and sight. For a few moments I was elevated to that exalted state of freedom - the foggy sleep state I walked around in lifted. My reverie was broken by the sound of children shuffling off to class. I trudged after them gathering what little energy I possessed.

Once inside, the familiar routine of a school day gave my shattered life a small thread of normality.

On the days I taught in the old school house I stood on the dais in front of the chalkboard, the rotting floorboards letting a cold wind blow up through the gaps. Down the back past the table and chairs the same four children sat at a long wooden desk. They filled up their inkwells, opened their exercise books while the other children rummaged in their tubs for their pencils and paper while I marked the roll. There was a rhythm to it that made that daily duty satisfying, bringing the children and I into our day as they answered to their names.

The four children down the back of the class room weren't on my roll but their names, written in fine copperplate writing, were in a faded blue attendance register locked in a filing cabinet in the Principal's office. Those four children were my mother and her siblings. These classmates from the Great Depression didn't belong in my current class but they were there in attendance each time I taught in the old weatherboard schoolhouse that leaned, was rotted, and absorbed the smell of children's stale sandwiches and their noisy squabbles.

I continued to watch the eagle circling over my tent. It hovered in the air, the wind pulling it over to the cave where it continued riding the thermals in easy circles. As I followed it there I made out a couple of small figures, their faces lit by the glow of a fire in the cave. I stood just inside the cave's entrance to have a better look expecting it to be Nana and her mother. It was.

I'd passed my great-grandmother's house each day I taught at this school, hard to spot despite my knowing where it was. Though I slowed down, the endless paddocks of long grass hid houses, sheds and rusted farm machinery that crossed worn driveways. Some days the white peeling shell with the sky blue trim sat up on the rise so was easy to see, on others, lost in the mists of a crisp autumn morning.

This daily pilgrimage to and from school breathed life into memories this old farmhouse held for my family. As I passed by I looked in through the rotting wooden frames, their glass full of holes, patching together a family picture with the few snippets I'd been told about them. The old, black iron kettle was boiling on the hob. The women laid the table while their mother stoked the stove and checked if the scones had risen to have with their tea. Fresh raspberry jam was scooped into a crystal cut dish, the cream fresh from their only cow, whipped with a hand beater. The cracked teapot still held the tea, the insides stained with tannin. The tea strainer sat in its saucer beside it, all ready to be served.

The blue dish with berries dotted on the top held a firm slab of butter that was easy to melt into a hot scone fresh from the oven.

My great-grandmother wiped her hands on her stained, starched apron, touching the tops of the scones to see if they were done. Satisfied, she picked up the tea towel, took them out of the oven, turning them over onto a wire rack on the bench. The rain beat down on the tin roof, the distant hills misty. The women were quiet like the day, deep in their own reflections. Steam rose from their cups as they sipped their tea and passed the scones, jam and cream around the table. Lil's sister May placed her hands over her growing belly, weary. Lil patted her hand and refilled her cup. These three women of the Great Depression warmed their hands by the stove and their hearts by being at the table with each other. Hard times called for soft hearts joined together if only for a little while.

The lusty cries of new life filled the front bedroom of the old house in a small country town on an autumn day, whose rooms were used as a hospital. On a cast iron bed, mother and child lay sweaty on bloodied sheets. Three weeks was scant raising of a child by its mother. Poisoned blood provided poor milk for this child to thrive on, and poisoned blood took a mother in infection and fever to an early death. This baby swaddled in loss, bathed in tears and raised in sorrow was my mother.

I watched Nana's face flickering in the firelight wanting to be with her but knowing I couldn't as I didn't belong in the cave. I ran out towards my tent and looked up into the sky for the eagle. I spotted it, a dot in the distance.

An eagle had flown over the old hall that matched the old schoolhouse in age and memory the day a uniformed policeman and policewoman from the Child Protection Services greeted me and my colleagues at the door.

That morning, we'd been given literature by them to read about the services they offered to assist vulnerable, at-risk children. A question and answer time followed. In the afternoon, a film was to be shown that presented scenarios these children might find themselves in.

As I waited for the projector to whir to life, an image flickered in my mind of Mum and her three siblings. They were sitting in the row in front of me, waiting to watch the afternoon matinee with a bag of lollies and a lemonade each from the general store just down the road from the hall. Auntie Eileen said they sometimes went to the afternoon matinee for a treat as children.

I watched the film. Tears started without my permission. Why was I crying? Why did I feel so strange? Why did I want to run and keep running? What was I running away from? I couldn't breathe. *'My cousins.*

They did this to me. And to my sister. I could see her. No. I don't want to see this. I don't want to remember. Make it stop, make it go away".

A gentle touch intercepted my memory, snapping my fright. The policewoman patted my shoulder and whispered in my ear, "There, there dear. It's all right. This happens a lot when people watch this. They remember. Don't be embarrassed. Cry. It will do you good. This has been locked inside you for a long time. It needs to come out".

I hung my head sobbing as the policewoman offered me some tissues. Taking a couple I blew my nose. I couldn't watch anymore of this. I didn't need to see any more to understand. I understood full well what it was like because it did happen to my sister and I. I'd buried it for all those years to survive. It was out now. No turning away from it though that is what I wanted to do.

The policewoman offered the box of tissues to another teacher, the tears welling up behind his glasses as she patted him on the shoulder and whispered in his ear. A box of tissues and some whispered words the only comfort allowed as her purpose was to educate us to help the children we taught, not to support us who'd been abused when we were children.

I returned to my class in the old school house, not able to bear looking at Mum and her siblings still there in their long wooden desk up the back of the classroom, squabbling with each other.

Now I was the continuing living presence of family teaching at that bush school Mum attended with her siblings. The significance to her was enough to finally allow me to see a photo of my birth grandmother I had begged her for years to see. Sitting on the couch at home I opened the envelope with shaking hands. A face lined with sweet sorrow slid out of it. I cradled its full expression in my hands. Ringlets of fair, curled, thick hair rippled down her shoulders caught by a pale blue satin headband. It matched her dreamy, large, round, blue eyes that looked up and away to the heavens. I scrutinised her image looking for traces of myself but saw nothing, not even the faintest expression. Mum, her sisters and my sister stared back at me. I held this angelic young woman dressed in pale blue satin with a hint of rouge on her delicate cheeks to my heart for a few moments. I kissed her on the cheek and placed the photo back in my lap. This joined me in a small knowing of her. I was complete.

After further begging once I'd seen the photo, Mum relented and told me where my grandmother was buried. The cemetery was an easy drive from the school just over the other side of the mountain. Her grave was hard to find but once found, it didn't take long for me to feel her presence as I stood there, the warm wind pouring through the spaces in the gum trees brushing my face and hair. A faint voice I strained to hear was attached to that wisp of her presence that lingered in the sunken, brown, cracked neglect that was her grave.

"I felt your longing to know me. Don't let abuse ruin your life".

Her thinning words were swallowed by the throaty warbles of a pair of magpies sitting in a tree branch; heads back, singing their song to the sky. Staring into that sunken, cracked stone where her young bones lay, I knew she was finally at rest as there wasn't even a whisper of her left now. Her words, "Don't let abuse ruin your life", seeped into me as I stood staring at her grave. "I won't", I promised her as I turned and walked back to the car.

Julie's budding child's daydreams of being a teacher when she grew up led her to the school in the bush her mother and her siblings attended as children. That day in the old hall unearthing the buried memories of abuse the broken child had suffered at the hands of their cousins twisted around Julie's memories of assault by the school principal and her father's friends. Though Julie was yet to know who exactly this other part of her was, now she could no longer ignore what was once a hazy presence of ill ease within her.

... scene 17 ...

the hole in my pyjamas

setting
in the broken child's cave of sorrows

Julie's broken child fled out of the cave. I the Temple Woman took her by the hand, parts of her left embedded in fright in situations she had no hope of mending as she tried to keep a step ahead of her fright. She ran down to the river and dropped her picnic basket at the water's edge. She ran along the rocky path tripping herself up, falling, then running some more. There was no way she would be able to keep a step ahead of her fright, no matter how hard she tried. Though she didn't want to go back, it was time to return the broken child and her picnic basket full of painful memories it contained to her cave realm, where all her unhealed pain and trauma resided to face it. In the cave she would find the lost pieces of herself and retrieve them by confronting those who had done her harm and giving them a piece of her mind.

After she had exhausted herself I took the golden triangle with the words; 'Beauty', 'Respect' and 'Care' in each corner out of the broken child's basket and handed it to her as they were the foundations on which The Lost Temple of Julie would be built. The number 11 affixed to the word 'Beauty' at the top of the triangle shone. Full of trepidation the broken child laid the triangle against the thick outer wall of the cave and entered with her basket. She hitched up her pyjama bottoms, the elastic in the top stretched loose, struggling with the lid of the basket as she tried to close it on the football that was sticking out of the top. She sat on the basket bowing the top of it further until the straps were buckled up. She dragged it further into the cave using it as a seat, unable to go any further.

Sitting hunched over on my picnic basket, I crossed one hand over my gaping pyjama top and wedged my other hand hard in between my legs, rocking back and forth and screamed until I was hoarse, "Why did my cousin turn on me like that?"

"You trusted me so I knew you weren't going to suspect a thing. It was perfect. I couldn't believe my luck. I knew it was bad but I so enjoyed having you".

I jumped up off my basket and spun around at the sound of his voice. Terror ripped through my body. I stood frozen in that moment of being ambushed, the screaming a constant echo on and on inside of me as I fled to the shelter of a rock.

That icy winter's morning I'd tiptoed out of my room to the spare room to see if my cousin Jack was awake. From the doorway I wasn't sure, so I went to the side of the bed. I was cold, so I decided to surprise him by hopping into bed to have a cuddle with him before breakfast. He stirred as I pulled the covers back. Sliding in beside him I laid my head on his shoulder thinking how nice it was to be cuddled up to my favourite cousin.

Putting his arm around me he said, "Good morning cuz". I liked it when he called me that. It made me feel special. Laying in the warmth of his words and his body about to turn over to snuggle in and sleep a little longer, he undid a couple of buttons, stuck his hand down the front of my pyjama top, grabbing my breast. What was he doing?

"You know you've got the breasts of a thirteen year-old", he said as he stroked one breast then the other. But I'm only ten I thought, as I tried to wriggle away. He held me tighter. He had a strange look on his face I didn't like and a funny smile that gave me the creeps. Rolling over on top of me he tugged down his pyjamas bottoms and pushed into the hole in my pyjamas. The harder I tried to push him off me, the harder he pushed inside of me, his weight trapping me. I squeezed my eyes shut, my body rigid, wondering when it would ever end as the voice inside me screamed and screamed '*no*'. I heard the kitchen door open. He rolled off me. I made a dash to the door opening it before Mum did, doing up the top buttons and twisting my pyjamas on straight before she saw me.

She said, "Good morning you two".

"Good morning", Jack said with his biggest, kindest smile.

I pushed past Mum and rushed to the bathroom. Locking the door, I tore off my pyjamas my heart pounding. Shivering, I ran the face washer under the hot water, rubbed lots of soap on it then wiped and scrubbed and dabbed between my legs knowing the stain he left inside me would never go away. My thoughts raced as I rubbed more soap on the face washer. It was my fault. I shouldn't have got into bed with him. What if Mum found out? I'd get into trouble. It was wrong and bad what he did. Mum had taken me to the talk at school. I knew it could make you pregnant. What if that stuff is still inside me and I am pregnant? He did something I didn't want him to even when I tried to stop him. Mum will be wondering what I'm doing in here, I'll have to go. I don't want her in here asking questions about what I'm doing, why I'm taking so long. I know she'll be wondering. I don't want to get into trouble. Hastily I rubbed the towel between my legs then opened the cabinet above the vanity basin looking for the lavender talc shaking lots and lots of it between my legs. Lavender was Nana's smell. I wanted Nana. I wanted to snuggle into my Nana, have her hug me, stroke my hair and kiss my cheek. I wanted her to make it go away. I had to make it go away. He's my cousin. He's supposed to look after me. He tricked me pretending to be a nice, kind, gentleman cousin but he wasn't.

Auntie Joyce had told her boys the same thing every time our family drove over to visit our cousin's interstate, "Play nicely with your cousins. Look after them. They are your guests while they are here".

They escorted my sister and I to the park then let us have first turn on the monkey bars walking alongside us ready to catch us if we fell. The eldest, Jack, helped us up the big slide steps telling his middle brother Colin to wait at the bottom to stop us falling off the end. The boys didn't mind if we dropped the ball or couldn't throw it far enough. They threw the ball so it was easy for us to catch, gave us first pick of their toys. They asked us what we'd like to watch on TV, moving their chubby baby brother Terry out of the way while Jack changed channels. I was so excited when Mum told me they were coming to live nearby. Auntie Joyce missed all her family so much that Uncle Alan arranged to be transferred back home with his job in a bank. Mum invited Jack to come and stay a few nights in the spare room to give the family a break. They'd been living in a small motel room until their new home was ready to move into.

I picked up the rusty tin with a picture of faded lavender flowers on it, opened the holes at the top, giving it a good shake to see if there was any talc left in it. A few granules filtered out, their perfume long gone.

A dirty towel poked through the split white plastic weave of Mum's tall, dirty wash basket she'd missed when she loaded up her washing machine in the dim corner of the cave. I bunched the thinning elastic round the waist of my pyjamas in tight making a flap of material to cover the hole in my pyjamas.

It was just a tiny hole when I'd first asked Mum to mend my pyjama's but she didn't so it got bigger. They were my favourites. I didn't want to throw them out. Mum didn't like sewing, only mending things if she had to, to make them last longer. If only she had. I wondered if my life would have turned out differently if she'd done such a simple thing as darn that hole in my favourite pyjamas. I hurled the tin of talc as hard as I could across the cave, fell to my knees on that dirty towel with that filthy stain still inside me and wept.

"I knew I needed to be quick in case your mother caught us. You have to be ready to pounce when you get the chance. I got my way. It made me feel big and powerful and strong to have had my way over you. All I wanted was to get my way".

Sobbing, I peeked out from behind the rock at the sound of Jack's voice fearing he was still close but he'd slunk away into the shadows of the cave before Nana could see him.

I hitched up my pyjama bottoms, did up the buttons of my top, tucking it into my pants. Flopping on to the lid of my picnic basket I wedged my hands back hard between my legs to cover the hole in the crotch, hung my head and wept some more.

... scene 18 ...

the family picnic

I watched Nana and my great-grandmother having a cosy little picnic together sitting on a tartan blanket they had spread over the large flat rock. Nana had relit the fire by the stream that trickled through the cave, a blackened kettle boiling on it. She opened her tin of tea with the red rose on it, dropped a couple of spoonful's into the small metal teapot then poured the hot water in. Her mother put the lid on the teapot then turned it a couple of times. She set down a couple of enamel mugs on a wide log and poured the fresh brew into them. Nana chose a rock cake from her mother's hamper and nibbled at a corner, the two of them enjoying their little picnic.

Unlike her Nana and her mother, Julie's broken child felt distressed when she heard there was a family picnic coming up.

That blanket came out on family picnics and was well used. My picnic basket had stood in the middle of that green and yellow tartan rug at the foot of a big, old, gum tree. There were biscuit and cake crumbs strewn across the rug and the marks of folding chairs on one edge that had pressed into it over the course of the picnic where the shade of the tree was sought. Empty beer bottles were stacked up against its side along with half-drunk cups of orange cordial. The water rode up over the weir in a continuous motion creating a shiny mini waterfall, splashing down to the next dip in the stream and on through the picnic ground, its banks lined with tree ferns of various heights.

My cousins were taking my sister by the hand up over the hill way up the back away from the adults. I ran as fast as I could after them until I got a stitch shouting her name but she didn't answer me. Taking a big breath I kept running. I heard noises in the bush. I found them in a dirt patch under a gum tree over to one side of the path. She was standing there with her underpants down around her knees, Jack and Colin circling her. I ran to her throwing myself against them catching them offside, pulled her pants up, grabbed her and shouted, "RUN !", but she was stuck to the spot. I tried to pick her up but I was too little to carry her. Those boys just watched with that horrible smile on their faces.

I tugged at her again. This time she moved. I dragged her along with me as fast as her legs could go until I could see the grown-ups sitting in their chairs in the distance.

Gripping my sister's hand, we walked to the toilet blocks. I stood her at the open door of the toilet closest to the basin, found my white hankie with the pretty pink and blue flowers on it Nana had given me, and ran it under the tap. Kneeling down I lifted my sister's dress and slid her white underpants down to her ankles gently wiping the blood from between her legs rinsing my hankie out under the tap again. I dabbed at the blood on her underpants hoping it would disappear, then I wiped the dust off her shiny black patent shoes. My sister held on to my shoulder while I pulled up her pants for her. I patted down her dress, adjusted the lacy tops of her white socks, then smoothed down her fringe turning her ponytail back straight, tying the blue bow back around it. Stuffing my handkerchief with the splashes of blood all over it into my cardigan pocket we walked out the door of the toilet block hand in hand until we reached the grown-ups. Seeing Mum I asked when we were going home.

"Not for a while yet, go off and play".

I wanted to scream at her, *"No! I know what kind of games they want to play"*.

I spied those horrible cousins in the cave over behind the washing machines, shooting hoops near Mum's basket jostling and pushing each other to get at the ball to throw it in the ring.

Jack threw me a look as he ran past Colin and called out to me, "I like the game. It's all about the game. Getting away with it. The thrill of it and not getting caught. How many times can I do this? So many I will never be caught. You know why? It's the shame. They wouldn't dare talk about it. You would never be believed and better still, if you were no-one would do a thing about it. There are secrets to protect, right! Made it so easy".

I pressed my hands over my ears and crouched down behind a rock, treading on the blood stained hankie. He bounced the ball on the rock and shouted over me, "Can't you see, you and your sister were just part of my little experiments to see how far I could go and what I could get away with. You had no one to protect you, so I could go ahead and do what I liked with both of you. I got away with so much and no-one knew a thing".

His voice echoed on and on, mingling with the screams that echoed on and on inside me. He threw the ball to Colin who missed the ring, running up close to me to retrieve it.

Colin held the ball to his chest as he stood on the rock above me. "I had to do what Jack told me or else he would hurt me too. He threatened me with so many bad things if I didn't do what he said".

"You hurt my sister. All I cared about was keeping her safe. Get away from me and my sister, leave us alone!" I swept the blood stained hankie up off the cave floor and balled it into my fist, too scared to move as he threw the ball to his brother and ran off to continue shooting hoops with him.

"Why won't you play with your cousins?"

I jumped up at the sound of Mum's voice. She must have been watching those cousins and me while she did the washing. I put the bloodied hankie behind my back, letting it drop to the ground. She asked that same question over and over, one I would never answer, too scared to tell her the truth. One day it flew out of my mouth before I could stop it. I was standing in the kitchen after school while Mum busied herself preparing the evening meal. She asked me yet again, "Why won't you play with your cousins?"

She went to her pill bottles lined up like soldiers on parade on the kitchen bench and shook a pill out of each. She looked at me as she tied her apron round her waist, waiting for an answer.

"I don't like them".

"Why?"

"I just don't".

"They are your cousins. You have to play with them".

"No I don't. I don't want to play the games they want to play. They hurt us".

"What are you talking about?"

"They do things to us on purpose to hurt us that makes me sick. I have to get my sister away from them. I hopped in bed with Jack for a cuddle when he stayed that time and he stuck his thing inside me, and that can get you pregnant. He and Colin hurt us in all sorts of nasty ways when we are with them. I try to stop them hurting my sister but I can't. They hurt me when I try. They jump on me and punch me and won't let me get to her. They pull her pants down and do things to her. I hate them and never want to see them again. There, you know now, are you happy?"

The green, white and yellow pills sat in a little heap on the bench with the glass of water, forgotten in my confession.

"I have to protect your Nana and Auntie Joyce".

What sort of an answer was that? Mum turned her back, walked over to the stove and stirred the casserole with a wooden spoon. I turned on my heel slamming my bedroom door on the confrontation, shut in the room where I'd been got at for my cousin's pleasure and thrills. I kicked off my sweaty school shoes, tossed my long grey socks on the floor and flopped back on the bed, playing with the zipper on the front of my high school uniform. I'd told her now. At least I didn't get into trouble but what sort of a response was that? 'She had to protect Nana and Auntie Joyce over us?' What was going to happen to us? I wished I'd never told her. It wasn't going to change a thing. Why did she have to protect my Nana and Auntie Joyce over me and my sister? That unanswered question hovered over me like an ill wind for years and years and years.

A flicker of movement alerted me that someone was watching me. It was my sister, crouched in a hollow she'd found for herself looking too frightened to come out of her hidey hole in the cave. A pretty little cane basket painted blue, sat at her feet with matching blue feathers and some little yellow chickens stuck to the handle. Empty Easter egg wrappers in gay stripes lay scattered about, some swept up in the wind stuck to a large piece of driftwood. Her copy of the photo of our birth grandmother in its white envelope lay between the Easter eggs in her basket. She took some pink geraniums and yellow daisy weeds from her basket, pierced the juicy stems with her fingers threading the flowers and weeds together around herself on the rock. When she'd finished she took out a clear plastic sugar bowl with a crack in the top. She lifted the lid, took out the silver teaspoon and sprinkled the magic dust into the middle of her fairy ring, making a wish, a ritual our mother knew well. She used to come to the back door at home and call my sister, the sugar bowl in her hand. She'd been watching her make a fairy ring from the kitchen window while I played on the swing. After the ring was made my sister went inside, sat in front of the TV waiting for the fairies to leave her something. Mum always obliged, leaving some lollies in the ring. She'd tear herself away from the TV long enough to check if they'd been, gather up the lollies and return to the lounge room to eat them while watching cartoons.

My sister lifted a bag of lollies out of her basket, choosing a red jelly snake. She stretched it out as long as it would go before it broke, and bit its head off. For now she'd forgotten about the bloodstained underpants that belonged in her basket. Mum had returned it to her own dirty wash basket in the cave, puzzled that after washing them the blood stains remained. For now my sister had forgotten the cousins who lurked in the shadows nearby. All she saw was her fairy ring and the magic of a wish.

Nana gathered up the gaily colored striped foil wrappers glistening on some driftwood to throw on the fire when she needed another cup of tea.

With tenderness my sister lifted her golden teddy bear out of her basket, rubbing her face across his worn, black buttoned nose. His scent, the essence of her innocence. No matter how many times she buried her face in his familiar scent, her innocence was long gone.

Jack and his father stood on the outer edge of the circle of men in the cave, keeping an eye on the women by the fire. They must have seen me running out from behind the rock because Uncle Alan stopped me before I could reach the safety of the fire where Nana sat.

He put a firm hand on my shoulder, then his fingers to his lips and whispered to me, "Ssh. We know what's going on but we can't tell anyone okay?"

"No. It's not okay. It never will be okay. He raped me. That dirty, stinking son of yours raped me".

"I know. I know. Ssh, keep it down. It was a very bad thing that happened to you but you have to keep quiet about it even if you're upset and angry, okay?"

"No it's not okay".

"There are some things a little girl can never understand until they are grown up and then they do. Lots of bad things happen to grown-ups too that they don't like and have to put up with. It's just a part of life".

"I don't care. I am a little girl. Bad things aren't supposed to happen to little girls. Grown-ups are supposed to take care of us and keep us safe no matter what. That's their job. I need to be taken care of. I need to feel safe. I am scared now. So scared. How am I supposed to fight a bully like him? He likes to fight. It makes him want to hurt me more. I can't make it go away and all I want is for it to go away. All I want is for it never to have happened. I am so alone".

"Chin up. Smile. Get on with it, that's the girl".

That was all very well for him to say but how do you get on with it when you have no idea how to get over it? All I wanted to do was to get over it and get that rotten, stinking snake's poison out of me for good.

"You have to look after the family first, remember that. The family always comes first".

"I am part of the family. If this is what being a family is, I don't want any part of it. This is not my family. My family takes care of all the children and each other and always, always love each other no matter what. I am going to find my family and I am never coming back again".

"Ssh."

"No. I will never be quiet again".

"No-one can know what happened to you. It would destroy our family and its reputation in the world. Protecting the family reputation is more important than protecting you".

Mum must have noticed us talking as she came over and asked, full of bright smiles, "What's going on here?"

"Julie and I are having a little chat about her school work". Uncle Alan ruffled my hair and had a sip of his beer.

"Oh that's nice. Now go off and play. The grown-ups want to be left in peace for a while".

I clawed at my hair in a vain attempt to wipe away my uncle's phony affection and did as Mum asked me but not to play; to hide in another part of the cave where I couldn't be found by any of the family. That didn't last for long, my agitation evicting me from my hidey hole sending me flying towards Mum. I marched up to her and put my hands on my hips. She was emptying the contents of her dirty wash basket into the washing machine.

I yelled, "Bad things aren't supposed to happen to little girls. Grown-ups are supposed to take care of them and keep them safe no matter what. That's their job. I need to be taken care of. I need to feel safe". I kicked Mum's basket over and stood in front of her, repeating what I'd just said, "Bad things aren't supposed to happen to little girls. Grown-ups are supposed to take care of us and keep us safe no matter what. That's their job. I need to be taken care of. I need to feel safe".

Mum glared at me. "You have to look after the family first, remember that. The family always comes first".

She turned back to her dirty washing. I pressed my hands over my ears and screamed and screamed trying to bury the thoughts about what would happen next time I had to see those cousins. Nana and her mother hearing sounds coming from over behind the fire hopped up to see what was happening. I ran to them and sat beside Nana, trying to take her hand. She didn't notice me as they were already lost in their moment of togetherness again.

Nana turned to her mother. "You know we agreed that after you died I had to let all May's children to live their own lives. I was just a guide, a soft place to fall, a shoulder to cry on for all of them. I wanted to help strengthen their bond with each other. That is why Sunday night tea, family picnics, Christmas were so important. I fostered in them the importance of these family gatherings to give a chance for the wounds to heal, to bring the family together with their children so they would continue when I wasn't there any longer". Her mother nodded in agreement.

Nana went over to her sister May's children and offered them a little cake, just baked, out of an old toffee tin. They each chose one from the tin and bit into its warmth. That was the best thing of all about going to stay at Nana's, helping her make the little cakes. The white patty pans crackled in my fingers as I'd pushed them into the holes in the baking tray. She let me sift the flour into the large ceramic bowl then stir in the milk with her big wooden spoon as she added the butter. I helped spoon the mixture into the patty pans then she put them in the oven. When the puffy, golden cakes had cooled I added the pink food color to the icing sugar. We stirred it in and Nana knifed the icing over the cakes.

She made those cakes when our side of the family visited for Sunday lunch. She smoothed chocolate icing on the other half for those boy cousins just to be fair as that was their favourite icing before she sprinkled them with hundreds and thousands. I didn't like sharing her little cakes with them. They didn't deserve nice things from Nana.

"Boys, put those cakes down now, you don't grab cakes and run around your grandmother's dining table like that. Where are your manners? Sit down now and finish your cakes at the table at once". Jack and Colin ignored their mother but Terry sat down when Auntie Joyce asked them to.

I went to Nana's bedroom to get away from them after we'd all shared a Sunday lunch lamb roast at the large dining room table. Nana let me go in there and read her women's magazines. I liked sitting on the low chair with the velvet cover and curled mahogany legs that sat by her bed. I felt like a princess.

The door kept slamming to the guest room. It was getting on my nerves. I put the magazine down on the chair and went to have a look. Jack had his back against the door. I went to open it but he pushed his body against it and smiled that horrible smile. I could hear Colin laughing in there. My sister! I tried to push him away to grab the doorknob. When I went to turn it, he jabbed me in the ribs hard with his elbow. He opened the door ajar. I saw my sister lying on the far bed, Colin's legs straddled over her. Now I was in total panic. I needed to get in there and get her out. I pretended to play along with the game so he'd let me in. I pushed on the door. He opened it then closed it, until I pushed on it so hard, that he opened it. I fell inside the door, his laughter all over my back. Colin stood at the end of the bed laughing too; Terry wedged up against the wardrobe trying to keep out of their way. My sister was lying on top of the pink chenille bedspread, her face white, not moving. They jumped on her. She just lay there. I pulled at both of them yelling at them to get off. The boys started pushing at each other. The room was too small for all of us. They banged up against the wardrobe door. It sounded like they'd just broken it.

Uncle Alan stormed in the door. "What's going on in here?" I sat on the other bed, pretending nothing had happened. I didn't want Uncle Alan to yell at me too. I couldn't think about what had happened and that I wasn't there to stop it.

"Nothing Dad", Jack answered.

"Get out of here now. Go outside and stay there until I say you can come in".

"Yes Dad", the boys replied and walked out of the room leaving Terry standing there at first but he decided to follow them too.

I closed the door, rushed over to my sister and helped her up off the bed giving her a hug she didn't return. I smoothed her hair and clothes down, led her out of there by the hand, closing the door behind us.

I wanted to go home.

In the cave, Nana put the tin back in her wash basket after offering a little cake to her own mother who chose one with pink icing. She peeled back the paper and dropped it into her apron pocket, biting deep into her little cake. I wriggled closer to Nana and snuggled in to her neck, the faint smell of lavender providing a little comfort.

The sound of a bell made us all look up. Grandad waved as he arrived on his postie bike then leaned it against a large boulder. Nana jumped up and kissed him on his weathered cheek.

He said, "Look what I found propped up against a rock when I went for a bit of a walk".

Nana smiled. The metal basket attached to the handles, had telegrams and letters, his war medals and a thin tin mug with a metal dog tag inside it. He saw the blackened kettle on the fire so got out his mug, shaking the tag from it which fell to the ground. He took his cigarette papers and tobacco pouch out of his shirt pocket, pushed a wad of tobacco from his pouch into the paper, rolled it then ran his tongue along the edge of the paper to seal it. He reached into his trouser pockets for some matches and lit up. A smoke and some tea and time to reflect. In Changi, it was a smoke, some tea, toothpaste and with little else to survive on until he and his boys were liberated; emaciated, diseased and spent after three long years.

Nana filled the kettle, blew on the fire to stir the embers and poked it with a stick. She threw some of the empty wrappers from my sister's basket on the fire and it sparked up. Grandad stared into the distance, a single glow of red lighting his worn face as he sucked on his cigarette. Nana took some telegrams and letters out of her basket and thumbed through them, stopping to read a line or two. Her mouth tightened and the tears came. She cuddled me as she told me why she was crying.

"I had to run the post office while your grandfather was away at the war. People in my community, many friends, lost their sons. Young wives were left widowed, many with children and in financial hardship. But in spite of the bad times we all pulled together. We all had our families to raise, war or no war". She hugged me tight as she put the telegrams and letters back in her basket and wiped away her tears with the back of her hand. Grandad came up behind her and put his hand on her shoulder.

I looked up at him. "I didn't feel you liked me or had much time for me, you just went along because Nana wanted you to".

"You were always a bright little girl and very perceptive. Whatever I felt about the goodness of my fellow man was butted out in Changi. I needed to stick with my mates who'd been through what I had and support them, keep strong for each other just like we did in camp. I saw young boys die and I could do nothing to help them. It burned me bad. I drank the memories away and tried to keep going as before; hold down a job at the post office, provide for the family, return to community life but it was hard. It got me down, real down. Lil was a strong woman and kept the family together. She tried to be there for me while I recovered, hoping the man she knew before I went to war would come back, but I never did. I tried to give Lil some good times, travelling overseas and staying the winter up north to keep old age at bay for a bit longer, keep her comfortable and provide for her after all she did for me".

Grandad took his medals out of his basket. Nana pinned them on the lapel of his tweed jacket and kissed him on the cheek like she did each year on Anzac Day before he left for the march. Nana and I sat and watched it together on TV each year while Mum prepared lunch because that day was her birthday. Nana leaned forward in her chair when Grandad's battalion was announced and waited to see him march past, doing a quick roll call of who out of the POW's were marching with him that year. She waved full of pride as they marched by.

Jack, his namesake, marched with Grandad. He would inherit those medals when Grandad died. Auntie Joyce would make sure of it as she claimed him to be the rightful inheritor, being her eldest son. I could think of no-one more undeserving of such an honour.

I jumped off Nana's lap, snatched a medal out of Grandad's hand, stood in front of him and shouted, "Anzac Day made me so angry. We were all supposed to be proud but all I saw was another bunch of men getting drunk. I had no respect for that and for war if that was the end result of fighting for our freedom; having children being raised by angry, drunk, distant men. You would have been better off dead!" I glared at Grandad waiting for an answer.

All he could say was, "Despite putting on a happy face I know you struggled with your relationship with me but there was nothing I could do to fix that after what I saw in the war. It changed me." Grandad rolled another smoke and lit it, throwing the dregs of his mug of tea into the fire making it hiss.

The strident notes of a bugle rang throughout the cave; The Last Post. Grandad sucked on his cigarette, lost in a war that was never over despite peace being declared a long time ago. Over at the circle of men Jack stood to attention and saluted as a sign of respect. He looked over to see if Grandad had noticed. Dad and my uncles bowed their heads, beers in one hand, cigarettes in the other just as they did at the annual Prisoner of War picnic. There with the POW's they stood in a circle by their cars at a park by the beach and drank beer, smoked cigarettes and talked about the war. The car bonnets covered in empty bottles glistened in the sunlight. I kept away. I didn't like the smell of beer on their breath. Jack and Colin were allowed to join them. Good. I hoped they stayed there all day. No such luck.

All the Mums had told us to go away and play. I'd stalled for as long as I could. I sat down in a chair with Nana and my aunties and started talking to Nana but Mum told me to go. She was cross now.

Where had my sister gone? I started walking away from the picnic area up over the sandy hill. I saw her in a small clearing in the thick tea-tree forest with Auntie Eileen's children from the other side of the family. Oh no! Jack and Colin were coming over.

Jack said, "Let's play chasey".

"I don't want to".

I crossed my arms and stared at him. I should've known better. He threw me to the ground and stomped on me. He walked away as I struggled to get up and dusted myself down, my desert boots full of sand. It stuck to my mohair cardigan, my hair was full of it. I wanted to run away but I couldn't, I had to look after my sister. Colin had opened his fly and pulled his thing out. He was yanking on it with that horrible look in his eye, laughing hard. It was little and stiff with a purple vein wrapped around it. Jack watched all of us with a pleased smile on his face, as we watched Colin. Terry was crouched down in the sand against some tea-tree bushes, his eyes half closed. I gagged. Auntie Eileen's children from the other side of the family were rooted to the spot, stunned. They'd never seen this side of their other cousins before. Jack egged Colin on, laughing along with him, their little brother Terry looking up into the tea-tree trying to ignore what was happening. It was disgusting. They were disgusting. What was wrong with them!

I grabbed my sister's hand and yelled to the others, "Let's get out of here". That jolted them out of their shock. They followed me out of the thick tangle of trees into the daylight. We didn't speak about it. Ever.

Nana emptied the teapot while her mother poured the rest of the water from the kettle over the fire to dampen it down. It was time for Nana to get back to her work amongst the dirty wash baskets in the cave. I returned to my own basket.

I rummaged around inside it looking for a clean cup to get a drink of water from the stream. I found some sticks and stones, a couple of wooden spoons, and some knives that didn't belong in my picnic set and most peculiarly, Grandad's toothbrush he used to clean his dentures with, that hadn't been in my basket before.

My sister!

I ran to the hollow I'd seen her crouched in too frightened to come out. She wasn't there. An awful rhyme I couldn't shake swirled around inside my head, *"Sticks and stones can break your bones and inserted between your legs do hurt you"*. And so did the other utilitarian instruments resourcefully lifted by Jack and Colin from our grandparent's home or at a picnic, to be used for my sister's torture and their titillation. They had lain in her pretty little cane basket hidden under her teddy bear and Easter eggs, now empty as she had deposited them into mine.

I ran back to my picnic basket, tipped it upside down violently shaking it until they all fell out. My sister's bloodied underpants and the hankie fell out too, along with the photo of our birth grandmother in its clean white envelope. I turned my picnic basket over and looked inside. Some sticks and stones still remained stuck to the weave. I hunted through the cave for a long stick and flicked them out onto the floor of the cave with it. I wrapped all the bloodied instruments of torture with the underpants and hankie in the laundered towel Mum had put in my basket. Though laundered many times it was still impregnated with the filth of my cousin I'd tried to wipe from inside myself in vain. I ran the contents to the fire and threw them all on it, making it splutter and smoke. I ran back to the hidey hole to see if I'd missed my sister hiding there in the shadows in my rage but she was nowhere to be seen. I picked up the sugar bowl with the cracked lid, spilled of its remaining contents my sister had left by her fairy ring where she'd hidden away. I scooped up a few granules of sugar with my finger and licked it but its sweetness had long gone, along with the magic of a wish. I bent down gathering up some of the flowers from the ring twirling their stalks between my fingers.

If I could be granted one wish it would be to wind back time before my sister was seven years old when Jack and Colin had inserted an instrument of torture inside her for the first time. Because on that day, when they decided my sister was just a body to be used for their perverted thrills and titillation, she was lost to me for good.

... scene 19 ...

a new squabble

As the next generation skipped over, under, in and out of the family lies, these well-worn stories that tied this family together and were hard to break, were told to the next generation hardening their basket of hurts to their hearts.

Auntie Eileen picked up my cousin's skipping rope and dropped it into her wash basket. I watched Jane and Kathy walk along the path that cut through the middle of the cave looking for it. They found a deflated basketball, a rusted shooting hoop and the remnants of the liner of an above ground pool, its sides all beaten in. Broken records made stepping stones, rusted bikes lay on their sides, their tyres flat. Their two brothers Phil and Ian joined them. They all continued the search. It led them to a dark corner where cousin Jack jumped out of the shadows. Jane and Kathy ran off together, Phil and Ian the other way, the skipping rope forgotten for now. Colin wouldn't be far behind ready to assist him with what ugly game he planned to play next; like the one in Jack's bedroom.

I'd run in under Auntie Joyce's house to a dark corner to escape from a game of hidey Jack decided we would all play, knowing that it would be for his own twisted ends. I didn't want him to find me. I held my breath hoping my hiding place was safe enough.

Above me in Jack's bedroom, over Jack's laughter I could hear thumping and banging like furniture being moved. I heard a chair fall: Colin's voice in all this commotion muffled by the floorboards above me.

My sister!

Aren't there any adults in the house? They must be able to hear the racket going on in Jack's room, all the coming and going to get more drinks and food. I heard footsteps. I felt sick. Please don't let Jack find me. The door to under the house opened. Someone was coming in.

"Julie?"

Phew. It was Phil. We heard Jack calling my name. Phil put his arm around me squeezing me tight. I buried my face in his chest. I could feel our two hearts thudding together. Jack's shadow swept past our hiding place. I was safe.

I said, "I want to get out of here. Help me".

"Okay". He crawled out first. "It's clear". I followed him out into the daylight and dusted myself off. I rushed into the house looking for my sister. She was standing outside the door of Jack's bedroom staring, white faced. I clutched her shaking hand and found a chair near my parents, sat her on it, watching Jack and Colin's every move until it was time to go home at last.

Before that day, Phil was just Jane and Kathy's big brother I played with when I went over to stay when Mum was ill and needed a break. From that day on Phil became my protector.

I watched Auntie Eileen take a seat on a rock with her side of the family, across the stream from my side of the family. Nana stoked the small fire, lighting the cave walls a little. Weary, she put her basket down and waved me over patting the rock beside hers, so I sat down.

She turned to me. "I hardly knew your mother and she never felt like a sister to me in the way Joyce did".

Uncle Bob looked up at the sound of the quiet voice of his sister, nodding in agreement as he continued sifting through some photos he'd found in a basket under some empty beer bottles. "Your mother looked so much like our mother as she got older it was painful for Bob and I to see as it reminded us of what we lost. It hurt that your mother didn't tell you the truth as my children were told when they asked me about my upbringing; that you were all first cousins".

I did eventually find out the truth after another bout of pleurisy sent Mum to her bed with her laboured breathing. She sent me to Auntie Eileen's to stay again on a folding bed between Jane and Kathy in their bedroom. We talked for hours after Auntie Eileen kissed us goodnight and turned the light off. She'd been very kind to me, treating me more like a daughter than a niece. I supposed it was because I'd stayed at her place so many times before, I'd become part of the family. I liked that feeling.

Friday night was lolly night. When Uncle Harry came home from the pub, he gave us ten cents each to buy a bag full from the milk bar across the road. Bananas, snakes, chocolate freckles, raspberries, milk bottles and strawberry kisses. We watched TV on the big couch, munching away until bedtime.

The next day Jane and Kathy turned an end of the skipping rope on the lawn in their front yard. They chanted together, "Over, under, in, out, over, under, in, out". I kept time with the chant until Phil and Ian jumped in, flat footed and got caught up. Jane and Kathy dropped rope making their brothers take an end each. They joined in the rhythm with me until Phil and Ian's arms tired from turning the rope and Jane and Kathy's legs agreed. We all flopped on the lawn, resting near the above ground pool. Phil shot me a glance and blurted out what was on his mind as us children tend to do.

"You know we're first cousins too".

"No we're not. I asked Mum about it. She said you are all second cousins because your Mum and Uncle Bob are brother and sister. Auntie Joyce is Mum's sister so her boys are my first cousins".

"No. They are all brothers and sisters. And there's one who died when they were young. She was called Grace".

Now I was getting confused. I'd never heard of her before. I argued, "So why does your Mum call Nana, Auntie? Nana would be Mum to all of them".

"Their mother died a long time ago".

"I don't believe you!"

"Why do you think my Mum and Uncle Bob lived with their Nana when they were growing up?"

"I didn't know that".

"Well they did. Ask Mum".

"I will". I was getting really upset now. I didn't like this conversation at all. It wasn't adding up even when I tried hard to match it all up in my mind. Like the problem I had with Maths at school. I needed to find Auntie Eileen. I was trying hard not to cry. I walked around the back. She was hanging clothes on the line by the chook shed. She smiled when she saw me. I stood there, passing her the wooden pegs working up the courage to ask her. "Is it true you and Mum are sisters?"

Her smile turned to a frown as she said, "Yes it's true".

"But Mum says you're not".

"I know, but we are". I watched Auntie Eileen string the white sheets out between the two wooden poles, her back to me, trying to decide if it was her or Mum who was lying to me. This was too much. I went inside and lay on my bed. I tried and tried to work it out but it didn't add up. I needed to know before I came to stay at Auntie Eileen's again. I had to ask Mum about it when I got home.

Mum lay back on the white pillows her face as white as them, her breathing still uneasy despite the rest. I stood at the end of her bed summoning up the courage to ask her about she and Auntie Eileen being sisters.

When I asked she said, "We're just relatives".

"But Auntie Eileen said …".

"That's enough talk about this all right. I don't want to hear another word".

"But I want to know".

"I said I don't want to hear another word. Now go".

Mum issued a volley of coughs that sent me from her room with the unanswered question hanging in the air, 'who was lying to me, and why'? I didn't like being lied to.

Phil would never lie to me. He was my protector, strong, tall and fierce like a lion. He stood up to Jack and Colin when they tried to push him around and get in his face at a family get-together. He had a mean stare that told them to back off, he meant business. If they didn't listen, he punched them hard. Sometimes they had to be broken up by my uncles when it went too far, so Jack and Colin knew he wasn't a pushover. Phil followed after them, calling them nasty names. That made me happy because they deserved it. He saved his smiles and his kind eyes for me; sometimes a kiss on the cheek, sometimes on the lips. It made me feel special, loved.

Mum wanted to put an end to Phil's protection.

After school, getting the orange juice out of the fridge and a glass to pour it into, Mum swung round from the stove her mouth set in anger and snarled, "You keep away from your cousin".

"No".

"Did you hear what I said? Keep away from him".

"I don't want to".

"Your auntie and I know what you're both up to. He is your cousin. You can't see your cousin in that way".

"I'm not doing anything wrong".

"Yes you are. You can't marry a cousin. The children turn out deformed and retarded because the genes are too close. You don't want that".

"You said that only happens to first cousins. We're second cousins so what's the problem? We're not doing anything wrong. Who said anything about marrying him? I don't want to marry him. So are we first cousins or not? I want to know the truth!"

"It's Nana. You won't think the same of her".

"What's Nana got to do with it?"

"If you knew she's not your real grandmother you won't love her the same".

"What a load of absolute rubbish. What difference does it make? She's the only one I've known. You lied to me!"

So Auntie Eileen was telling the truth all along. That left a bitter taste in my mouth the sweet orange juice I gulped down didn't take away. I slammed the sliding door to my room shut on my mother's tears and flopped down on the bed flinging my school shoes at the wall. I turned on the radio above my bed and opened my Dolly magazine trying hard to forget the conversation. Tears spilt onto the pages as I turned them. It was going to be hard but I'd have to distance myself from Phil now. It wasn't fair to either of us now I knew the truth. It was wrong to kiss a first cousin on the lips. What an awful mess this was. How was I going to stop this without hurting his feelings?

There was a dull haze over both sides of the family from the dusty light penetrating the cave. Mum sitting on a kitchen chair beside her washing machine reached into her basket. She took out a bottle of pills. Unscrewing the lid she threw a couple in her mouth swallowing hard. Uncle Bob took the top off a beer, running his hands through his thick, wavy hair. He poured himself and his brother-in-law Uncle Harry a glass, whose blue singlet and work shorts were covered in bits of hay from working at the produce store. Uncle Bob rolled up the sleeves of his khaki work shirt and between sips of beer checked off his delivery sheet from another round he'd made in his truck. Auntie Eileen put her wash basket down, leaned in, took her pills out from under the clean washing and undid the lid of the bottle. She sat on a rock, swallowed a couple, gulping them down. Empty pill bottles were rolling about making lazy circles around Uncle Bob's and his sisters' feet in the slight breeze but none of them noticed. They were bonded in their own emptiness that could never be dulled, no matter how many pills the sisters swallowed or how many beers their brother drank; an emptiness only the constant love of a mother could fill. Uncle Harry put down his beer, sat beside Auntie Eileen then turned to me. "Eileen wanted you to have the love we had in our family. Couldn't really afford to feed another mouth when you came to stay but we made do".

A rusted tin labelled 'Apricot Jam' rolled into my feet. After an evening meal we didn't finish, Auntie Eileen caught Jane, Kathy and I tucking in to generous helpings of bread and jam. She was furious. She said she couldn't afford for us to eat extra food. That was all there was for the week; if we didn't eat our tea we could go without. I picked the tin up and handed it to Auntie Eileen who tossed it back on the ground.

I looked at Uncle Harry. "That's how it was", he said.

Uncle Bob put down the loose change he'd been counting and looked at me kicking at the jam tin between my feet. "Eileen was a good auntie to my children. They loved her. The split in the family caused Eileen pain, so I supported her. We and all our kids were close".

Uncle Harry had another sip of his beer and chimed in. "I wanted to help Bob as the family's continual fighting with the other side of the family caused him grief".

Uncle Bob poked his hands into his pockets and played with the rest of the loose change in them. His wife Auntie Gwen marched up to them with a frown on her wide face her brown eyes narrowed. She ran one hand through her permed hair, the other banged against her hip as I continued rolling the jam tin between my feet.

She kicked it away. "I thought you got far too much attention from the rest of the family. A lot of that was your mother's doing. My kids were good kids too. They just got on with their lives without a fuss but Joyce, your mother and their kids had to be the best. Bragging about how well liked and smart you were, your grades at school, ballet, all the medals and competitions you won at dancing. It drove Eileen and I up the wall. We talked about it for hours on the phone. I just played along for Bob's sake as he was a good man and I loved him and so did our children".

The voices of the other side of the family had travelled across the cave to my side of the family. Ever vigilant when it came to protecting her idea of a perfect family Mum dropped her pegs and left the washing dangling on the line, striding over with a worried look on her face. She bent down to me. "Your aunties might have seen it as bragging but it was my protection. All your achievements, how well you were doing at school, how well liked, how smart you were. You were the perfect daughter to have to keep up the family reputation and I was going to remind others of that any way I could. I know you didn't like it. You saw it as blabbing, you couldn't trust me to keep things quiet you shared in confidence but I did what I needed to do. It was very exhausting keeping all that up but everyone had to see I was doing it right. We were the perfect family having the perfect family life".

Auntie Gwen rolled her eyes as Uncle Bob put his arm around her and kissed her cheek. She growled at Mum, "Go back to your sister, I've heard enough of this. Leave our family alone".

Mum went to defend herself some more but Auntie Gwen waved her away. Mum left me sitting on the rock, crushed. Auntie Gwen looked at me. "Sure Bob had a chip on his shoulder, like Eileen being raised by their grandparents. He felt he got a bad deal too. Joyce and your mother often reminded Eileen and Bob they were the ones with the mother and the advantages it came with, so they were difficult in-laws. Your grandmother tried to smooth over the arguments and bring both sides of the family together as best she could. Bob and I, and Eileen and Harry tried to support her".

Uncle Bob put his hand on my shoulder and Auntie Eileen put her arm around me hugging me close. She said, "This mess all started when Joyce came back here to live. We had to see more of your side of the family for your Nana's sake. At first I thought Joyce's boys were nice children even though I thought Joyce was too overbearing with them. But as Jack and Colin grew they had a streak in them I didn't like, aggressive and rough; bullies. I didn't encourage my children to play with them other than at family picnics. Joyce didn't like we were more of a family like cousins should be with you and your family, and wanted her boys to be as close, but that was never going to happen".

Jane had taken the rope out of her mother's basket. She called to her other cousins on their side of the family to come and play with them. They were happy to join in the game.

Auntie Eileen said, "You knew how your cousins felt about Joyce's boys; you all made fun of them. You all made fun of Joyce too because you didn't like her telling you what to do either. She isolated herself from the very thing she wanted; to be loved and respected like your Nana".

I pushed Auntie Eileen away and sobbed, "I wish Jack and Colin were dead. Then no-one would have to protect anyone from anything and we would all be free to love each other like a proper family". I looked over to my protector Phil, playing happily with the cousins on his side of the family. I covered my face with my hands, exhausted from shedding the tears that no matter how much I wept I never felt any better and nothing changed after I dried my eyes.

Auntie Eileen picked up her cane wash basket. The photo of her mother was caught by a gust of wind and swirled around in it before settling at the bottom again. She plonked the skipping rope Jane had left on the ground at her feet on top of it to stop it blowing away. She looked over to her two sister's sitting together by the fire having a cup of tea and walked away, her husband and children following behind her. Her grandmother called after her but she didn't hear her. Uncle Bob put a lid on his memories, and he and Auntie Gwen waved goodbye to them.

Left alone, I looked around the cave to see where Jack and Colin were. Risking them jumping out of the shadows I crept back to my basket as there was something left in it I wanted to look at. I lifted the football off the clean white envelope containing the photo of my birth grandmother and slid it out of its envelope. I circled her face with my finger taking in every little detail of her features, lost in thought about her. I felt someone behind me. I leapt up ready to run.

"I found a basket you might like to have. I saw you looking at the photo of May". Nana handed the shallow woven basket to me by its thin, high handle. "May used to collect flowers in it from our mother's garden. My sister was pretty and popular with the boys. She was a dreamer, happier living in a fantasy world of her own. She expected to marry, have children and that would be her lot. Your mother is very like her".

I slid the photo of my birth grandmother back in its envelope, laid it in her basket and gave Nana a hug. She appeared out of the shadows dressed just as she was in the photo. She walked up to Nana took her hands, kissing her on the cheek. In that moment my birth grandmother and the one I knew as Nana threaded hearts and hands together. I felt their love for each other flow into my heart.

My birth grandmother turned to me, "You got the perfect Nana. She loved you, cared for you as if you were her own granddaughter and that is all that matters in the end; not who gives the love but that you feel loved by the person who gives it to you. The rest is just a name. She was warm, giving, loving and had a big heart. She cared for us all. Mum was harder but fair. Between them they gave my children a good life".

As I put my birth grandmother's basket down beside mine, my great-grandmother laid the cloth back over her basket and stood, tears in her eyes and walked away hand in hand with her daughter May.

... scene 20 ...

something really bad happened to me

Julie's broken child stared at her battered picnic basket, her birth grandmother's words 'don't let abuse ruin your life' still uppermost in her mind. Those words increased her desire to shed the rotting seeds of hurts from her basket for good. It was the reason why she had returned to the cave even though she had wanted to flee from it and never return. It was her Auntie Joyce who provided the opportunity to do so if she was courageous enough to seize that opportunity given to her.

Jack and Colin stood in the cave with long faces watching their mother fuss over me, Terry behind them playing with some toy cars. Auntie Joyce had called me over to sit with her while she continued her mending. She must have seen me over with the other side of the family and wondered why her sister had rushed over there all of a sudden, not looking happy when she returned to the washing. She brushed my long hair and parted it down the middle, one side for the girls she didn't have and the other for the boys she did. "You were the little girl I never had. I always wanted girls. I would have loved three little girls to dress up. They would have had the prettiest clothes and the nicest bedrooms. But I kept getting boys. I so hoped the last one would be a girl but it wasn't and I was so disappointed. I had to hide it but it was hard. So instead I was going to give you things I could only give to girls". She plaited each side of my hair with her plump fingers and tied them at the bottom with pink bows. She tapped me on the shoulder to say she'd finished. I turned around as she leaned her chubby face close and smiled at me taking one of my plaits twirling it in her fingers. "If you were my girl we would have gone shopping and I'd have bought you pretty dresses and made dresses for your dolls then we'd dress them together. Girls were a waste on your mother. She would have been much better with boys". She placed a rag doll in my arms and kissed me on the cheek. "Your mother spent lots of time in her room, day dreaming we all said. I was dreaming about getting married and the house I was going to have and how nice I was going to make it. And the girls I was going to teach how to help me look after it. You need to be a very good home maker to raise girls. Such a waste on boys. They just want a maid to cook and clean and wash for them. Your mother would have been perfect with boys; don't have to teach them a thing, just look after them and the man does the rest. Your mother doesn't appreciate how special you are. I do. I would have sewn all your ballet costumes with love. She was always complaining to me about all she had to do for your ballet and all those other things I would have loved to do for you".

"Well, Mum did get grumpy at concert time. She couldn't sew like the other mothers but she did sew the sequins on my costumes by hand. And she wouldn't let me help in the kitchen when I asked her if I could. She said I had years and years ahead of me to cook, iron and clean and to make the most of the time when I didn't have to do it".

"It makes me so sad to hear that. I would have taught you to cook and sew. We would have had such fun doing that and sharing the chores together".

Auntie Joyce found a button and some thread in her sewing basket to sew back on the rag doll's dress, the rocking chair keeping time with the in and out of the threading of the needle through the button hole.

Mum squeezed the towel she'd found smouldering on the fire amongst the items of torture through an old wringer she'd found lying in the cave and dropped it into the wash basket, butting in to the conversation. "Joyce had to be the expert and authority on everything. She kept up a running commentary on my life to Mum. I couldn't get a word in. Joyce knew best, it drove me up the wall. It was very wearing. She did it to everyone in the family but she was my sister so I put up with it. Mum wanted us to be friends so I did my best to please her, so I went along with her telling me what to do. Mum loved us as her own so we couldn't let her down in any way. Everyone in the family wanted Mum to be happy as she was such a special woman".

Auntie Joyce nodded in agreement singing to herself and to the three little girls she never had. She took off her glasses and broke the end of the cotton off with her teeth. She snipped the ends of the thread on the button and laid the dress in her lap.

As Mum stirred the washing with the stick in a disused copper so she stirred my resolve to tell Auntie Joyce what was on my mind. I sat on a kitchen chair beside her and took a deep breath.

"Auntie Joyce?".

"Yes Jue".

"Your big boys are so mean".

The boys, tired of standing there, started to push at each other. Terry took a step back as he knew what was going to happen next and didn't want to be caught up in another one of their skirmishes.

"No they're just boys. They wrestle and fight because they have a lot of energy they need to get rid of".

"They are nasty boys, your boys".

"They're not that bad".

"Yes they are. Remember you told them to play nicely with me and my sister. Well they don't play nicely at all when we go on picnics and go to Nana's house and when we go down to the school to play".

"I'm sure that's not right. They might get rough with each other but I have taught them good manners and they are very polite".

The boys were now facing off, their arms locked across each other's shoulders staring each other down, eyes narrowed.

"I don't call it polite when they grab Nana's little cakes off the table without asking and go rushing around the room leaving cake crumbs all over the floor".

"They're just being high spirited. You're just not used to having boys around you all the time so you get a bit confused about their behaviour".

"No I don't. When we went to the basketball courts at their school I ran with the boys trying to get the ball off them so I could have a turn to shoot for goal. They held the ball out and when I tried to take it they snatched it back and ran off laughing".

The boys moved into a headlock pushing at each other hard and yelling at each other. Terry, his toy cars in his short's pockets retreated and sat beside my sister. They both watched them from the false security of distance high up on a big rock.

"They were just having some fun with you. You have to learn to take a joke".

"I don't think it's funny when they throw the ball at my back real hard and then laugh. I want to cry but I don't want to show them they've hurt me".

"Well if you had they might have stopped doing it".

Auntie Joyce laid down her needle and thread, folded her hands over the rag doll's dress, rocking back and forth singing softly to herself.

"I tried to run away from them but Jack grabbed my arm so hard it burned. He wouldn't let go when I tried to get his hand off me. He threw me on the asphalt and jumped on top of me. He started bouncing the ball on my chest very hard. I tried to hit him and I was screaming at him to let me go but he just laughed and so did Colin. He got handfuls of stones and dropped them on my face. They were sharp and it stung. I was trying to get up to look for my sister. I couldn't find her. I don't know what they'd been doing to her. Lucky for me some grown-ups and their children came around the corner. When he saw them he jumped off me pretending nothing happened".

"They would have been playing with her on the climbing frames on the outdoor course they go on for sport, giving her a hand up and letting her have a go". Jack and Colin were now writhing on the floor of the cave butting up against rocks, sharp stones in their backs but they only felt their rage and the grit of the fine gravel between their teeth. "Oh, Jue. You're a silly girl. Jack was just wrestling with you trying different moves on you. You know the boys like to watch the wrestling on TV. You've heard them shouting and laughing when those wrestlers throw each other about". My sister and Terry moved a little closer to each other their eyes locked on those two boys as they butted heads.

"Auntie Eileen's boys don't fight like that when I go to their place. They play nicely, they are gentlemen".

"So are my boys".

"No they're not. If they were they would stop fighting when you told them to and not have to wait for Uncle Alan to come home and deal with them".

"Jue, I told you. They are just being high spirited boys when they wrestle like that. All boys do it. Sometimes they just need their father to remind them not to get too carried away. It doesn't mean my boys aren't gentlemen".

I jumped out of my chair at the sound of Uncle Alan's voice, not daring to move. "When Jack misbehaved with Colin, he had to be taught a lesson. I needed to keep on at him all the time so he didn't get out of control". He got his tattered black leather belt out of his basket and stroked his hand with it as he glanced over at his two sons locked in combat. "I had to break Jack's will and his spirit so he knew I was the boss".

Uncle Alan exerted his will over all his household. I dreaded him coming home from work the times I was over at their place for tea and the boys had misbehaved. Auntie Joyce would say to them, "Just wait till your father gets home". She'd rung Uncle Alan at work and told him they'd been fighting again. He stormed in the front door throwing his briefcase and jacket on the couch. His face whitened and his eyes greyed as rage filled him. He pulled his belt from the loops of his suit trousers. It warmed up against his side with threatening strikes. He hit Colin on the back of the head with his open hand and marched him off to his room by the shirt collar yelling at him and hitting him.

I followed Auntie Joyce into the kitchen trembling and saw Jack in his bedroom. Uncle Alan had tied Jack's hands behind his back to the chair with belts from Jack's wardrobe. He whipped and whipped him with his belt and his tongue. Jack's screams escalated with each lash. They went right through me and made me tremble more and more. I heard Colin in his room crying waiting for his turn as we returned to the lounge room with cake and lemonade. Jack begged him to stop but his father's ears were too full of rage to give him mercy. I fought back the tears and put on my bravest face as Auntie Joyce chatted away to me in front of the TV, my stomach in knots unable to eat the cake. I wanted to run out of there and never go back. Uncle Alan was as mean as Jack and Colin. Why didn't Auntie Joyce do something? Terry was watching TV his eyes not moving from the screen. Uncle Alan's belt was now slack by his side. It slid out of his grip and curled at his feet like a snake, his rage spent with Jack. He didn't notice any of us in the lounge room as he marched into Colin's room.

Auntie Joyce had been going through her sewing basket looking for another matching button to sew back on the rag doll's dress. She didn't even look up appearing not to have heard or seen a thing as her two boys rolled over the cave floor still locked together under the cold eyes of their father, his belt at his side waiting to strike again.

"Why didn't you do something to stop Uncle Alan beating the boys?"

"It wasn't that bad. Boys need to be punished like that. They need to know their father is the boss and a good whipping makes them stronger".

"But Jack begged him to stop. It must have hurt him so much. He screamed louder and louder but Uncle Alan didn't take any notice. He was so angry he just kept whipping him. It's so bad to hurt other people like that. You just let it happen. How could you let that happen when he was hurting Jack like that?"

The boys were pulling each other's hair and gouging at each other's eyes. In their efforts to maim each other primal grunts turned into screams that wailed through the spaces and bounced off the walls of the cave. My sister and Terry were now huddled up together. My sister clutched at her teddy bear rubbing her face across his black buttoned nose, her eyes pressed shut.

"Your uncle is the head of the household and I have to support him in what he needs to do to discipline the boys. With boys you've got to toughen them up to face life. They have to be big and strong and brave and take care of the women. So a bit of a whipping isn't going to do them any harm in the long run".

"It's not right to hurt your children like that to punish them. Uncle Harry tells his boys off and makes them go to their room when they've been naughty and they're not allowed out until he says so. That makes them behave".

"Well your uncle does that too but we run a different household here, not all families work things out the same way".

"I don't see anything being worked out. Miss Rowe hit my hand with a ruler every time I used my left one. She even tied it behind my back to stop me using it. I can't help it if I'm a left hander. It just made me scared about when I was going to be hit next. Even though I tried so hard to use the other hand because I was so scared of being hit I could only write properly with my left hand. Mum marched up to the school and told her to stop after I came home crying and I told her what Miss Rowe was doing".

"Well girls are different. If you were my girl I'd be up at the school too".

Uncle Alan stood in the cave clenching and unclenching his hands as his two sons attempted to exhaust their rage too.

"I needed Mum's approval just as much as Joyce did".

Mum was lost in the rumination of her sisterly rivalry, oblivious to what was going on around her so she hadn't heard what I'd told Auntie Joyce about her boys. They'd exhausted themselves from their struggle lying on the floor of the cave on their backs well away from each other gasping for air.

Frustrated with Auntie Joyce's lack of understanding with what I was trying to tell her about her nasty horrible boys and their father I ran at him. Uncle Alan picked up his belt, flicked it across the cave and I shouted at him. "You tied me up in your arms when you dragged me onto your knee and groped me in front of Mum and Dad and Auntie Joyce when you visited us. I tried to pull away and you gripped me harder".

I rushed at Mum and startled her out of her rumination with a jolt shouting at her, "You and Dad watched and did nothing to rescue me".

"What?"

"Uncle Alan groping me in front of you".

"Groping? I don't know what you're talking about. It was all just a bit of fun". Mum threw me a look indicating I'd made up what I'd just told her.

"It was not!"

I swung around to Uncle Alan and screamed at him. "I was so scared of you and what you might do if I didn't play along".

"In front of the family was the best place to do it. It was perfect to play and flirt in front of others. I got away with it, didn't I!"

"You dirty, filthy man. Mum, are you going to say something?" I turned around but she wasn't there. She was over at the clothesline pegging the washing on it where the daylight penetrated the cave.

Uncle Alan picked me up and held me in a firm grip as I kicked out at him, my rage unleashed. "Do you know how heady it is to get away with things in front of others? I could give Jack a whipping and get away with it right under your nose while Joyce went on like nothing had happened. I could grope you whenever I wanted to and no one did a thing".

"I wasn't yours to touch and control!"

Uncle Alan shrugged his shoulders and let me back down indifferent to my tongue lashing, which further enraged me as I paced in front of him. My sister peeked out from behind her teddy bear, pink geranium petals fluttering around her basket stirred in the unleashed rage flying about the cave. There was no relief from my attempt to try and appease my pain. It just rubbed the hurts in deeper.

Auntie Joyce looked up from her mending and saw Uncle Alan standing there. She waved him over. He walked over to her with slumped shoulders and the same long face his three sons bore. My sister and Terry remained high up on the rock not daring to move.

Colin, still winded from another losing battle with his big brother, limped towards my broken child and sat askew on the kitchen chair. "You saw how scared and upset I got and how I fought Jack. It made no difference what I did. I was stuck. You saw the beatings I got. They didn't make a man of me and they didn't make me strong, they destroyed me. Jack was so cruel to me, crueller than Dad. Dad got him first then Jack got me. I hated what Jack made me do at family picnics and when we visited Nana's with you. I just wanted it all to stop and go away but it never did".

Colin had been talking to my turned back. I was too wounded to have any compassion other than for myself and my sister I'd tried so hard to protect.

"Those bloody boys of Joyce's. Bloody nuisances the pair of them". Dad strode past Mum's family and threw open a large bottled glass door that led into a public bar behind the kitchen table further in the cave. He slammed it shut behind him having seen the tail end of their skirmish. How many times I'd heard Dad say that to Mum after Auntie Joyce and Uncle Alan had gone after a regular visit on the weekend.

I could make out shapes of men through the door as I got closer. One of the men opened it on me with a beer in his hand. I recognized him straight away, one of the police boys. He left it open and returned to the crowded bar.

Dad was holding court drink in hand, a semi-circle of his police boys in front of him laughing at his jokes and indulging his tall stories of heroics on the job.

I marched up to him tugged on his trouser leg. "Why were the boys a nuisance?" Dad looked down surprised to see me there and that I'd overheard what he'd said about Jack and Colin.

"Your mother pressured me to do something about it when Jack got into trouble for his twisted ways. So I used my connections and the charges were dropped. Galled me as he was doing the very thing I was locking those other bastards like him up for. And he did it more than once".

I reeled at the offensive truth. I rushed after Dad on his way to the bar for another round of drinks. I waited while he was served. I needed to tell him what had happened.

"Something really bad happened to me".

"What?" I trailed after him drinks high up in the air as he pushed his way through the crowd.

"I got into bed with Jack for a cuddle and his snake bit me."

"What do you mean his snake bit you?"

"It got into the hole between my legs and left an awful mess".

"Well there's not much I can do about it. He's your cousin. I can't send him away. You have to see him whether you like it or not. I can't even give him a warning because he is a part of our family. It would upset things in the family too much if I arrested him. Think of all the problems it would cause. Families have to stick together no matter what. Those are the rules so there's not a lot I can do I'm afraid. Just try to keep away from him as much as possible". Dad joined his police boys back in his space in the semi-circle and passed one of them another beer.

I looked up at him, tears welling in my eyes. "That's not fair. What about me? He did that to me and you are protecting that monster for the sake of the family. The family is more important than what happened to me? You are a policeman. You are the law. You have the power to do something to make this stop and you're telling me you're not going to?" Dad turned his back on me and took a cigarette and light from one of his police boys. I crossed in front of him and said, "He didn't have my permission to touch me like that. He did something I didn't want him to. He did it even when I tried to stop him. I don't like people playing tricks on me. It's so nasty and cruel. I don't think tricks are funny. I feel so dirty. I don't like feeling dirty. I like things to be clean and tidy, my room and my clothes and my body all fresh and clean like the air and the sunshine. Only the doctor and Mum are allowed to look at and touch my private parts. I don't like the doctor looking but sometimes he has to because I get worms but Mum stands beside him while he examines me".

"I told you. He's your cousin so you have to see him whether you like it or not. Families have to stick together no matter what. Now go away. I'm busy".

I wiped away my tears on the back of my pyjama sleeve as I voiced to Dad the lament that eddied around and around the empty beer bottles stacked on the slippery pyramid against the cave wall; "When are you coming home?"

"Later".

"When later?"

"Just later. I forget my other world when I'm with the boys. That's why you never knew when I was coming home. Neither did I half the time. Getting off duty I was off for a drink and lost all track of time. I slept in the watch house if I didn't make it home. I didn't care but I knew your mother did. We fought about it a lot".

"But you had me and I needed you and you weren't there".

Dad turned his back on me again and took the beer one of the police boys thrust in his hand, taking a long drag on his cigarette. I hung my head and walked out the door of the bar past my father's family, past my mother's family and past my grandparents sitting by the fire looking puzzled as they removed the objects I'd thrown on it so they could light the fire to make a cup of tea. I looked for my sister I tried so hard to protect but she was nowhere to be seen, the harm done to her unfixable - she irretrievable. I walked past my empty picnic basket, the football beside it and past my birth grandmother's basket which held the white envelope with her photo in it.

... scene 21 ...

befriending the broken child

setting
julie's camp by the river

Julie's broken child kept walking knowing she would always be alone in a family riddled with secrets, a family who believed the family reputation was more important to protect than her sister and herself.

I walked out the mouth of the cave, removed the triangle from where I'd propped it against the cave wall and kept walking towards a tent I noticed down by the river hoping whoever was inside might offer me shelter. I parted the doorway and asked if I could enter.

Julie made room on her mattress and waved her in taking the golden triangle from the broken child and laid it on top of her backpack.

I recognised her straight away. It was the child in the pyjamas I'd seen in the cave once before. I took her hand as she laid her head on my shoulder and stroked her hair until I felt her settle.
"Here, choose something to wear".
The child went through the clothes in my back pack. After a good look she sat back taking out a pair of clean, white underpants. She leaned over me shook out my wedding dress and smiled. I smiled too.
"Now I know who you are. I saw you in my cave with Neil's mother once where the laundry was being done. You were arguing with her. You wore this pretty white dress. Now I am going to wear it". When she changed into it, it was too big for her. It didn't seem to matter as she was beaming that she'd shed her pyjamas with the hole in the crotch at last. I rolled them in a ball and threw those filthy clothes out of the tent.
The child crawled out of the tent with my picture hat and parasol. I followed her with the golden triangle and hung it from the top of what

was now our tent, the number 11 at the top of it glowing in the sun. She put the hat on, hung the parasol off her arm and looked around at her new surroundings.

Leaving her to settle in I took the kettle to the river to get some water to make tea for the two of us. On my return I noticed she'd found the white silk pouch embossed with stars. She was twirling an eagle feather in her fingers, the tarot cards spread over the ends of my old wedding dress.

Seeing me she said, "I had a feather like this in my basket but it got tipped out when I threw the things out of it onto the fire in the cave. I lost it".

I pointed up to the sky at the eagle that was always there when I looked up, doing easy circles over my tent. Holding on to her hat, the child watched its path taking it higher and higher. When we lost sight of it I sat down on the ground beside her and put the kettle on. I gathered up the cards and went through them until I found The Tower, The Hanged Man and the Death card putting them in a row on the ground.

The child asked, "What are these cards?".

"Tarot cards".

"They don't look very nice".

"They tell a story about our life if you know how to read them and I do now. I taught myself with a lot of practice".

"Will you teach me?" I nodded as I picked them up and shuffled them ready to do a spread for us. She put her eagle feather in her picture hat and made herself comfortable. I made some tea and handed her a mug.

We sipped it as I dealt the cards. The helmeted skeleton in his armour grinned at us with hollow eyes as I pointed to the Death card.

"There was the sound of a hammer. I was in the shower. I turned it off, grabbed a towel, wrapped it around myself, my hair dripping and rushed to the direction of the noise. I peeked through the curtains in the spare room and saw a truck parked outside. A man was banging the 'For Sale' board into the front lawn. Each bang pounded into the dirt an end to my hopes and dreams I'd had for a life with Neil. That was it. It was all over. I flinched with each strike of the hammer and pulled the towel tighter round me. I had to move to a new place, a strange place and start again on my own. It wasn't right. I was a married woman. Neil was my husband. I loved him. He was with Louise, my best friend. I didn't have any emotional or mental framework built into my mind I could use to comprehend let alone deal with this truth. I went over and over it but there was no comfort though I craved it so much".

The child said with surprise, "I used to hang out with her. She was at that run down bar with the rest of my drinking friends in the cave partying with us till all hours".

"I saw her there at the bar with Neil's family when I sought shelter in your cave after I got married".

She took another sip of her tea as I picked up the Hanged Man and continued with my story. "I was left to hang upside down in Neil's family still unable to turn myself right way up in my life though they were no longer in it. As I lay in bed at night still awake well after midnight all my fears swam in my head about a future alone. There was a mortgage to pay. I didn't have a permanent job. I wasn't going back to full time teaching. What else could I do? How was I going to buy a new house with no permanent job? How was I going to afford to pay a mortgage on my own? Would I get enough from the sale of the house to pay a deposit for another one? Where was I going to live? How was I going to pay off the large credit card debt Neil left me to pay? How was I going to pay my bills? I was struggling to meet the basics of living. I didn't have any savings other than the $7.43 left in our joint account. All those questions I couldn't answer pulled the hangman's noose tighter and tighter round my neck as I realised I was responsible for everything in my life."

The child picked up the card. "I had a noose around my neck too. She looked at it with tears in her eyes. She put her arm round me and lay her head on my shoulder. "I was so choked up with fright, I couldn't speak out about what happened to me with those horrible cousins of ours. Even when I did our mother wouldn't listen. She said I had to keep quiet about it for the sake of the family's reputation. So I let them all have it. I said what I'd always wanted to say to the family I wouldn't dare say to their face because I knew they wouldn't listen, care or do anything about it. They would just hurt me more to try and keep me quiet. I'm so glad to be out of that cave and never having to go back in there again".

"Yes, keeping up with the Jones's. Our mother was so focused on that, that's for sure. Always comparing who was doing what and trying to keep up with those she thought were of a suitable social standing in the community. She cried when she told me Mr and Mrs Jones were moving to a more upmarket suburb. She said they wouldn't want to mix with us anymore. You did the right thing letting the family have it, giving them a piece of your mind. They deserved it!"

The child sat back and looked at me, both of us taking in what we'd just shared. I gave us a few moments, then I continued telling her my story.

"*What am I going to do?* Those words swam in my head over and over as I lay in bed tossing and turning night after night suffocated by my circumstances and feeling emotionally destitute. The house was filled with the sound of all the fights Neil and I had before he left. Snippets of conversation went around and around my head hunting me down.

'I can't go on in this marriage'- 'Neil will make a great father for Jason'- 'I have to think of myself first' – 'What about me, we're best friends' – 'We're just friends' – 'She's nice and slim and not too esoteric'. I could hear the word *'run!'* punctuating these thoughts.

The child sitting cross legged on the ground started jigging her knee up and down clasping her hands tight, her knuckles white. She closed her eyes, her jaw clenched. I put my hand on her knee and waited for her to calm down. She opened her eyes, tears spilling down her face. "That was me saying *'run!'*. I was trying to tell you I was there and the pain I was in. I needed help. I was so alone".

Though it was difficult for both us it was important I told her all of my story.

"Tonia, the dog Neil wanted, lay in the space he once occupied, snoring. Even her bulk and her attentiveness to my desperate state she tried to soothe with big slobbery kisses didn't reach into this bereft place in my heart. I got up and wandered about the house lost, the same thoughts continuing unabated. I kept watching out the windows scared of being attacked. One night a prowler shone a torch through my window and banged on it. Tonia flew off the bed to the window jumping up and barking. Her weight and the noise of her fierce barks made the window rattle. She was my only protection and I was fearful of losing her too.

Neil had said on one of his last visits, "I want to share Tonia with you if you won't let me have her. I want to take her on the weekends and take her on holidays".

I exploded. "You've got to be joking. You leave me for my best friend, the two of you get what you want and now you want me to share Tonia with you? Tonia is all I have now. We need to be left to settle and adjust to a life without you. You want to make it harder than it already is? No way". I called Tonia and she followed me inside. I slammed the front door, fell against it sliding to the floor weeping.

The child was watching the water gurgle along the river over the rocks eddying in little pools in various spots. "I know what it's like to be scared liked that." She tapped her finger at the Tower card. "I lived in such darkness my world crashing down around me with no way to get back up even though I tried. I had to get away, to do something. Nothing was working. I escaped from the cave on the day you remembered what happened to me during the film at the school where you were teaching. I had to get out, go and never go back. I wanted to run and keep on running until the pain went away. I made your insides catch on fire like the Tower in this card on that night when you'd had enough after your marriage ended. I was the one driving you to get dressed into your tracksuit, not even bothering to take off your nightie first, tucking it in and lacing up your runners so you could get to the highway as fast as you could through the cold and fog. I was the one who pushed you onto the road as the glare of headlights approached as that car sped towards you".

I searched the child's eyes that stared at me full of pain. "A force pulled me back onto the footpath. I snapped out of the trance I was in and realised what I'd just done. My legs buckled under me and I collapsed on the kerb. The cold and rain that had started to fall hitting my face until it stung, which I hadn't been able to feel until that moment. I heard the words *'You owe it to yourself to find the meaning of life, you owe yourself the chance to live life truly and fully'*. I half ran, half stumbled back home on leaden legs with those words ringing in my ears. I fell back into bed exhausted and snuggled up beside Tonia. I stroked her head while I stared at the foot of the bed, still unable to settle. I still couldn't believe what I'd just done. Out of the darkness a cream and tortoise shell comb appeared in front of my eyes; the one Nana used to comb her hair with. As I focused on it she appeared at the foot of my bed bathed in white light, her luminous glow blinding me for just a moment. I opened and closed my eyes thinking they were playing tricks on me. When I looked again she was there as clear as day with her shiny blue eyes and silver hair, that loving smile of acceptance I missed so much. It lit up the room and bathed me in its glow. I had never felt so loved in my life. I felt the swish of air as she glided to my head and stroked my hair. I cried tears of solace and elation, this time bathed in the peace and comfort of her caresses, no longer feeling all alone.

I heard her say, *"I have been waiting patiently for you to be ready for me to visit. I will look after you until you can look after yourself. I will guide you to the world of spirit. That is where you belong. There you will find the peace you seek. It is inside of you. You will find it"*. The white glow started to fade and she disappeared from the foot of my bed and the room was dark again. My bedroom felt very empty as I lay there. "Thank you Nana. I will find this world within me no matter what it takes". I knew I could trust Nana to take care of me so I would be all right, which I'd find the strength to keep living. She'd stayed close by me since her death waiting to help me. She'd felt my grief and answered my pleas for a resolution to this suffering. She'd gone to the garden I created for her with words to comfort her as she waited to die. Now she was sharing the bountiful wisdom she'd gathered while walking in it since she joined her family there who had gone before her.

The child sat back from the cards as I finished telling her my story and said heatedly, "Those cousins, what they did to me and our sister!". She threw a look in the direction of the cave.

"I hate them". I nodded in agreement. "I love Nana, she looked after us and protected us. She tried so hard to look after all the family and love us all". I nodded again. "The drinking and the arguing, it never stopped". The child jumped up using the tip of her parasol for support and straightened her dress. Pointing the parasol at the cave she shouted, "All the grown-ups over there were doing mean nasty things to each other and to me just to protect their dirty little secrets and their lies".

This broken child who I now knew beyond a doubt was also a part of me too, started to run off so I grabbed her hand and strode over to the cave with her pyjama's thrust under my arm. While she waited at the entrance I marched towards the dim glow of the fire and tossed those pyjamas on it. The fire flared and smoke billowed over the cave. I could just make out the shapes of various family members, some trying to sleep off hangovers and others the disquiet of heart break that the walls of this cave contained.

"Come with me. I want to show you something". I led her to my weeping green world under the willow tree. "Come inside".

I parted the doorway letting her crawl inside first. Her eyes grew big as she looked around my world. She went through my jewellery box covering herself in my bangles, beads, the beaten golden Buddha and my pewter heart. Taking off her hat, she plonked my wig on her head and spun the globe of the world around and around. She picked up my ballet books, then put my 45 'Julie Do Ya Love Me' on the record player and while she danced to the tune I told her about my first kiss. Sliding into my desk she lifted the lid and emptied it of all the books inside. She scribbled on the chalkboard then erased it with the duster. Putting on my ballet shoes she danced about under my tree. Getting into the spirit of it all she put the bracelet on that Paul had given me and I gave her the doll that sat on my bed Tad had given me, hugging it and giving it a kiss. Opening my ballet case she squealed with delight seeing my Barbie doll and all her clothes. She put a soft green evening gown on Barbie and turned her around admiring it.

The letters and numbers of my Ouija game were moved about in her flurry of activity. I grabbed at them putting the Vegemite jar over them so they wouldn't fly off my desk. She asked me what they were. I told her about the game 'Ouija' I played with our sister. She asked me how to play it so I spread the letters and numbers out on the desk. She squealed when the jar flew to the letters under the guidance of our questions and our hands.

We lay down on my grey blanket snuggled up beside each other watching the sunlight dancing through the branches of the tree, giggling as the ends of the leaves tickled our faces and feet as they brushed back and forth over us. Cocooned in my world together we drifted off singing along to 'Julie Do Ya Love Me' she had kept playing since I told her about my first kiss. I didn't mind. I was happy that at last we'd become friends.

The needle was at the end of the record when I opened my eyes and realised where I was. I sat up, looked at my clothes and saw they were the ones I travelled overseas in, not my flower girl's dress. I took the needle off the record and slipped the record back into its cover. Then I remembered I'd brought the broken child here. She was nowhere to be seen.

I looked around at my budding child's world under the willow tree one last time, parted the branches, stepped outside and went looking for the broken child but she was nowhere to be found. I called at the cave's entrance, looked in my tent and walked along the path by the river but she'd gone.

What Julie didn't know was that I had taken the eagle feather out of the broken child's picture hat and trailed it across Julie's inner eye, coaxing it further awake as she'd slept under the willow tree with the broken child. As it opened, the broken child in her wedding dress faded away until only Julie lay on the grey blanket under the willow tree.

A waft of rose oil filled my nostrils, its sweet scent leading me back to the tent. I lifted the golden triangle off the top of it and read the words in its corners, 'Beauty,' 'Respect' and 'Care'. Nana. She was the one in my family who had shown me the greatest care.

I looked up into the sky above the tent my feather in hand and watched the eagle riding the thermals circling higher and higher. Night after night as I'd lain in bed trying to go off to sleep Nana would come to me, bathed in white light smiling, her blue eyes sharp and clear. I'd melt into her smile and the love in her eyes as she took my hand lifting me higher and higher away from my sleeping body. As I rose up with her the sky became clearer, the light whiter. I resisted at first. Nana tugged my hand gently so I went with her in trust, embracing the feeling of inner freedom this movement brought me. Winged white angels floated past me. Nana waved, smiled and pointed to them then smiled at me. My heart opened and I felt my body fill with light. Moving around in this new world beyond my body my inner sight opened. With that wider vision I understood what Nana was trying to show me. I had eagle eyes and if I used them I would see my life from a higher perspective. A step away from my heart break and from that perspective I could see a wider view of my life I hadn't been able to see before. With my eagle eyes I could hold the vision of a new life story and be able to create it for myself.

On the nights Nana's shining light was absent from my dream state Pa's voice of authority boomed out through it, waking me to sit bolt upright in bed.

"*I can see you are determined. Do not give up. You have a strong will. You will make it. You have to. Keep going. Go on. Do not give up*".

Together they carried me away from my distress, Nana steadying my flailing spirit and Pa helping to strengthen my will. I picked up the Hanged Man card. I was no longer hung upside down in my own life. Nana and Pa's continued support past their deaths, had righted me to the correct orientation of what was required within me to keep stepping forward into my own life story.

> Julie's grandmother had provided a bridge for her to cross so she would be able to find me and in so doing, The Lost Temple of Julie. She would learn to trust me now to lead her into the inner world of her temple as she had trusted her grandmother who led her to me.

As I hung the golden triangle back up on the top of my tent, I wondered who'd given it to this broken child who was a part of me. I was so focused on the tarot cards I'd found in the white pouch embossed with stars, and the difficult times they reflected in their symbols that I never stopped to think how the pouch got there at the side of my tent. I picked it up again and opened it to see if there was anything else in it beside the tarot cards and the eagle feather I'd already found. I put my hand inside and felt something sharp at the bottom with some bits of what felt like sand or fine gravel. I pulled out a small clear quartz crystal. Holding it up to the light all the colors of the rainbow sparked from its facets as I twirled it round in my fingers. The dancing light brought the same joy I'd felt when returning to my willow tree again to show the broken child what was contained within it. This light brought a sense of promise and hope to my heart. I tipped the rest of the contents on the ground finding tiny fragments of crystal dust that sparkled in the sunlight. I stood my crystal in the centre of it. I couldn't take my eyes off it.

As I continued to watch the colored light dancing a shape began to appear within the crystal. It was a woman. She was wearing a long, white shift that brushed her toes and a tiara made of eagle feathers and clear quartz crystals. Now I couldn't take my eyes off her. She carried a basket inlaid with mother-of-pearl with crystal handles. Putting her hand into the basket she threw a shower of fine dust toward me just like the crystal dust I'd found in the pouch. A blast of colors shot out all around her and she was gone. My inner knowing sensed she'd given me the pouch and the items it contained, and the broken child the golden triangle with the words 'Beauty', 'Respect' and 'Care' in each corner, and the golden number 11 at the top.

I crawled back into the tent and emptied my backpack. I put the tarot cards, crystal, eagle feather, the golden triangle and my astrology chart into it with a change of clothes, shoes and my raincoat. I dragged it out of the tent and strapped it over my shoulders.

Looking around one last time I headed for the path down by the river. I stopped at the cave wall and picked up the lotus blossom filled with the scent of rose oil and walked towards the sun, the eagle continuing to circle above me as I took each step.

Through the sharing of her temporary home, some of her story and inviting the broken child into her budding child's weeping green world to play Julie had managed to befriend the broken child. In that act of friendship Julie was now strong enough within herself to carry the remnants of the broken child's pain and bear it for them both.

In meeting I, the Temple Woman for the first time and sensing it was me who had given her the pouch and the broken child the golden triangle the two children's realms merged within Julie's heart bringing her another step closer to me.

... scene 22 ...

the women's circle

setting
the path by the river

Rays of sunshine filtered through the trees up ahead as I walked along the path by the river. The eagle hovered over these tall trees that reached up towards her before riding the spiral of air even higher. I could hear the voices of women I recognised echoing through the forest. There was one with a proper English accent - Lois.

Lois, the doorkeeper to Julie's soul's awakening provided Julie the next bridge to cross to bring her to me, The Temple Woman.

I picked up my pace and saw her and my esoteric study group sitting in a circle in a gap through the stand of mountain ash. Lois had suggested I join the group. I was greeted with hellos and hugs as I joined the circle putting my backpack down beside me.
Each woman had a basket beside them. Inside each basket were crystals, incense, books, flower essences, scented oils and nourishing food. In the centre of the circle there lay a pile of books. Anna, an earthy woman of Russian descent strong in physique and mind with a cheeky smile and sense of humour, was the teacher of this group and Lois's closest friend. She had a book in her lap and was reading to us.

Each woman carried a basket of hurts in their hearts. They weighed their basket against the knowledge that they were responsible for their own lives and how they wanted to live it. They were women committed to grow and heal from their past hurts. This created a common bond that strengthened each time they met and soon spread past its confines to offer support in friendship. This group of strangers gave Julie's life some sort of continuity and a sense of purpose when everything else in it had fallen apart. She felt at home with these strangers because she was able to share her thoughts and feelings without derision about what she was discovering in her inner world, because they were on the same journey of discovery too, as committed to it as Julie was. Unlike the other circle of friends Julie grew up with who were focused on their careers, children, and material aspirations, with these women Julie would begin to learn and understand the language of the temple. In doing so she'd use it to live her everyday life where she would rediscover her own life story.

Anna passed the book to Claudia, a vivacious middle aged woman with a contemplative nature. She took a box of incense out of her basket, put a fresh stick in the burner that sat in the middle of the circle and lit it. The scent of sandalwood rose up into the canopy of mountain ash. I took my lotus blossom out of my pack and laid it beside it, the scent of rose mingling with the scent of sandalwood.

She pulled her coral pink pashmina shawl around herself as she turned the page of the book and read the next page to the group in her Swiss accent. Finishing the page she passed it to Joan who spoke with a throaty inflection indicative of her older age and her Australian roots, her eyes sharp and wit to match. Next to read a page was bright and proper Alice from a conservative Australian country town. She had the same streak in her as Joan with her quick wit when she chose to show it.

The book 'Creative Visualisation', by Shakti Gawain was passed to me, a paragraph underlined on page sixty-one at the beginning of the chapter on prosperity. It was now my turn to read a page out to the group.

It said, 'A very important part of the whole creative visualisation process is developing a sense of prosperity. This means having the understanding, or consciously taking the point of view that the universe is abundant, that life is actually trying to bring us what our hearts and souls truly desire-spiritually, mentally, emotionally, as well as physically. Almost everything you truly need or want is there for the asking. You only need to believe that is so, truly desire it, and be willing to accept it'.

Before Alice had her turn to read the suggested affirmations for prosperity from the next page of the book, Anna asked the women to take a crystal out of their baskets to bring more light to the circle. I took my crystal out of my pouch and laid it with the citrines, rose quartz and amethysts laid down by the others. I'd needed to create a couple of my own affirmations that suited my changing life circumstances after my marriage ended. My marital home sold quickly leaving me two months to buy another one and find a permanent job. The income from emergency teaching was not able to support servicing a mortgage, my day to day living expenses, let alone having any left over for pleasurable pursuits.

The price range I could afford to buy in narrowed right down after the proceeds of the house sale were split in half and the associated costs to sell it paid out. I was told each time after initial enquiries at various estate agents in different areas in a wide radius from where I lived that I didn't have enough money for a deposit for a house.

Every night before I went to sleep I visualised going into a real estate agent's office and a salesman saying when I enquired, "Yes we have a property in your price range I can take you to look at today".

Late in the day after another Saturday enquiring at different agents and being told there was nothing available in my price range I walked into the last one in the area and the estate agent said, "Yes we have a property in your price range I can take you to look at today. What you can afford is the lowest the owner is prepared to go to sell".

He drove me to a street not far from the office. We pulled up outside a house called The Eyrie, a slate tiled, white stone cottage that sat high on a ridge at the fork of two roads providing me with a view to the mountains where my mother's family were born and raised. The name of this house confirmed to me this was to be my new home but before I could claim it as my own, I needed a bank loan.

I made an appointment to see a bank manager for the following week. Between then and the meeting, I kept visualizing myself across the desk, the bank manager handing me the paper work to sign for the loan. At our actual meeting, shaking inside as he looked at all the figures on the print out from my emergency teaching earnings I'd been asked to provide, I waited for his answer. He looked up over his glasses and said he would approve the money for the loan. I crossed the road to my car with a skip in my step, whooping with joy.

All that was left to do was find a permanent job. I repeated the affirmation I created, 'I have a wonderful new job with great pay', over and over every night before I went to sleep. This relaxed and calmed my churning thoughts allowing me to have a more restful sleep.

I'd been supplementing my sporadic emergency teaching income doing casual work at a store selling leather goods and luggage. The store manager Laurel and her second in charge Marion had been kind, giving me extra hours as they knew I needed the money. While Marion dusted the suitcases and I cleaned the glass cabinet the wallets were displayed in, she mentioned that a friend of hers said they were looking for people at a building company to be employed as marketing associates at their new display homes. I had two questions for her, "What did they do and what was the pay like?" Marion said they showed visitors over display homes and got leads for real estate agents to follow up to convert into sales. When Marion told me what the job paid, my next question was, how did I get an interview.

After the interview, I floated along the footpath back to the car knowing I had a full time, well paid job. I was hired the day before I moved in to my new home.

Now settled in, I stood on the back veranda of my new home, my own eyrie, looking at the embankment that defined the grassed level below where old fruit trees stood in rows in the large garden, keen to tidy up this neglected garden full of weeds, long grass and overgrown plants. They needed a good prune, fresh soil and some water. I decided to tackle the embankment first. Armed with a garbage bag, small hand shovel and some gardening gloves I walked down the steps and stood on the grass surrounded by empty beer bottles. The previous owner must have decided it was a perfect place to throw his empties from the back deck after having a quiet few beers after work.

Digging into the cracked, grey earth I hit something rough like broken concrete. I tugged at the weeds covering it and with them came shards of brown glass. As I dug deeper I found more, then more. I picked through the rubble bit by bit unearthing layers of soil filled with small pieces of broken beer bottles applying the painstaking skill of an archaeologist as I made my way along the embankment, ensuring I'd dug every last piece of glass out, not prepared to lay down fresh soil and plant a garden in the rubble of broken beer bottles. I put the empty beer bottles in the garbage bag along with the small pieces of glass I had unearthed from the soil, emptied the bag into the large recycle bin and wheeled it onto the nature strip ready for collection. I pulled off my gardening gloves, satisfied I'd made a start, even though there was still a lot of work to do before I could plant a fresh garden of my own.

... scene 23 ...

our picnic

I got up and stretched after Alice finished reading the rest of the prosperity affirmations at the end of the chapter, laying the book down on the grass. The others in the circle decided they needed a break too. I wandered down the path past the stand of mountain ash where the forest changed to open paddocks with grazing cattle. In the far paddock stood a tall dying tree, its sturdy, thick arms knotted and worn but still holding life; for in the fork of one of the top branches where they still had leaves, was a large, deep nest made of dried grasses and sticks. The eagle once a dot in the distance over my tent by the river spiralled down and landed beside the nest.

I could hear laughter coming from the other women drawing me back to them. They were having a picnic. Plates of food were spread out on an assortment of brightly colored Indian shawls. Alice took some cups and saucers out of her basket and poured hot tea from a tall silver flask. Claudia took a white china plate out of hers with a home-made poppy seed cake she sliced up on matching plates and placed them at their feet. Lois and Anna were discussing the numerology reading Lois had done for Anna while they sipped their tea. There was another woman there too I recognised; a vibrant, healthy woman with thick ringlets of hair and a smile that exuded confidence and warmth; Adele. I rushed up to her and hugged her. Alice offered me some tea and Claudia a piece of cake. I sat next to Adele and joined in the bright conversation. We'd all been to see her at her healing centre. She'd helped us improve our health through the use of herbs, aromatherapy oils, flower essences and diet.

The first time I'd met her she swept into the consulting room and sat on the leather couch opposite me. She let me talk through my tears about my marriage break up until I stopped.

She said, "You left him. You outgrew him and it was time to move on".

Her words slapped me awake and I sat up straight on the couch. It wasn't something I'd considered. The truth of her words pierced my boiling gut.

Over a series of consultations Adele gave me various combinations of herbs to regenerate my body and essential oils to have in a series of baths to promote emotional healing coupled with flower essences I'd put under my tongue. An eating program was devised to help with my various food allergies, sensitivity to certain grasses and the general lethargy I laboured under. She was able to ascertain what my body and mind needed and in what amounts by conducting a muscle test on my body. It involved asking my body what it needed. If it wanted herbs, an oil or a flower essence when Adele pushed down on my hand my arm stayed firm. If it didn't, my arm would drop indicating the body didn't want what she asked because the muscle had switched off. Within a short time I'd lost weight, felt more centred in myself and my overall health started to improve. Having the ability to ask my body what it needed to heal made sense to me, rather than relying as I'd done unwillingly through coercion in the past on the advice of my doctor and my mother to take pills. My mind had been dulled enough living through and then reliving all the traumatic experiences of my past after my marriage ended without it being further dulled with more pills. So I'd chosen not to seek help from a doctor this time.

After this initial course of successful treatment by Adele at her healing centre, I'd decided I wanted to learn to treat myself. I bought a kit with herbs, oils and flower essences for my own personal use and was taught how to muscle test myself to know what dosage and combination my body needed. I used muscle testing to find the food that would best nourish my body. I started to understand if my body said it needed these things, my mind did too to help focus with the process. An affirmation, a clear positive statement provided that focus; something I'd already learned worked for me in finding a new home and job.

Anna called out to the group,

"Who would like a tarot reading?". All eyes turned to me.

"You wouldn't mind?" Anna asked.

"Happy to". I opened my backpack, found my white pouch embossed with stars, tipped the cards out and spread them in front of me. Joan gave them a shuffle deciding she would be first to have a reading. She handed the cards back to me after she'd chosen three from the pack. I turned her cards over on the grass, the others in the circle eager to know what the cards said for Joan. As I gathered up the cards ready for the next reading the Death card fell onto my lap still casting its long shadow over my life. The divorce papers.

Filling out forms define our lives, a signature binds us to what we have read as understood within the jargon. Unspoken contracts between people are the ones that are the most binding, which no amount of legalese can set firm and no witness can be a party to. In my heart I had that contract with Neil. The papers had arrived in the mail informing me the divorce would take place at the local magistrate's court.

We met on the steps outside the courthouse on the designated day. At the desk in the foyer the young clerk asked me what we were there for. I hung my head trying not to cry. I couldn't tell him.

Neil said, "We're getting a divorce".

"Sit over there. Be with you in a minute".

We sat on the chairs he pointed to and watched a group of people stream out of the court and a new group enter after them, their legal team striding ahead of them. Detectives and uniformed police walked in and out with facts and figures about times and places alleged crimes were committed and alleged perpetrators were present.

I'd sat in courts like these with Mum and my sister on those hard backed benches that smelt of polish, sweat, fear and bad words, waiting for Dad to give his evidence. Mum passed boiled lollies and barley sugar in waxy white paper bags to us. We sucked on them waiting for Dad to get down out of the witness box in a courtroom on the way to a holiday in the country at Pa's. I peered into the courtroom, grimacing at the memory, glad this hearing wouldn't take place in there. It should have really because as far as I was concerned a crime had been committed by my husband and my best friend Louise.

"Okay". I jumped as the clerk's voice summoned us back to the desk. "Have you got the divorce papers?"

I nodded and took them out of my handbag with sweaty hands. I thought I would collapse. He looked them over.

"Right. It all seems to be in order". He reached under the desk and plonked a dusty bible on the counter.

"Place your hands on the bible".

He had to be joking. We're getting divorced right here in front of all these people coming and going and the ones standing behind us waiting to be served? What about some respect for our privacy? Isn't there an office? This matter is so personal. This can't be happening.

"Do you both solemnly swear…" I blanked out.

I muttered something, nodded and heard Neil do the same. The clerk removed the bible from under our hands, stamped the paperwork declaring, "You're divorced".

That was it. It was final even if it wasn't legally for another 12 months with the Decree Absolute. Afterwards we walked over the road to the pub for a counter lunch. Our conversation was subdued, asking each other about our jobs. Neil asked after the cats and Tonia. All such a familiar, comfortable conversation amidst the unfamiliarity of divorce. We both had a piece of paper that told us we were single people again. That didn't change the feeling he was still my husband. How could a piece of paper take ten years away eight of which were years of struggle after Neil chose his family over me when his father asked him to choose between us.

I came home and nestled up against some floral cushions on the seat under the bay window and stared out onto the highway, rolling the blocks of ice around and around my glass of gin squash with a slice of lemon in it, the ice clinking against the sides of the glass tossing the lemon about. I put the glass down beside me and held a couple of my clear quartz crystals that lay on the windowsill alongside some citrines, rose quartz and amethyst all filling with rays of the late afternoon sunlight. Above the fork of the two roads that lead to where my mother's family was born, lived and died, an eagle circled higher and higher into the sky. I needed to do something to lift myself out of this emotional pain I was drowning in. I decided to take a bath, muscle testing what oils and dosage I needed to put in the water and turned on the taps.

I lay back in my sunken bath, the edge lit by candles, the water filled with a blend of ylang-ylang, rose geranium and rosemary oil. My grey and white cat Billy perched on the edge watched the candlelight flicker on the walls. I closed my eyes and took deep, calming breaths. A sound bubbled up in my throat, then another, then another until they came out as a chant in a language I'd never heard before. It changed to tones of different pitches that vibrated in my body soothing it in some strange way. I didn't have a clue what was going on but I let it happen, the fear I'd felt initially now turned to fascination about what was locked away inside me.

As the sounds died away I immersed my whole body under the perfumed water feeling my heart beating evenly, my body buzzing full of life in a way exercising my physical body had never given me. I rested my head against the edge of the bath, Billy still watching me. Both of us relaxed, he purring as I stroked his head. He shook the water off and tucked his paws in.

I closed my eyes and with my inner sight saw a young Indian woman with a Newfoundland dog in a canoe on a lake. The water was still and with each stroke of the paddle, it lifted up the water along the side of the canoe with a little rush that pushed her on toward the shore of the camp. I sensed with my inner knowing that was where she lived. An eagle circled overhead and she talked to it in the way I'd been chanting while lying in the bath. It glided down closer and closer to her, her dog sitting still watching it too. She stopped paddling and let the canoe float opening her arms to the eagle. The eagle glided over the top of her head and climbed back up in to the sky. Two men who had been watching the eagle greeted her at the shore, steadying the canoe and helping her and her dog out. My inner knowing sensed the two men were her father and husband. I felt she was much loved by both men and respected for her shamanic powers by them and all her tribe because she was able to communicate with nature. That inner knowing was given to me as I watched the vision unfold and also that this was a peaceful, happy life where she was free to explore her true nature and spirit. The chanting continued and I joined in with her. As our voices merged into one I realised the young woman was me in a past life.

Billy's paw on my cheek brought me back, the bathwater now cold. I reached up for my towel and climbed out of the bath. Billy rubbed around my wet legs while I blew out the candles, the feeling of peace and happiness in that life I'd had as that woman still with me.

My tarot cards were passed to each woman in the circle, shuffled and dealt while we drank more tea and ate more cake. Anna stood and stretched inviting us to do some yoga poses. She was a yoga teacher and our circle had all attended yoga classes for many years. We did some rounds of 'Salute to the Sun' breathing and stretching deeply through each pose that made up each round. The shrill cry of lorikeets rang out as they flew over us in a sheet of rainbow colors. After the last round we sat again in our circle and Claudia suggested as a fitting end to our picnic she lead us through a guided meditation inspired by the ones we had followed in 'Creative Visualisation'. We closed our eyes, made ourselves comfortable and were led within to our inner worlds.

"You are walking along a path. It is made of crystal. There are green fields full of flowers swaying in the wind. The sky glows with light. There are domes made of crystals over rows of vegetables that are plump, juicy, full of goodness. Take your basket and pick what you need out of the garden. There are seats along the way; sit, rest, admire the view of the mountains, take in this luminous world".

The woman in the long white shift with the tiara made of eagle feathers and clear quartz crystal I'd met before was standing in a green field near the domed gardens in which stood a triangular structure made of fine quartz crystal. I felt my energy being pulled there. Stepping inside the triangle the scent of rose oil greeted me. At the top of the triangle was a golden number 11. I unlaced my white walking shoes and stood barefoot on soft, fine sand over which frangipani flowers were scattered having fallen from a large tree covered in them. Scooping up a big handful of them I cupped them to my face drinking in their sweet perfume then threw them in the air letting them fall over me catching one to tuck behind my ear. I ran onto the grass, sat under the tree and watched the waves rolling in to shore, the sea breeze catching my long hair. The sides of the triangle began to glow around me with golden light, rich and smooth like honey. A word formed in each corner out of the honey colored light, 'Beauty' at the top, then 'Respect' and 'Care' at each corner. Immersed in this inner world, I surrendered to the beauty and peace held within it and let it course through my energy field, opening my heart to the love that welled up in me as I sat there under my frangipani tree and watched the waves roll in. My inner knowing told me this world was my inner temple and I had finally found it.

I heard Claudia's voice telling us to come back and leave our garden, it would be there whenever we wanted to visit it. I now knew that was true because I carried my temple within me.

Julie knew of me more intimately now through the shared wisdom and support of her new circle of friends with whom she engaged in activities of a spiritual nature more suited to that of a Temple Woman. Reconnecting to the elements of nature and their use in healing the body and the mind through her time spent with Adele at her healing centre, she found the medicine of the Temple Woman. Soaking in a perfumed oil bath she remembered the first of what would be many stories from her past that were part of her history on the temple walk along the unhurried path of timelessness, its steady rhythm paving the way to help her know more of who she truly was; a Temple Woman.

Within that first remembered story as a Native American Indian woman, the memory of her shamanic roots and her spirit animal the eagle were revived within Julie. She now knew The Temple Woman within her had the sharp eyes of the eagle, whose inner sight allowed her to see the hard circumstances of her current life from a higher perspective, bringing healing and reorientation to her own life story.

Through the weighing and measuring of life's experience against the principles of beauty, respect and care, the three pillars of her temple, Julie now had the foundation to live within her own life story, one filled with inner beauty, self-respect and self-care.

... scene 24 ...

consulting my life map

We sat quietly in our circle, enjoying the peace that lay in this forest and between us. Lois and Adele broke it by deciding to say their goodbyes. Alice and Claudia started packing up the cups, saucers and plates then Joan and Claudia gathered up their crystals and brightly colored shawls and put them back in their baskets. Anna gathered up the books and put them back in hers. There were more hugs and goodbyes as the women left the clearing under the stand of mountain ash, knowing our circle would meet again soon. My crystal, cards and pouch were left in the middle of the circle along with my lotus flower infused with rose oil along with my basket. I sat back down in the clearing, the scent of rose oil spreading around me keeping my newly found inner temple close. Now found, my inner knowing sensed it was time for me to consult my life map again.

> On it she would find more of the co-ordinates that would guide her further along the path of her own life story, the one of I, the Temple Woman she carried within her.

I opened my back pack and took out the blue folder with my life map in it. The wind rifled through the pages of my map caressing my hair as the branches of the weeping willow tree had once done, offering me comfort. I found the part I was looking for. It said, 'You are at a very important phase in your life, the time of the Saturn Return. This means a new cycle is commencing. The Saturn Return commences at approximately twenty nine years of age but sometimes takes two to three years to be fully felt. It is the time where there can be an awareness of what one's destiny is and therefore what one has to do. You have to work to fulfil your role in a vast drama, even if you have no idea how you've come to be assigned the part you're now playing. Sometimes it might feel as if the Hand of Destiny picks you up and thrusts you into a particular fate which seems to 'happen' to you rather than you consciously choosing it. All in all, you are now in a cycle where there will be a definite change of course and things will never be the same again, and your karmic mission in life will unfold'.

I looked up from the life map and considered what I'd read. Saturn's heavy hand of destiny did crush my old life to little pieces thrusting me into a fate I didn't choose with the ending of my marriage. An enforced new cycle had commenced, requiring a change of course, one I was trying to negotiate as best I could. However much I wanted it be otherwise things would never be the same again. My life had changed for good. In all the turmoil it brought I was trying to forge a new way forward. Despite the uncertainty, my life had started to come together a little bit more, the worry, tension and fear easing a little and I started to actually enjoy my own company, pleasing myself about what I did and when. Being single again became a luxury to be enjoyed as I was no longer nervous living on my own. I budgeted my money. I was on my way.

Or so I thought.

I was called in to the office on a Monday morning with a group of other marketing associates and told we were being retrenched effective immediately, given a week's wages and escorted out of the office. Instead of going to work, I drove home worrying the whole way. How was I going to pay my mortgage? Interest rates had gone up since I bought my home and I needed to find an extra $120 a month to pay it. What was I going to do for a job?

As the fear rose in me, I returned to the power of affirmations to help centre my mind and calm my frazzled nerves. 'I have a wonderful new job with great pay'. I said the affirmation I'd created last time I was unemployed, over and over again, in the car, going to bed or taking Tonia for a walk. It had worked before so there was no reason it wouldn't work again.

It did.

When I'd been looking for full time work before I moved into my new home, I'd applied for various other jobs with no response. Within two weeks of being retrenched I received a call from the teacher's college I'd trained at offering me casual employment; lecturing in classroom management. My previous lecturers were now my peers including my adored Grade 6 teacher. When once I was nervous about a lecturer's visit to watch me teach on a teaching round my students felt that way about me visiting them on theirs.

I stood at the whiteboard in the same room I'd taken tutorials with Neil in classroom management. As my students made notes I gazed out the window over the buildings and looked down into the quadrangle where I'd laughed and joked with him, Louise, Carolyn and Kim on the way to the large hall to attend a morning lecture.

Walking in to the caff, I glanced over to the tables where I used to sit with Neil and our group and first had the vision of Neil and I in front of the fire, cosy together in our married life. I blinked back the tears and swallowed the regrets. The current intake of trainees entered in their tracksuits to get lunch, making their way out of the gym where I'd giggled with Louise about boys and was asked to leave by my teacher.

After lunch I sat outside his office next to the gym waiting for him to finish teaching a group of students. He invited me into his office to have a catch up. The last time we'd spoken on the phone I'd told him of my marriage break-up. We hadn't seen each other for quite a while. My heart opened when he looked at me with those kind eyes, smiled and said, "You're still as beautiful as you were as a girl".

I blushed, leaving his office with the same warm glow I had after I'd spent a day in his classroom when I was a child. I passed the student union room where I'd spent plenty of lunchtimes lounging on vinyl couches with the springs exposed, listening to a band, the room as full and the band just as loud, students with a drink in their hand, a cigarette dangling from their lips. Now I was on the other side walking past on the way to the lecturer's staffroom in our building.

I would have liked a permanent position at the college as I enjoyed teaching classroom management, but my degree and ten years of teaching experience wasn't enough to secure one without a lot of extra study for which I didn't have the time or the means.

At the end of my four-month tenure I drove for the last time past the football oval where I'd kicked a goal, no longer interested in football either to play or watch. With no job again I returned to emergency teaching until I could find another well paid permanent one.

From my eyrie high on the hill, the eagle made lazy circles over me while I picked lemons from the trees in the orchard on the lower terrace of my back garden to sell to the local greengrocer to make ends meet. I was now a vegetarian no longer able to afford to eat meat on the income from sporadic emergency teaching work. Tonia watched me as I sat on my bed and shook out the coins from the piggy bank. Whatever was in there that week paid for bread, milk and some cat food.

When the phone rang to say there was a day's work for me I had to ask the Vice- Principal to repeat what she'd just said. She'd asked me to teach the Grade 6 for the day at my childhood primary school.

I found a spot in the teacher's car park for my small red car. I made my way to the staff room over the asphalt where I'd lined up at assembly and received applause after my Grade 6 teacher's speech about my guts and determination. The teaching staff were preparing their lessons. A couple of the older students at a table against the wall helped staple worksheets together as I'd done when I was in Grade 6. The teachers sipped their cups of tea and nursed their mugs of coffee. To my surprise a couple of male teachers were still teaching there all those years after I'd left, their signatures in my autograph book.

I followed the Vice-Principal up the steps and was led to the door of my Grade 6 classroom. Sitting at the desk in the same spot where my teacher once sat, I opened the folder to the day's lessons plan, still in a daze. I wrote up the day's writing exercise on the board. Though the spelling champion box long gone it was still there in my mind. I lined up with my grade on the asphalt as my Grade 6 teacher had done with me and listened to the Principal address the assembly.

Two girls with pigtails taller than I was when I was a girl sat at my old desk. As I walked up and down the aisles marking the children's work I looked out the window to the building supply yard at the school fence line. The sound of pipes clanging being offloaded in the storage area startled me as they had when I was daydreaming as a child. There were posters on the wall but not of surfboards upended in the sand, hula girls and palm trees, or sunsets over big waves and volcanoes spewing lava. Coming from a tape recorder there was no sound of the sea at their local beach with the children of our sister class playing and laughing in the background. Instead there was the muffled shuffle of feet and banging of desk lids as books were taken out and returned just like when I played school, after school with my sister.

After the children were dismissed I sat at the desk and looked around the classroom one last time where my dreams to travel overseas had begun and were later realised with Neil. Like the last day of school it was just as hard to leave as I knew this time it was to say one last goodbye to a part of my past where I'd been happy.

Returning to her Grade 6 classroom this time as the teacher woke up Julie's dreaming once again, the spirit of the hula that had called her since she was a budding child entering Julie's dreams at night.
Though her old friendship circle had collapsed beyond repair, there was still a childhood friend Jenny left she once played 'Around The World' with on the bottom oval at school at lunchtime. Julie and Jenny had kept in touch over the years. In between overseas postings Jenny and her family had returned to Australia for her husband Rob's work, living not far from where they had gone to school.

'I have a wonderful new job with great pay'. I kept saying this affirmation while walking Tonia, working in the garden and going off to sleep at night. It finally worked. Jenny, knowing I was looking for a job, rang one evening after my day's teaching to say Rob had seen one on the notice board at work he thought I would be suitable for with my teaching skills.

I was out of my depth working in middle management of an oil company, though I was grateful for a permanent job and the friendship of my small team. It made the long daily commute to the city and back each day bearable. It felt more like a wonderful new opportunity to start afresh than a wonderful new job. The last part of my affirmation was realised; it was great pay, enough to afford a trip to Hawaii.

> This personally tailored dream tour was perfectly suited to a Temple Woman. By visiting Hawaii Julie would find another story from her past that was part of her history on her temple walk upon the Earth.

... scene 25 ...

my dream tour

Arriving as the sun rose over the volcanic mountains of Oahu I was greeted with the traditional "Aloha" and lei made of shells put round my neck by a women in a tropical print muumuu then driven to my high rise hotel across from Waikiki.

Standing on the balcony looking over the turquoise ocean and feeling the sandy warmth of the tropics trickle into me I recognised the aqua chairs placed on the balconies of the high rise opposite. Though obscure, they were the first point of interest on my dream tour.

Too keyed up to be sleeping though I should have been, I headed for the Ala Moana shopping centre where I recognised the car park, another obscure point of interest on day one of my dream tour. The Japanese tea shop where I sipped green tea out of tiny ceramic cups after looking at the shops was another dream tour stop I recognised. Collapsing into bed I was lulled to sleep by the waves crashing onto the shore I'd heard on a tape as a child in my Grade 6 classroom while drawing in my Social Studies book.

The next day I sat on Waikiki beach. I had a swim in the ocean that was once just a poster on the wall of my classroom the children in my sister class swam in, the verdant green Diamond Head jutting out to meet the pounding waves. The surf was rough, the current strong tossing me about quickly tiring me so I rode a wave in and scrambled out of the water, happy. I strolled back to the hotel along the boulevard admiring the rows of surfboards in every color of the rainbow dug into the sand, amused to see them even outside the police station.

A short plane flight amongst passengers with clucking chickens in cages, small wooden crates of coconuts and pineapples, sunny colored decorated straw bags filled with bananas and hibiscus plants, brought me to Maui for the day. I drove my hire car along a stretch of coastline lined with coconut palms and pineapple plantations dotted in amongst small villages with thatched dwellings alongside luxurious resorts with large swimming pools.

I stopped in the tourist strip, walking inside a gallery I recognised was the next stop on my dream tour. It had polished dark brown floorboards and white weatherboard walls on which hung vibrant paintings of tropical fish swimming through coral reefs and dolphins flipping out of the ocean in play. Enormous amethyst geodes were placed in rooms throughout the gallery. I bought rose oil and a small pack of affirmation cards.

The drive up the narrow winding road had little between it and the cliff edge. I looked down to the valley of green plains and forests of fir trees way below that became smaller and smaller as I climbed up through thick, dense cloud into sunshine at the top of Haleakala Crater. The air was thin and icy making it difficult to breathe at first. I stood on the mountain top and looked down on the wide path the lava flow took to the sea and the tips of the distant islands that poked out of the clouds, taking it all in. I sat on a massive flat volcanic rock and meditated; the sun on my face the wind ruffling my hair, dropping down into the silence as I did when I sat with my circle in Anna's lounge room on a Friday night.

The next morning walking through the marketplace close to my hotel, I admired the curvaceous women with figures like ours clothed in muumuu's that looked stylish on them. Fleshy men with bright floral shirts and shorts made their way to and from their stalls to get boxes of goods to stock them with.

I found a small beauty salon where one of those curvaceous women from the island of Kona, named Venus did my make-up and hair; a splash of indulgence. A ruffle of teal and lavender tulle was placed over my chest and a large yellow hibiscus flower pinned into my styled hair. After my makeup was done I looked like a Hawaiian princess. The day ended after lunch with a tour of the palace where the history of the Hawaiian lineage of kings and queens was explained to me by a guide and their elaborate artefacts admired.

On the island of Kauai driving over a single lane bridge lined with hedges of purple and red bougainvillea, yellow and pink frangipani and orange lantana, I slowed down to avoid some chooks that had free range on this island. Philodendron and banana trees pushed their way up into the rainforest canopy. Taro and guava plantations stretched out to the sea on either side of the town. I turned in to a rundown garage with an old petrol pump and filled up the hire car.

The sun had come out after a sudden downpour leaving this verdant world dripping, rivers of water pouring down the channels of the huge leaves of the various plants. I noticed a bookshop. I went inside to browse. My Australian accent engaged me in conversation with the owners as they liked the sound of it. The wife told me about the ruins of a temple to Laka, the Goddess of hula at an ancient Lemurian site; a local secret not shared with many tourists she said. She also told me that according to the Hawaiian people Lemuria was a lost continent with an advanced civilisation that had sunk under the Pacific Ocean after a cataclysmic earthquake thousands of years ago and they believed they are descendants of these people. She gave me directions to the site that wasn't far from her bookshop but not apparent unless you had local knowledge of where to find it, she said.

I parked the car in a small clearing spread with thick twisted roots of fig and pandanus trees. I found and followed a rocky track that hid the ocean though I could hear the pounding of the surf close by. Turning a corner I found another clearing spread with big, flat boulders that went down to the shoreline. The tide was right in so the beach wasn't accessible. I watched the grey-green waves throw themselves onto the rocks. The shape of a woman formed out of a wave, a grey-green crystal ball in her hands. I heard her say, "Look at it". As I did I felt the rock under me begin to vibrate, its energy moving through my body. The woman's shape turned silvery grey, her body shining like the crystal ball she held, reflecting the colors of the ocean. Her features formed into a Hawaiian woman with tanned skin and clear green eyes, her face draped in a long tangle of seaweed that cascaded through her long brown hair.

I closed my eyes and with my inner sight I saw taps turn on at points up my spine and black water pouring out of them as I breathed in rhythm with the life force of the waves pounding on to the shore. This woman handed me small crystal cups of colored liquid indicating to drink from them. "Cleanse and purify your insides". Anger erupted out of my stomach flowing like lava to the sea. She grabbed the debris of my anger throwing it out over the waves. "Only make decisions as they are needed in your life, don't project and make decisions on things that haven't happened yet". Empty of the anger I felt elated, inspired, at One. The pounding waves of energy of the ocean swell flowed into my inner eye allowing me to see the ancestors of the Hawaiian people walking over the rocks and hear them singing to their music. The woman with the grey-green crystal ball joined in, in a light, tinkly voice that was distant then faded as did the music, the ancestors gone.

I opened my eyes. A skinny, tan dog approached, sat by me and looked out over the waves drawn to the energy of this woman too. I picked up three small rocks and placed them in my lap, and lay my hands over them as I watched her merge with the surf, her voice swallowed by its pounding. And then she was gone. I sat and watched the waves crash onto the rocks, not wanting to leave but there was a car to return and a plane to catch.

The next day back on Oahu I did some window shopping along the streets back from the beach. I came across a shop called 'The Wedding

Ring', its window display and awnings being another stop I recognised from my dream tour. I met a Hungarian man at the bus stop outside the shop who hadn't been on my dream tour, going back to Canada. I chatted to him while I waited for the bus. That night I dreamt all my guests had gathered for my wedding but I didn't have a groom.

The last day, I hired a car to drive around the island. I stopped at a beach further north where the tropical fish swam close in to shore and tourists could feed them. As I paddled in the shallows some striped fish in fluorescent colors approached swimming between my legs. I sprinkled some food in the water from a paper bag emptying it, bringing many more fish like I'd seen on the posters on the wall of my Grade 6 classroom. I dived into this oceanic tropical fish aquarium, my dream tour now at an end.

... scene 26 ...

moving on

My crystal glowed in the sunlight coming through the branches of the stand of mountain ash by the river. I picked it up, its warmth in my hand soothing. I watched the colors change as they danced with each other. I could see within the dance an aqua ocean and the fine, golden sand of a long stretch of beach dotted with coconut palms, volcanic mountains behind it, aqua light filling my crystal. In that moment I knew aqua was the color of my temple. The aqua light faded and with it the dancing colored light in the crystal disappeared.

Uplifted by this inner knowing I put the crystal back in the pouch with the eagle feather and pack of tarot cards, picked up the lotus flower then zipped up my back pack. The eagle flew down low over the path ahead beckoning me to follow her. I hesitated.

I felt drawn to consult my life map again to find the next co-ordinate to help guide me first. I sat back down on the log by the river to read what it said.

'Accentuated with the Saturn Return is Saturn entering your First House. This in itself brings with it a period of being more realistic about yourself, of trying to get a perspective on what kind of 'you', you want to create. You will begin to build this new you through concentrated effort and self-appraisal. It is a time of paying attention to yourself with considerable seriousness, a time when you begin to know yourself more deeply and a time to know more about your individual capabilities. It is a time of one of the major transitions in life. You may start working on some study, interest or long term goal which will grow into a full time vocation or major ambition. You will certainly be looking at yourself and at your values. You could feel guided to specific types of work even if you feel a definite resistance to pursuing such activities'.

I put my life map back in its blue folder. It was clear Saturn's heavy hand still hadn't finished coursing through my life. The icy cold water flowing over the pebbles and rocks of the river bed was refreshing as I scooped up some in my cupped hands, splashing it over my face. I took another scoop of water with my red mug I'd taken out of my backpack and sipped it looking out to the distant mountains, reflecting on what I'd read. Refreshed, I stood, put my mug away, picked up my backpack and continued walking along the path.

Looking up at the eyrie in the dying tree I saw the eagle sitting next to it. She opened her beak and three little heads popped up, their beaks open ready to receive the nourishment their mother had brought them. As she had her job to do to feed her young, my job to feed myself and my animal family and put a roof over our heads left me with little energy or time to socialise other than with my circle of women friends at our esoteric study group on a Friday night. As my enthusiasm for my job waned and my enthusiasm for pursuits of a spiritual nature grew, I sought avenues to make an income from them driven by necessity as the better pay my new job afforded me eroded over time. Bigger mortgage repayments, the added financial strain of a long commute by car and train into head office in the city to work, made it necessary to find extra income outside of my job to meet my financial commitments. Having shared my spiritual interests with certain work colleagues led to forming a weekly meditation group held after work at home.

Looking in my letterbox one night after work I found a brochure with courses being offered at local community centres in the area where I lived. As I looked through what was on offer it occurred to me I could teach some of the courses as I had experience with tarot, creative visualisation, dream journaling and aromatherapy.

On a weekend with no classes to teach I was meditating on the seat under the bay window at home, the warmth of the sun on my face when the phone rang. It was Neil.

"I'm ringing to let you know Louise and I are getting married. Thought it would be better if you heard it from me than from the others".

It would never be better no matter who told me the news. I wanted to shout at him. I gritted my teeth. "Are you?" and hung up.

In my mind I went through what his news meant. It was a seamless exchange for him then; just a matter of swapping Louise and I over. And a seamless exchange for her too when I thought about it. Now she was going to be the daughter-in-law, not the friend of the daughter-in-law. She will be Neil's wife to our mutual friends. And who would I be? The ex-wife, the ex-daughter-in-law with the ex-husband.

Shards of anger glowed in my gut, pricking my insides. I did what I was taught to do in Adele's course to release pent up anger. Grabbing the cushions off the seat by the window I pummelled them hard and stomped my feet. My anger still unspent, I snatched Tonia's lead off the back of the door and hopped in the car. On the highway that led to the mountains of my mother's family home I wound the windows down and yelled myself hoarse. Tonia's big head stuck out the window of my little red car, rivers of her slobber raining down onto the road.

Not long after Neil's news my next caller Mandy had more bad news; my ex-husband and ex-best friend's wedding ceremony and reception was to take place at the venue across the highway I had a clear view of from my bay window. I still couldn't grasp how our mutual friends could accept these two as a couple formalising it by attending their wedding knowing how much hurt and pain they had caused me. Nor could I grasp why Neil and Louise would choose to have their wedding at a venue they knew I could see out my lounge room window.

On the night before the wedding, I loaded my camping gear into the back of the 4WD of friends who hadn't been invited to the wedding. They were sensitive enough to ask me to go away with them and their two children for the weekend.

I walked for miles along the deserted beach, staring into the choppy water knowing that across the highway at home the wedding was taking place.

The words pounded in my head, '*Is there anyone who can give a reason that this union should not take place? Speak now or forever hold your peace*'. I stepped forward. '*Yes. This is my husband my best friend is marrying. She stole him from me with total knowledge of what she planned to do*'. All the wedding guests would be shocked wishing I'd go away. The tears came. I gave them to the biting wind that was whipping the sand around my legs as I kept walking into an uncertain future.

Julie stopped, adjusting her pack heavy on her back after all the walking she'd done; her budding child's willow tree and the cave of her befriended broken child beside it now far behind her, yet she still carried the fragments of those two places in her heart. Her growing realisation that a Temple Woman resided within her encouraged her through the activities of a spiritual nature she was now pursuing with her new circle of women friends and through teaching others that voice became stronger within her. However that voice was still outstripped by her mother's that demanded the family came first at all costs. Though her mother remained in the cave with the rest of her siblings, the broken child within each of them crying out in pain, her mother's strident voice carried out from it into Julie's life. It became shriller as she felt the loosening of her influence on her daughter's life as Julie moved a step further away into a story her mother could never be a part of as she lived her life within her family story. Julie had already discovered the three pillars on which her temple was built; respect and care its foundation, beauty its apex, contained within its walls her own life story. The two stories clashed as did mother and daughter.

... scene 27 ...

back in the cave of sorrows

I lay down on a patch of grass beside the path, weary, using my pack as a pillow I was happy to have off my back. I turned to one side and tucked myself in to a ball, seeing only the view of a fern forest, the emerald green fronds bowing to a gentle breeze. I closed my eyes and felt the presence of my befriended broken child in my heart as I saw a picnic basket lying on a tartan rug under a big old tree beside a weir in a fern forest. The issue of my non-attendance at the continuing regular family picnics caused ongoing tension between my mother and I well before my marriage ended. I'd lost count of how many times in various ways over the years she'd tried to cajole me to attending the next family picnic hoping I'd change my answer from a 'no'. They tumbled through my mind my head tossing from side to side as I tried to rest.

"Are you coming to the family picnic? Your cousins are expecting you".

"Your cousins would like to see you. They always ask after you and why you're not there".

"What am I going to say when they ask why you're not there?"

"Your cousins are asking after you."

"Your cousins want to see you".

"Your cousins are wondering why you won't come on a picnic. What am I supposed to tell them?"

"Your cousins miss not seeing you at the picnics".

"There's a family picnic coming up next weekend, your cousins would love to see you".

My mother's insistence that the family tradition continue regardless of the further trauma it would cause me by maintaining it; my childhood confession of the abuse my sister and I endured at the hands of our two cousins long buried in her mind, drove her to attain the outcome she desired. When her pleas didn't elicit the response she wanted she tried another tactic over a meal on the way home after work to ensure I had contact with the very family members I never wanted to see again in my life.

"Joyce said Jack was looking for a tree fern for his garden so I've organised for him and Uncle Alan to come over and dig out the one that you want taken out of your garden".

"I have organised my next door neighbour who wants it to dig it out".

"Well you can't say no after I've organised it".

"I want my neighbour to have it, she has done a lot to help me since I moved in and it is a small way of saying thank you".

Unsettled hearing my mother's insistent voice tumbling through my head I sat up and leaned back against my pack gazing out into the distant mountains and sighed. Despite my protest, I'd held my squirming befriended broken child firm in my heart as Jack, Auntie Joyce and Uncle Alan pulled up outside my home the following weekend. I turned over away from the fern forest settling my head down on the other side of my pack and closed my eyes again still seeking rest, but my memories wouldn't allow it.

"Hi cuz", Jack had said with his biggest smile.

I turned to my aunt and uncle, said hello to them and vowed to myself Jack wouldn't step foot inside my home. I showed him and my uncle the shed. They found the spades and started to dig. My uncle soon tired of the hard work, leaving Jack to continue to grind and tug at the root of the tree fern just as he'd tugged at my pyjamas and ground himself inside me against my will. Jack peeled off his shirt exposing his sweaty hairy back and chest. I fled, retching over the kitchen sink while I filled up a glass with water. Auntie Joyce followed me inside eager to share the ingredients and method of a new recipe she wanted me to try. She asked if I needed help to get drinks for them assuming that was what I was doing inside and helped me take them out.

Jack sat on the front step telling jokes and arguing with his father about the best way to get the fern out. Auntie Joyce involved herself in the discussion while I stayed silent willing them to leave, my arms wrapped round Tonia who'd been lying there watching them working.

After more digging, tugging and pulling Jack and Uncle Alan gave up on being able to get the fern out. Leaving it there with its roots exposed in the dry dirt in my front yard they left, Auntie Joyce unhappy Jack wasn't able to dig it out to take home.

That was the last time I saw Jack.

My befriended broken child's memories were as insistent as my mother's voice that cut across them, flinging me back to the entrance of the cave again. My parents stood there with Neil, their faces grim, their baskets still tied tight to their hearts filled with the unripened seeds that never bore fruit; a worn and deflated football between my father and Neil's feet. Louise joined them and gave Neil a kiss on the cheek. He put his arm around her waist and he brightened. I winced and looked away seeing them all together. I had winced the time I'd demanded to know why she and Dad were still seeing Neil after they married. Mum said, "Well he's nice to talk to as a friend". I threw back my chair from the kitchen table and stood glaring at her. The inane reason she gave me and her impassive expression that went with it incensing me further.

"He left me for Louise, saw her behind my back. He betrayed me, broke my heart. I am your daughter, you are supposed to support *me*, be loyal to *me*. How could you see him knowing what he and Louise did; she set out to get him, you told me that at the beginning and she did. They're married and you still want to see him after all the hurt and pain he caused me, *your daughter - your daughter*!"

The word daughter didn't seem to have any weight even with the added emphasis I put on the word and repeated to make the point. Mum, her face still impassive, changed the subject as if she hadn't heard a word of what I'd said. I burst in to tears, grabbed my car keys and sped down the road still fuming. There was no respect for me, no care for my feelings, no acknowledgement of the impact the aftermath of my marriage ending had on *me*, her daughter. I sobbed all the way home knowing that at my expense and my feelings my mother's greater need was to keep the son she and my father never had, even if Neil was no longer their son-in-law.

My sister who had told me our parents were still seeing Neil, stepped forward out of the shadows carrying her empty basket and joined them; Neil and Louise. Though it pained me to see them together knowing I would always be the outsider now even in my own family and that my sister was lost to me long ago, if she reached out to me I would respond because of what had happened at the hands of our cousins.

Auntie Win's laughter broke the silence in the cave, her face lit by the glow of a cigarette as she shared a smoke and a beer around the kitchen table. The sound of her huge bunch of keys jangling in the pocket of her red cardigan startled me as she walked over to the fridge to get another bottle of beer.

The hospital.

My sister had rung to ask me to visit her there; my last visit being to say goodbye to Nana on the day she died. Unease filtered through my body as I stopped in the car park and looked up to the psychiatric wing. The familiar airless smell of a mental health institution closed in on me as I rode the elevator up to my sister's locked ward. I rang the bell and looked through the small, thick, mesh covered glass window in the door. As I waited to be let in I was as reluctant to enter it as much as I had been standing behind Auntie Win as she found the key to the ward and let us in locking it behind her. I am an adult now. I could handle this I told myself as this nurse did the same thing and led me to the common room.

I saw my sister in the corner talking to a middle aged man with a three-day growth. He had the dull eyes of a person who was taking a cocktail of medication, my sister sharing that look. Her medication for the pain of a disease of the nervous system left her to hobble with the aid of a stick. Many others with the same condition she knew in her support group already wheelchair bound.

When my sister saw me she smiled and invited me to sit on a worn, green vinyl couch with other men and women seated in this corner of the room who had the same dull eyes that stared through me as a child walking around a ward with Auntie Win.

I swallowed hard, smiled at them all and said, "Hi. Nice to meet you".

"I've been telling the others you don't think any of us are mad". My sister turned to the man with the three-day growth. "Tell her what you told me". He looked unsure. "Go on tell her", she encouraged.

"I see swallows flying on a path they follow every day. I feel I am part of them, they know who I am. They talk to me and I talk back to them". He started making swooping motions with his arms to denote the flight of these birds.

"I believe you", I said.

He looked relieved. It was true. I did believe him. I'd had some unusual experiences since I joined the circle of women I met with every Friday night at our esoteric study group. The only difference I could see was that this man had no context in which to place his experiences like I did. I could see why my sister didn't think he was mad. That must have been her purpose asking me to visit, to prove to him he wasn't, even though he felt he must be if he was having this recurring experience that led him to end up in a psychiatric ward. Our shared experience of being forced to enter the confines of madness housed within the walls of an asylum on the way to Pa's house as children forged an acute sensitivity to the states of the mentally ill. Our shared experience of our own mental illness as a result of the abuse we endured as children only heightened that sensitivity. Going back down in the elevator I was reminded there was a very fine line between staying sane and going insane and you don't always know when you've crossed it.

Julie had hovered in that grey area a couple of times when suicidal as the pressures of her parents' story she lived within threatened to swallow her up in its continual distress. Her sister was now hovering in that grey area too. Her memories of the abuse she endured as a child were well hidden from her only to surface when like Julie, circumstances forced their recovery. And when that day came it would be time for Julie to confront the family about what happened to her and her sister, not as a broken child once hidden in her cave but as an empowered Temple Woman in charge of her own life.

... scene 28 ...

the christmas tree

I stood and stretched, slinging my pack over my shoulders ready to continue along the path I had followed since my budding child left her willow tree behind to begin life as a married woman and my befriended broken child freed herself from the confines of her cave. The scenery changed along this part of the path; up ahead a new forest, the fresh scent of pine needles damp under my feet once I entered it. I smiled with both amusement and delight on seeing one of the trees covered in snow shimmering with traditional European Christmas decorations. I rushed up to it twirling a snowman in my fingers admiring the silver angel at the top. The blinking, colored fairy lights beamed their light into the forest. This was the Christmas tree I'd seen in a dream the first November after my divorce from Neil, with an accompanying message, "You'll be proposed to by Christmas".

    I'd sat up in bed still aware of the tree and the message. I dismissed the dream. I did want to remarry but I wasn't ready so soon. Besides it would be impossible to meet someone and agree to marry them that quickly with hardly knowing them. I was still enjoying the peace and quiet of my new home and the freedom to please myself what I did and when. I wasn't keen to start dating again after all those years of being married. Remarriage had been in my mother's plans for me when she realised there was no hope of Neil and I reuniting.

    She had bought me a ticket to a 'Desperate and Dateless' Ball in the city where I'd been matched with someone I'd meet on the night. This was not a date, it was more like a one sided arranged marriage where two sets of parent's decide their children will meet and later marry. Her unwanted dating advice had amounted to reminding me I had better lose some weight if I was to have any hope of meeting and marrying another man. I gave my current bed mate Tonia a pat, quite happy for it to stay that way for now, laying down and snuggling in to her.

    As next November approached I wondered if the Christmas tree and message would appear in my dreams again. It did. Though still happy on my own and dateless by choice I wondered if the dream would come true. It didn't. After that dream through the following year, I started to fill in time idly in my lunch hour browsing in shops in the arcade close to my office for a break and some fresh air. A new shop opened later in the year that sold antique jewellery. From time to time I'd look in the window to see if they had any new pieces as I loved antique jewellery. This lunch hour a ring caught my eye. It was rose gold with a pale blue sapphire with two diamonds on either side. I went in, asked to look at it and tried it on. The jeweller said it was an Edwardian ring circa 1910, with a Ceylonese sapphire. I'd walk past and look in the shop window every now and then to see if it was there, pleased to see it was even though I knew I couldn't afford to buy it. My thoughts turned to remarrying again on seeing that beautiful ring but I dismissed them as I still didn't feel ready for a relationship.

A week after the appearance of the Christmas tree and the message in the November of that year I'd seen the ring, the course co-ordinator at the community centre called to say my tarot class was cancelled due to lack of numbers to fill their enrolment quota. She suggested I might like to take the class at home. Reading out the names and phone numbers of three women and one man I wrote them down then rang to see if they were interested in having a class at my place. They were, so I arranged a class for the following week.

As I gobbled down my tea after getting home late from work on the night of the class, the three women I'd contacted rang within minutes of each other to cancel fifteen minutes before it was to start. There was no answer when I rang the man to tell him they'd cancelled.

He'd been on his way over, the sound of a motorbike indicating he'd arrived. I dashed to the kitchen, washed my plate and cutlery and stood near the door anxiously waiting for the knock. I opened it to a short, dark man of European descent with brown eyes and a beard. He was dressed in green army fatigues, black bike boots, a green and yellow scarf tucked into a blue bike jacket.

Smiling politely he said, "Hello, my name is Les".

He was my 'caff dreaming man' so I knew straight away I was going to marry him. Trying to disguise my shock I asked him to take a seat, which he did on a chair opposite me. I sat crossed legged on the couch dressed in my aqua dress with the palm tree and sunset with the word Hawaii across it I'd bought there. He took his cards out of a camphorwood box with his initials engraved on it, the same deck as mine and put them on the table.

He explained, "I'm a computer programmer. For the last couple of years I've been writing a tarot card program on my computer at home. I want to learn how to read the cards so I could complete the program".

We talked a little about our jobs, the other classes I was teaching as we went through the suites of cards, discussing how we interpreted their meanings. I listened carefully as he gave his thoughts on the Hanged Man, The Tower and the Death cards.

The second week he arrived at my front door with a blue lace agate handing it to me with a warm smile and a kiss on the cheek. I was touched by his kind gesture. The stone was smooth in the palm of my hand.

As we settled on the couch he took his cards out of their box. "My father found this as a raw stone in a river bed and polished and cut it in to this shape. He's called Les too. He and his third wife Annamaria who is Hungarian also, have taken up lapidary as a hobby in their retirement".

"Ah, so you're Hungarian. I was wondering where you were born".

"Me, my younger brother and parents are all refugees. We escaped from Hungary in the uprising when I was a young boy when the Russians tried to take over our country. My parents had a choice of Canada, New Zealand and Australia to emigrate to. They decided on Australia. Dad and I had our names anglicised to Les to help us fit in better here".

"What's your real name?"

"Laszlo".

"That suits you much better. You don't look like a Les. I bet your Dad doesn't either. I'm going to call you Laszlo".

"Call me Laci. It's what my family call me. It's like being called Andrew but having it shortened to Andy".

I must have had a puzzled look on my face. "How do you pronounce that again?"

"Lot- see". He enunciated the sounds so I got it. Laci.

I shuffled his deck of cards and handed them to him. "Let's do a ten card spread. I learned this from an American woman I met when I was staying in Amsterdam".

As we delved into the meaning of the cards, he saw a strong relationship between two people in them.

The third week he arrived at my front door and handed me a tape of Vivaldi's Four Seasons with a smile on his face and a brief kiss on the lips.

"It's one of my favourite pieces of classical music. I feel it is one of yours too".

I smiled and nodded. We listened to it as we went through and discussed the meanings of the numbers for the suite of cups over a mug of green tea.

One night after work I arrived home tired as usual to find the lawns mown, the front garden bed weeded and new soil added to it. Freshly watered carnations in deep reds, pale pink, yellow with orange streaks were planted in it alongside clumps of impatiens in similar hues. His loving gesture touched my heart.

On the fourth week, I was invited to his place for the first time for the last class. I stood at the large window looking out over the orchard and vegetable plot in the back garden.

Laci came up behind me, put his arms around my waist and whispered in my ear, "Will you marry me?"

"Yes". I turned to him and we kissed. He said, "I knew I was going to marry you the first time we spoke on the phone. I remembered your little red car from my drive to work when I saw it parked in the driveway the first time I came to your house".

"I remember seeing you on your motorbike passing me on the road on the way to the data centre when I worked there before it was moved into head office in the city. I want to invite you to Christmas lunch to meet my parents. Will you come?". He nodded.

I stood in the pine forest and stared in wonder at the shimmering Christmas tree of my yearly dream and the message that went with it - a proposal by Christmas. The tree was as magical as the way my caff dreaming man was brought to my doorstep one evening in mid-November making my dream come true that I'd be proposed to by Christmas. My mother's cool response to the news when I'd called in on the way home from work to tell her that we were getting married and I wanted to invite Laci to Christmas lunch was, "I suppose you know what you're doing, you're not nineteen anymore".

After meeting Laci at Christmas lunch she said, "I suppose I'll get to like him when I get to know him".

One lunch hour after Christmas, Laci and I met outside the antique jewellery shop in the arcade near my office building. I showed him the ring I'd chosen before we met and we went inside. He got out his cheque book and paid for the ring, sliding the box into his shirt pocket saying he would give it to me soon.

After the summer holiday season was over Laci invited me over for tea. When I walked into his lounge room I walked into a garden. The forest green shag pile carpet was dotted with large white daisies with sunny yellow centres. On the tiled hearth sat a large cane basket filled with more of them. I tiptoed between the flowers bending to look under one of them as Laci said my ring lay under one of them. I found it under a daisy near the hearth, turning to show him with a smile. We met in the middle of the daisy garden where he placed the ring on my finger and we kissed, now engaged. I picked up the basket and gathered the daisies into it one by one handing it to Laci. He placed it in the middle of the kitchen table where a simple meal he'd prepared was laid.

The colors in Julie's ring sparkled in the candlelight as did their eyes as they sat across the basket of daisies. They clinked glasses of champagne and got to know each other a little better over dinner. In that tender-hearted moment of great beauty standing in the daisy garden, I, The Temple Woman took the tarot cards and put them back in my basket inlaid with mother-of-pearl. The cards had fulfilled their purpose as through them, Julie had returned to the realm of the Temple Woman who dwelt inside her and found the man she was to share the rest of her life with.

... scene 29 ...

meeting the temple woman within

Morning sunlight filtered through the spaces between the pine trees drawing me towards its warmth, the Christmas tree now gone. Beyond the trees I could see a clearing, the energy coming from it enticing me. I broke into a jog, eager to reach it.

On the edge of the forest I saw the eagle riding the thermals. She was circling over the field in which my inner temple stood. I ran toward it. The woman in a long white shift with a tiara made of eagle feathers and clear quartz crystal I had seen before, stood at the entrance holding her basket. In it were clear quartz crystal pots with healthy young plants growing out of them, an eagle feather and some clear quartz crystal points. I dropped my backpack to the ground and hastily unzipped it, tipping its contents on the ground at the woman's feet. I placed my white pouch embossed with stars and eagle feather in amongst the crystal pots, my inner knowing sensing that is where they belonged. The woman handed the basket to me with a smile and followed me into my inner temple carrying the lotus flower infused with rose oil she had given me in one hand and my life map I had been given by the astrologer on my current Earth walk, in the other. Tonia, my Newfoundland bounded up to her and stood beside her, looking up at her with big brown eyes full of love. I began to chant in a language other than my own and felt a rush of air as the eagle swooped down low over me and lifted back into the sky. The resonance of the chant died away and I felt my body still. I opened my eyes and Tonia was standing beside me looking up at me, her eyes filled with love. In the palm of my hand was a crystal. The aqua light of the ocean, the pink light of rose oil the yellow and white light of the frangipani flower burst out through my fingers. My inner temple glowed with golden light.

I dug my hand into the pocket of my long white shift and pulled out a small clear heart shaped crystal. I tapped it against the crystal point on my tiara and looked up to the fading stars in a dawn sky. Infused with this colored light, a frangipani burst open into full flower in one of the pots in the basket. I took it out. I knelt on the grass amongst a carpet of frangipani flowers. I dug my hands into the soft, sandy soil and planted this sapling that grew from the seed of my essence in my garden, the Temple Woman within now found.

Julie stepped out of her red tracksuit paints and pulled her windcheater with the koala on it over her head then untied her shoes and slipped them off her feet next to her pack. She stripped off her underwear at her temple's ocean's edge and dove into the water. When she finished drying herself and had changed into clean underwear, I handed her, her long white chiffon wedding dress embossed with a large silver astrological sun, the fingers of light spreading over her chest. I arranged her long train that was attached to silver clips on each shoulder while she buckled up her silver sandals. Bending down to my basket I slid my hand under her crown of pink and mauve azaleas woven with jasmine and placed it on her head.

A year to the day they met, as the sun was rising, Julie and Laci stood in a forest of mountain ash amongst acres of gardens, the hillsides awash with mauve, pink, orange, yellow and white azalea and rhododendron blooms. The sun's rays filtered through the trees onto the circle of guests who had gathered around them as they said their vows.

At the wedding breakfast held on the lawn they mingled with their guests as the string quartet played Vivaldi, the bees buzzed and the kookaburras laughed. As they cut their sponge cake covered in strawberries with the words 'Beginning A New Life' written on it, their guests with champagne flutes in hand, raised their glasses to toast its promise.

... scene 30 ...

the final betrayal

setting
Julie's childhood home years later

The phone rang. My sister's voice on the other end shaking and broken. "I've got something to tell you but I don't know how to say it". I knew what it was. I'd been waiting for this day for a very long time. I gave her the space to speak. "We were abused by those cousins of ours when we were children".
"I know".
"You do?"
"I remembered when I was teaching at the school Mum and our aunts and uncle went to. There was a talk from Children's Protective Services about child neglect. I have been waiting for you to remember".
"Why didn't you tell me?"
"I wanted you to remember when you were ready to". She burst into tears, her sobs tearing at my heart knowing she was only at the very beginning of what was going to be an arduous path of healing ahead. "I have a lot to share about what happened if and when you are ready if it will help you heal".
Her choking sobs escalated. "Thanks".

My sister and I sat on the couch in the lounge room of our childhood home, our parents sitting across from one another in their armchairs, stony-faced. We waited for one of them to speak, both our faces flushed with anger. We had told them the details of the abuse we endured at the hands of our cousins. Their response was to confront them about it to hear their side of the story so they could decide if what we were saying was true. Our mother spoke first. "You father and I talked to your cousins and they said, "Oh no we didn't do anything. We didn't touch them. How could they accuse of us such a thing?"
"We believe them."

I looked to my father not surprised by my mother's response but still infuriated by it.

He hung his head and mumbled, "I thought something was going on".

"Why didn't you do something then?", I said coolly.

My mother threw him a withering look, turned to me and said,

"It was only a little rape…."

---------------------- *** -------------------

About the Author

A love of words as a child, spelling them and forming them into sentences using the rules of language fostered a desire to record the world around me in a daily diary. This passion for the written word translated into a teaching career where I delighted in imparting my love of language to primary school students through my 20's.

As an adult it was to words I turned when my life demanded understanding of the trauma I remembered I had endured as a child in my family. Now I recorded the world inside me by keeping a daily journal of my thoughts, feelings and insights that came through dreams and contemplation of the trauma. This rich narrative was very different to the one I'd been raised in as a child. It contained a vaster story, one more aligned with my own true nature expressed as my own personal myth.

Most days are spent at my desk trawling through my journals delving further into my rich inner narrative to create stories for future books that I hope will inspire others to find their own stories. If I'm not at my desk I can be found somewhere in nature. On the back of the motorbike with my husband or walking our two dogs, preferably at a nearby beach with a dog friendly café to enjoy a coffee after our walk.

www.ingramcontent.com/pod-product-compliance
Lightning Source LLC
Chambersburg PA
CBHW020319010526
44107CB00054B/1898